NEW YORK TIMES BESTSELLER

M. WILLIAM
PHELPS

MURDERERS' ROW
A COLLECTION OF SHOCKING
TRUE CRIME STORIES
VOLUME ONE

WILDBLUE
PRESS

WildBluePress.com

MURDERERS' ROW published by:
WILDBLUE PRESS
P.O. Box 102440
Denver, Colorado 80250

WILDBLUE PRESS is registered at the U.S. Patent and Trademark Offices.
ISBN 978-1-942266-71-6   Trade Paperback
ISBN 978-1-942266-70-9   eBook

Interior Formatting/Book Cover Design by Elijah Toten
www.totencreative.com

CONTENTS

FORENSIC FILES AND THE
ELECTRIC KILL MACHINE
-1-

MURDER IN MASSACHUSETTS
-34-

BLOOD ON SESEAME STREET
-83-

NOTHING THIS EVIL EVER DIES
THE LOST LETTERS OF SON OF SAM
-115-

DANCE WITH THE DEVIL
BEHIND THE SCENES OF INVESTIGATION
DISCOVERY'S "DARK MINDS"
-152-

THE EASTBOUND STRANGLER
BEHIND THE SCENES OF INVESTIGATION
DISCOVERY'S "DARK MINDS"
-221-

DEAD PEOPLE WON'T WALK AWAY
INSIDE THE REAL WORLD OF FORENSIC
SCIENCE WITH DR. HENRY LEE
-258-

PUBLISHER'S NOTE: The short stories appearing in this volume of Murderers' Row have been previously published but are being brought to you here for the first time as a collection, plus a "bonus" interview the author conducted with Dr. Henry Lee.

FORENSIC FILES AND THE ELECTRIC KILL MACHINE

EIGHTEEN-YEAR-OLD JIM MOREL went out jogging one afternoon, not long after the ordeal he had gone through with his childhood friends was over. Jim was running in the country air of Massachusetts, trying to clear his head. He was thinking about the future. Jim had turned on his friends, some would say. He was a rat, others would proclaim. He was a hero, still others would argue. Either way, Jim wanted to forget about the past year and move on with his life.

As he jogged in a secluded area in Norton, Massachusetts, a "big blue car," as Jim would later describe it, pulled up behind him to catch up with him, and then stopped.

This got Jim's attention. He had been looking over his shoulder lately.

"Are you Jim Morel?" one of the two guys in the car asked. They were hulking men, big and brawny. Jim had never seen them before.

"Yeah, yeah … why? What's up?" Jim was sweating, and out of breath.

Jim thought maybe they were old friends. *Grammar school? Junior high?* It was getting late in the day, darker. He couldn't really make out their faces.

According to Jim, however, these men were not there to reminisce about the glory days—they were there to hurt him. Hurt him bad.

One of the guys, Jim said, ran toward him with a "kitchen knife" and started stabbing into the air before hitting Jim in the arm.

"What the heck are you—" Jim said. He had no idea what was happening—but he knew why.

Before Jim could say anything else, the guy with the knife went for Jim's face and started slashing.

Feeling the warm trickle of blood running down his cheeks and arm, Jim took off as fast as he could into the nearby woods, literally running for his life.

THEY HAD A NAME THAT WAS hardcore. A lot to swallow if you didn't "get it:" *Electronic Kill Machine.* But then, "hardcore" was an appropriate term to describe this group of teens who made up the band and the posse hanging around to watch rehearsals and attend gigs.

Jim Morel was seventeen then. This was long before he was viciously attacked that Sunday evening while out jogging. Jim played keyboards. He had a clean-cut appearance: light hair, skinny, tall, baby face. He wasn't some head banger who walked around with a chain hanging from his ear to his nose, tattoos, studded bracelets, ripped jeans, black Harley boots, metal dotted about his face. Jim just loved the music. For him, it was all about the music.

"That band was a cross between electronic and, like, a heavier rock," Jim said, "but it was more abstract, kind of dark."

Old-school Marylyn Manson meets a contemporary SlipKnot, in other words.

That darkness Jim associated with the music had also infected the lives of some of Electronic Kill Machine's members—especially the drummer, Jason Weir. Thomas Lally and Anthony Calabro, along with Weir, were kids Jim had grown up with in Norton. As friends go, they were tight.

"Ant," as Anthony Calabro was called by his crew, Weir and Lally, Jim said, loved nothing more than "getting high and watching hours upon hours of *Forensic Files.*"

They lived in Quincy. They liked to sit around, drink, smoke weed, and watch hours of the show, intrigued by the mere stupidity of some criminals.

"It got to the point where they were actually taking down notes," Jim recalled.

They not only watched the show and other forensic crime shows like it, but they'd go online afterward and study each of the cases like they were students. They'd pull up witness statements, photographs, and court files and dissect each case as if it were some sort of high school assignment.

"Towards the end," Jim recalled, "they were just *obsessed* with the show."

It got to the point where Lally, Ant, and Weir looked at Jim and other kids in the group and, with smiles on their faces, said things as bizarre as, "We could kill somebody and get away with it."

Jim and the others would shake it off, maybe have a laugh.

Yeah, right. You guys—killers? No way.

THE NEIGHBORHOOD JIM MOREL and his buddies—Lally, Weir, and Ant Calabro—grew up in forty miles south of Boston, in and around Norton, was not so much rough as it was working-class. Norton, Brockton, Foxboro (home of the New England Patriots), Canton, these towns are suburbs: outside the confines of places like Quincy, Brookline, and Chelsea, where the streets are a little more hardscrabble and rough in some sections to walk around.

Still, for Jim and his friends, living amid white picket fences and lawn mowers and cul-de-sacs didn't change things at home. "We all kind of came from broken homes,"

Jim remembered. "We all kind of, like, moved in together and became each other's families."

It was the summer of 2001, as Jim told it. Ant was eighteen then. Lally was twenty-one, and Weir, like Jim, was seventeen. Jason was talented, Jim claimed. A solid drummer. Lally just hung around with the band; one of those wannabes or groupies. And Ant, well, Anthony Calabro was the band's self-proclaimed "manager." He was the kid who was going to take the group over the top, to the next level, get them a record deal.

Ant lived with his great aunt, 84-year-old Marina Calabro. Marina owned a triplex, a large three-decker in Quincy. Marina and Ant lived on the third floor. Weir and Lally soon moved in after leaving home, and having nowhere to go, and no one to turn to. Ant loved his great aunt. Jim said he talked about her a lot. About how kind, gentle, and outgoing the old woman had been.

Marina agreed to allow the kids to live with her. After all, she had a lot of money stowed away and owned property worth some serious coin.

"Whatever Ant needed, she bought it for him," Jim said. Ant crashed up a car up once. Marina stepped in and bought him a new one, then paid for his insurance, too. "I don't remember Ant ever having to work. Most of us had jobs. He didn't. She just paid for everything."

Marina adored Ant to the point of telling him that she was willing her entire estate—everything she owned, near of $1.2 million—to him. Ant was sitting on a hefty inheritance. He was young. Even if Marina lived to be 94 years old, it would only be ten years until then.

Jim Morel and his three buddies were recluses; they didn't much travel beyond the comfort zone of their own group or neighborhood. They didn't really make new friends. Jim's friend, Jason Weir, was a pretty bright kid, Jim recalled. "He, like the rest of us, came from a broken family. He'd done his fair share—like all of us—of petty crimes, but nothing too major."

They'd all been busted with drugs or in trouble for one reason or another. It was part of being a teen in suburban Boston and not having much direction or drive in life.

"The cops knew all our names," Jim said. "I was by no means an angel."

Jim went to high school with Thomas Lally. They were in a special program. They didn't go to classes with the other kids. There were a certain number of "troubled" kids, Jim admitted, who attended classes in the basement of the school. Out of the entire group, Lally was the first of the bunch to take things to an extreme level. Ant would soon take the title from Lally, however, in high school and even right after, Lally was known as the "crazy kid" who would do just about anything.

"He was very obsessed with, like, explosives," Jim remembered.

Lally liked to wear army fatigues and was into blowing things up for fun.

"He was odd. He did a lot of bizarre things."

Lally suffered from Tourette's Syndrome, which, according to the National Institute of Neurological Disorders and Stroke, is "a neurological disorder characterized by repetitive, stereotyped, involuntary movements and vocalizations called tics. ..." People with Tourette will often shout obscenities uncontrollably and experience violent body twitching and sharp jerks of the arms and shoulders and head.

This made Lally stand out.

For anyone who has suffered from the disorder, it's a debilitating condition. Lally was a big guy back then, over six foot tall and at least 250 pounds. Not too many people screwed with Lally or questioned the bizarre behavior brought on by his Tourette's. His profile would shrink later, but back when the Norton gang ran together, Lally was the monster of the clan.

"He blew up a dog house once, it was wild," Jim explained. "We had like grenade launchers and stuff like that. Where other kids might have had, like, 9mms and .38s, we had *bombs*."

LALLY, JASON AND ANT became so obsessed with *Forensic Files* that they sat around the Quincy apartment they shared during the summer of 2000 and on into 2001 discussing the various ways in which they could kill someone and get away with it. It became like a game. Smoke some weed and then come up with the best scenario you could to kill a person and still walk away a free man.

"They would talk about chemicals," Jim said. "How they could dip their fingers in certain chemicals and acids and it wouldn't destroy certain parts of their fingers, but would still take off their finger prints."

They also talked about the best way to commit the murder. For example, what would the chosen weapon be, the most sensible with which to kill someone?

Not a gun, obviously, which, according to them, would leave a path for authorities to track down the perp—aka, trace evidence such as gunshot residue or ballistic evidence.

A knife would leave the same.

Strangulation or asphyxiation?

No. Finger impressions could be matched up to bruises.

But an accident ... yes! That was it, the threesome decided. To murder someone and get away with it, the best way would be to make it look like an accident.

Stage the scene.

It seemed evil to break murder down to such a clichéd

MURDERERS' ROW: VOLUME ONE

way of thinking, but how many murders were committed where the killers didn't follow a few simple rules? Every crime show had made this point at one time or another. Lally, Weir and Ant, often stoned out of their minds, had figured this out while watching *Forensic Files*. On certain nights, in fact, perhaps when boredom overcame the value of good drugs, they'd act out certain crimes. Jim Morel said he'd show up at the apartment Ant lived in with Marina, Lally and Weir, and they'd be sitting around—bong on the table—discussing how to do it right.

"Hit a person this way and it would work."

"It would! Yes."

They dissected murders to the point where they believed the best way to understand the perfect murder was to look at it backwards. Take the result—in other words—and walk through backwards to see how to do it perfectly and without making one mistake. It took only one mishap and you were caught, the three of them knew by watching television. Every murderer in prison made that one mistake—oftentimes it was something simple—that pointed police in his direction.

They talked about it over and over, night after night—and then ... well, and then they came up with it.

A faultless plan.

"A frying pan," one of them said.

"A frying pan wrapped in a towel," another added.

Yes!

That's it.

MARINA CALABRO HAD RECENTLY retired from her hairdressing job. She was a sharp woman, not some docile old lady ready for a walker with tennis balls guiding the legs down the waxed hallway of a convalescent home. Marina cooked dinner, washed clothes, watched television, and made Ant and his friends' beds every day. For some reason, she had never married. She had no children—which was probably one of the reasons why she took Ant into her home—along with his two friends—and treated Ant as her own.

Many claimed that Ant, as time went on, started to despise the woman for some reason. When Marina was away, her house became a party zone, with Ant, Lally, and Weir playing hosts.

Ant, like the other two, was a professional slacker. They were pot-smoking, alcohol-drinking kids who thought they had all the answers, doing nothing more than playing video games all day long, watching television, eating McDonalds, or hanging out at the local mall.

None of them even wanted to work.

Marina put up with it. She might have expressed her feelings from time to time, she had allowed the behavior to continue.

Margaret Menz had known Ant for quite some time. She and Ant often traded stories when they ran into each other in the hallway of the three-decker, or outside in the driveway. During the afternoon of December 19, 2001, Menz left work early and returned home to the same building Marina shared with Ant and his buddies.

As Menz came up the street, at about 3:00 o'clock in the afternoon, as she recalled later, she spied Ant sitting in Lally's truck in the driveway outside the building. The door to the truck was open, and Ant sat there, with his dog by his side, appearing to be nervous, just not himself.

"Hey," Margaret said, startling Ant. Apparently, he hadn't expected Menz to come home at that time.

"Hey," Ant said, surprised to see her.

"What are you doin' sitting here in your truck?"

"I'm nervous," Ant said. "I got into an accident with my

car."

Ant had totaled the car Marina had bought him and, he said, he didn't know how to go upstairs and tell her. She was going to be livid. She had purchased the ride for him and here he had gone and destroyed the thing.

After ten minutes of what Menz later called "small talk," she and Ant walked into the building from the backyard. As they made their way to the door to get into the building itself, Ant said, "You see that?"

"What?"

He pointed to his dog. "My dog senses something," Ant added.

It was an off-the-wall comment. Menz didn't know what to make of it.

As she and Ant approached what was the second level of the house from the back stairs, Menz asked Ant, "Is Marina in there?"

Ant had heard Menz's question and understood it, because he looked toward her after she asked, but he never answered. Instead, Ant walked into his second-story apartment without saying a word, closing the door behind him.

Menz thought the whole thing had been strange. Ant was just not acting like himself; something was definitely different about him.

By 3:40 P.M. that same day, Menz left her apartment to meet up with her boyfriend. Menz recalled that the truck Ant had been sitting in earlier when she encountered him was still in the driveway when she walked out of the yard and down the block.

About 10:45 P.M. that night, after returning home from dinner, Menz heard a commotion in Marina's apartment. The walls and floors were paper-thin. She didn't have much trouble making out what Ant said (she lived directly below), but couldn't believe what she was hearing.

Dead ... go home, Menz heard Ant mutter.

"Dead, go home?"

What did it mean?

It was near midnight on that same somber night when the Quincy Police Department (QPD) received a call from Ant. Marina was dead, he said. She had fallen down the stairs, at least that's what it looked like, according to Ant. Perhaps she had tried to carry a bag of trash down the narrow, steep flight of stairs inside the three-decker and had somehow tripped? Perhaps she had a stroke? Maybe a heart attack?

Due to her advanced age of being in her mid-eighties, Marina's fall had been too much on her fragile body, Ant suggested, as he proclaimed that she was dead.

Ant explained to the police that he and Thomas Lally had found Marina at the base of the stairs when they came home. Ant appeared to be in a state of disbelief, and seemed appropriately saddened, even walking around in a daze in the days that followed, those who knew him later confirmed. His great aunt, the one woman who had rescued him from the streets and his broken home, had fallen and died, and he hadn't been there to stop it. He was upset with himself, it seemed, because he hadn't been there to help Marina when she needed him most.

Menz didn't think much of the *dead ... go home* comment she had heard through the floor. It could have been anything, or nothing, after all. Maybe Ant had been watching television or horsing around with his buddies. Who the hell knew? But that all changed near midnight, an hour after Ant called police, when Menz got a phone call from another Calabro relative living in the same building on the first floor.

"Marina's dead," the relative explained.

"What?"

"There's blood everywhere ..." the woman was hysterical.

"Someone'll be right there."

Margaret woke up her boyfriend, she couldn't bear to look. He rushed out of the house and down the stairs. .

A minute later, he was back. "It looks like Marina fell down the stairs."

Menz sensed that something was wrong. As her boyfriend described the scene, she thought, "That's odd, Marina is always so extremely careful going up and down the stairs."

It was close to the midnight hour when cops arrived at Marina's Quincy three-decker. There, at the bottom of the interior stairs, was the badly bruised and twisted body of Marina Calabro, Ant's 84-year-old great aunt. She looked terrible, and it appeared her body had suffered extensive injuries. .

People were mingling about outside.

"What's going on?" someone asked.

Ant had called in Marina's death, but Thomas Lally was with him. One of the cops on the scene noticed that Lally had fresh scratches on his face as well as what appeared to be a bite mark on his forearm.

"What's that from?" the cop asked.

"We were horsing around," Lally explained, "me and Anthony. We got a little rough and fought last night."

The cop seemed to accept his explanation.

Ant and Lally said they had returned home after a night out only to find Marina at the bottom of the stairs. They both seemed to be very upset by this horrible turn of events.

Two police officers sat with Ant in the kitchen while another cop walked Lally into the living room. In two separate interviews, they were asked to explain what had happened in more detail than simply "we went out." Step by step. Hour by hour. The cops wanted to know everything the two young men had done that night.

"I last saw Marina about 3:00 o'clock," Ant told police.

"She was inside the apartment. Tom [Lally] was here."

The cop took notes, as Ant kept looking into the living room where another officer questioned Lally.

"Was she on any medications or anything?"

"No," Anthony said.

"How was she feeling?"

"As far as I know, pretty good."

"What'd you and Mr. Lally do today?"

"We left about 3:00 and, in Tom's truck, took a ride over to the Emerald Square Mall. I drove."

"Why?"

"Tom's license is suspended."

"What did you buy at the mall?"

"We went there to get some more minutes for my cell phone."

The apartment was clean. Tidy. Picked up. Marina was no neat freak, but she liked to keep her place organized, that's for sure. Nothing seemed out of place, and nothing appeared to be missing. From the looks of it, Marina had taken a misstep and had fallen several flights of stairs to a painful death.

The cops weren't satisfied with Ant's answers just yet. They wanted more, so Ant was asked again what time he and Lally got home.

"It was around 10:30," he said. By routine, he and Lally entered the apartment the same way they exited, through the back stairs. "When we walked in, the kitchen and parlor lights were both on. The door to Marina's bedroom was closed. Nothing seemed unusual. You know."

Same as any other night.

There was a time difference, however. Emergency dispatch hadn't received the call from Ant until 11:53 PM. To that, Ant said, "We realized when we got home that we had forgotten to get cigarettes. So we went back out to the

7-11 on Adams Street"—right around the corner—"and then stopped at Nick's Sub Shop," nearby, "to get a submarine sandwich."

"What time did you get back?"

"Oh, about 11:00. Tom watched television and I went to make my bed and saw that the blanket was gone." Ant said his bed hadn't been made, which was odd. "Marina usually makes the beds."

When Ant realized his bed wasn't made, he explained, he and Lally started looking for Marina. They felt something was wrong. So Ant said he called his grandmother, who lived downstairs, to ask if she had seen Marina.

"I haven't heard from her," Ant's grandmother said.

"She's not here, either."

"She might be with some friends in New Hampshire."

Ant said he called his father in Plymouth next, saying, "I haven't seen her."

"Check the hallway," Anthony said his father told him.

Ant said he held the phone. "Tom," Ant called out, after telling his father to hold on, "check the hallway for Marina."

Tom returned. "She's at the bottom of the stairs."

LALLY SAT IN THE living room and waited for Ant's interview to conclude before his turn to talk came. One little discrepancy, one tiny piece of the story that didn't juxtapose with Ant's and the jig was up: they were heading downtown.

"We left around 3:00 and went to the Emerald Square Mall because Anthony had to fill his cell phone minutes," Lally began. "I was going to check on a job at Wal-Mart, but we left the mall instead."

Ant hadn't mentioned Wal-Mart.

"We stopped at several dealerships and looked at cars in the Attleboro area. We headed back to Quincy about 9:00 but there was a lot a traffic for some reason."

All easy enough to check out.

"When did you guys return?" (Such a seemingly easy and innocent question—but one to which the answer would reveal quite a lot to the investigator.)

"Around 10:30."

"Did you notice anything out of the ordinary in the apartment?

"No. The kitchen light was on and Marina's bedroom doors were closed."

"Did you guys stay home?"

"No. I forgot that I needed cigarettes, so we went out to the 7-11 and then to Nick's Sub Shop."

Lally kept to the story pretty much word for word, including the calls Ant had made, opening the door, and seeing Marina at the bottom of the stairs. Lally, though, ladled on the emotion. He said he ran down the stairs and looked at Marina. "I touched her hand to see if she was okay. I ran back up the stairs and told Anthony and we both started crying."

"Tell me about those scratches and bite marks," the cop asked, looking at Lally's arm and face.

Lally looked down. "Oh, yeah ... Anthony was drinking vodka right out of the bottle, he was pretty shitfaced. Marina asked me to get the bottle from him. When I grabbed the bottle, Ant grabbed me and pushed me and we argued, and Ant scratched me in the face and bit me on the arm. Here, look ..." He showed the cop his arm. "See?"

Both police officers went back into the kitchen and asked Ant about the incident.

His version seemed to confirm Lally's story.

As one of the officers took a look at Marina's body, he observed many things. Marina was lying face down on the bottom stairway. She was wearing a white shirt, green stretch pants, black socks, and white sneakers. Her left sneaker was torn and her ankles were crossed at the bottom.

From initial appearances, it certainly appeared to be an accidental fall.

In front of Marina's face was a "small pool of blood ... there were two cuts on her head and some blood under her fingernails."

Another officer, a trooper with the Massachusetts State Police (MSP), came over just then and pointed something out to the officer. There was "dust that had been removed from the hallway on both sides, which was consistent with a fall," the trooper later wrote. In other words, the hallway was dusty. The force and the air from Marina's "fall" had made an imprint on the floor much like, say, a book might make if you were to drop it on a dusty table. The air from the force of the book going down would push out the dust on all sides.

Another trooper photographed the scene and the mortuary came and removed Marina's body.

After conducting a rather routine post mortem autopsy, the medical examiner uncovered nothing out of the ordinary. Marina had apparently fallen down several flights of stairs and, during the process of that violent tumble, sustained multiple injuries that all contributed to her death. Among those injuries noted on the report were "head and neck trauma, facial abrasions, lacerations of the scalp, cervical vertebrae fracture, soft tissue hemorrhage, chest and abdominal trauma, three right rib fractures, five left rib fractures, contusions of the back and extremity contusions. ... The cause of her death was blunt neck trauma," said the report.

"... [T]he manner of her death was ruled an accident."

ANT SHOWED UP AT band practice the day after Marina was found dead to watch rehearsals. He seemed pretty much out of it, down and depressed, not talking much, "Jim Morel later recalled.

Ant had lost his someone he loved, so nobody gave him a hard time.

"It wasn't for very long," Jim added, "but at first he was very upset."

Everyone gathered around Ant and showed support. Even though, Jim said, "We all had our suspicions."

Suspicions ... because for the past year or more, here were three friends bragging and carrying on about how they could pull off the perfect murder and, lo and behold, Marina had turned up dead. Coincidence? Self-fulfilling prophesy?

For Jim, the thought occurred to him that Ant, Lally, and Weir murdered Marina, but, "I knew these guys, grew up with them. I couldn't believe that they would do something like that. It was all about the friend you had in high school: 'Oh, I'm a big tough guy.' But, you know, whenever it came down to it, where someone like Ant would actually get into a fight, whatever, he'd kind of, like, wuss out."

Jim explained that it was the norm for the three of them to talk tough to one another. At one time, they talked of opening up a hit man service. They spoke about murder as though it could become a hobby. Jim Morel believed there was no way that "the boys," as he called them, had the stomach or the guts to carry it out.

Over the course of the next few days (which would soon turn into months), Ant turned inwards even more. He wouldn't make eye contact with anyone, and always came across as being depressed. Despite all this, only a week after Marina's death, Ant was already spending the inheritance he had received from her, and on the most bizarre things imaginable. As he walked up to Jim Morel one day, Ant said, "I want to do some investments with you and the band."

"Huh?" Jim was stunned, thinking Ant was grieving and maybe this was his way of mourning the woman.")

The band had had a few record labels sniffing around,

but nothing had come through. Some cash to get the band's brand out there, maybe finance a tour, help to purchase equipment, would certainly facilitate that dream of making it big.

And so, a partnership was born.

As time went by, Ant became more and more invested, both financially and emotionally, in Electronic Kill Machine, as did many of Jim Morel's other childhood friends. In fact, the entire clan, Lally, Weir, Ant, and everyone around them, soon played a part in the band: promotions, producing, marketing, whatever was needed. Ant was the bank, of course, because he had more money now than he knew what to do with. According to Jim, Ant wouldn't even take rent from the tenants at the three-decker. They were all living there rent-free.

There were also hot rods and sports cars, bling, flashy clothes, and games. Ant kept wads of Ben Franklins rolled up in his pockets as though he was some thug rapper starring in a music video, walking around flipping people money. *Here, entertain me.* There was one occasion, when Ant went up to someone and said, "Here," tossing her a few hundred bucks, "make me smile."

Ant Calabro was Mr. Big Shot with all the dough.

According to Jim Morel, Ant was one of about five friends who, "Networking out, you must understand: we created our own family atmosphere. Our own place. Our own ideals. Our own rules. And our own standards on *every*thing. We became our *own* family. We trusted each other with our lives. We weren't just friends—we were brothers."

MARGARET MENZ WAS WATCHING television one day not long after Marina had suffered her fatal fall down the stairs. Rumors were rampant that Ant had had something to do with Marina's death, but the cops had investigated and closed the case. Officially, Marina's death was ruled a tragic accident.

As Menz watched television, hearing a ruckus outside her window, she got up and went over to the window to look out, where she observed Ant smashing many of Marina's things, including her furniture and some knickknacks..

Strange, Menz thought, as she looked on.

Ant finished busting up Marina's belongings, and then put the broken remains out with the rubbish.

That's so impersonal, Menz thought to herself, wondering if the guy just didn't have any respect for the woman's memory?

As the days turned into weeks, Ant began to host music and parties inside his portion of the three-decker, get-togethers which lasted well into the wee hours of the morning and into the next day. Parties full of yelling and screaming and things such as TVs, Radios, Beer bottles, being thrown out the windows.

They were living like they thought they were rock stars. All on Marina's money.

Within approximately a month after Marina's death, Jim Morel was hanging out a lot in Quincy at "the house," the three-decker Marina had left Ant. The apartment was in shambles: holes in the walls, empty bottles of booze everywhere, people sleeping here and there. One morning, at around 3:00 a.m., the place resembled a real-life animal house, as there were about fifteen people in the apartment being out of control, making a lot of noise with their shouting, drinking, smoking, and blaring loud music.

"We were all just singing this random song, chanting, loudly … singing … drunk out of our minds," Jim Morel recalled. "I remember thinking, God, the neighbors must *hate* us."

Jim reported that he even mentioned something about it

at the time to Jason Weir.

"Who cares," Weir said. "They won't say anything. They live here for free. Ant doesn't even charge them rent, he just doesn't care."

Jim and Ant sat down to go over that business partnership they had entered into. "Believe it or not," Jim said, "Ant was intelligent. He knew percentages and business. He understood that the money he was giving me for the band was paying him back with a good profit margin."

The drugs and the alcohol were getting to Ant, however, it did little to deaden an obvious pain growing within. For Jim, the question was, *Where was all that pain coming from—Marina's death?*

The mourning was over. Jim couldn't help but wonder what was bothering Ant? What was he running from?

The money, Jim realized, gave Ant a sense of power because he seemed to believe he could buy anything he wanted. It wasn't unlike him to have one hundred thousand dollars in cash hanging around the house. Meanwhile, he knew that when the cash was gone, he could get at least another $500K for the house itself, so if he needed the money, he'd just sell the house.

One day, Ant had an epiphany, and told Morel of his plan to start his own business.

"Mercenaries," Jim Morel said. "Yes, *mercenaries*. I thought it was completely, totally ridiculous."

Yes, Ant was about to put into action his dream of starting a professional hit man service. Jim explained, "With the kind of guys, like, you see in the movies. Basically, you go there and you pay the guy and he comes in and he either really scares the person, or kills them, or whatever the person orders."

Ant approached Jim one day with a concept for the business, saying, "I want to create a website."

"Look," Jim told him, "I don't want *anything* to do with this, man. I think it's kind of, well, stupid."

"Okay."

Jim couldn't help but think that a professional contract killer, as Ant had said he wanted to be, would never create a website and advertise his intentions.

"It just seemed like a really *stupid* idea." Then again, according to Morel, part of him believed that Ant couldn't have really been serious. More likely, he was just bored with his life. He was rich and could have anything he wanted. He just needed something to keep himself occupied.

Like everyone else around them, Jim was certain Ant, Lally and Weir had deliberately killed Marina, and in doing so, had reached their high point, especially Ant. They had killed someone and gotten away with it. What more was there?

"My personal theory," Jim pondered, "is that [Ant] felt that he's had his high, high up: they had just killed somebody and got away with it." Part of that "high" involved Ant taking Marina's knickknacks and placing them in the house next to the walls, lined up like targeted apples or cans, then they'd take knives or crossbows and aim for them. At the time, Jim believed it was just a strange way that Ant was showing his grief. "It wasn't my place to judge how the guy mourned his aunt's passing."

Their behavior escalated and they even bought a grenade launcher and went out into the woods and started to launch grenades. Grenades! Scary, sure. Crazy, absolutely. Maybe just another way, Jim considered, of a grieving kid with too much money to act out in an attempt at finding something to entertain himself. Jim believed that Ant was discovering that happiness was not for sale.

There came a time during the summer of 2002 when Ant became quiet and everything changed. When the money did little to stimulate him anymore, and the toys he bought became boring, Ant went in search for a new incentive for getting up every morning.

"It was like this role playing game," Jim explained. "That none of us"—Lally and Weir, included—"were all that interested in."

At one point, Jim went over to Ant's apartment and, "I counted like twenty-five spiral-bound notebooks in where [Ant] was writing all these stories."

Those stories would soon turn into Ant's new reality. He'd gather a group of "thirty to forty people at a time," Jim said, "and head out into the woods. They'd all sit down together. They all had ranks." It was an imaginary *Lord of the Flies* world Ant had created all by himself. "It was like this weird cult type of thing ... pretty messed up."

What Jim learned was that Ant had made up this "gothic, dark world, in which he was the leader ... people would come to him and ask to be part of this world ... part of another world."

Ant's version of Dungeons and Dragons.

Sometimes Ant's pawns would go into the woods, Jim said, early in the morning, and sit in the same place until midnight, all under Ant's orders.

"Ant had crazy manipulation powers."

With the arrival of the Fall of 2002, Ant's money was almost gone. He had basically blown hundreds of thousands of dollars on nothing much more than a Corvette, booze, drugs, parties, and an ultimate reality game.

"He bought insane amounts of mercenary equipment," Jim said. "He used to have all these fatigues, they would tie each other up and say, 'OK, you have a minute-and-a-half to get out of it.' They'd practically rip their skin off just to get out of it."

With little money left, Ant started thinking about selling

Marina's house. He was out of cash and out of his mind.

At the same time, Jason Weir wanted to exit the group. According to Jim, Weir was looking to get his life back on track. Weir sat with Jim in a TGIF restaurant on October 13, 2002, as the two discussed their mutual desire for a more meaningful future. . To Jim, the dinner was like old times, the two of them hangin out, talking about life. The chaos of Ant and his wild life was outside the door, an arm's length away, but inside that restaurant, they were two friends discussing their futures—and none of that crazy behavior of Ant's mattered in that moment. They talked about how good things were going with the band. Maybe they'd score a recording deal, perhaps even tour, thinking of the women, the fun of it all.

But Ant still managed to occupy their thoughts and their conversation. It was like he was always there. They both commented on how crazy all their lives had gotten since Marina's death. It had been almost ten months by then. Ant was out of control.

"My little sister," Jason Weir told Jim, "I need to be a good role model for her."

Jim nodded his head in agreement. It was heartbreaking for him to hear such a thing. He knew how deep the group had gotten themselves. Jason Weir wanted to get out of it all and lead a somewhat normal life, but Jim felt that he, himself, could not.

As they discussed Ant more in depth, Jim could tell Weir was harboring a secret that weighed heavily on him. Ant, Jim soon learned from Weir, had a good reason for the role-playing quasi Dungeons and Dragons/*Lord of the Flies* type of club he had started.

"He wanted to escape reality," Jim said. "I knew this once Jay [Weir] started telling me about what happened to Marina."

"He spent all his money," Weir said.

"Damn," Jim responded. "We need to get you on track, though, Jay."

Weir had an odd look about him. "Marina," he said quietly, leaning in toward Jim, looking around the restaurant to see if anyone was watching or listening, "she didn't exactly die on her own."

"What? What do you mean?" Jim was "floored" by the comment. At first, he thought, *I don't want to know anything more ... don't tell me anything ... I don't want to know.*

"Tom [Lally] ...," Weir whispered, "he beat her to death."

"Huh?" The thoughts running through Jim's mind were of his own grandmother, a fragile woman, like Marina, being beaten by three kids. What Marina must have gone through. The pain. The terror. Her last moments, realizing that her grandson's friends were beating her to death.

"What happened?" Jim asked.

"Tom hit her with a frying pan."

"What were *you* doing?" Jim wanted to know.

"I was just freaked out."

After talking more about what had happened the night Marina died, Jim was in a rough spot when he left TGIF's in Norton with Jason Weir on October 13, 2002. If he didn't tell someone, he was now part of it.

What should I do? Turn in my friends?

When Jim got home, he went straight to his father.

" I knew inside that he was going to go to the police if *I* didn't."

"I was thinking I was going to do this all anonymously, no one would ever know anything about me—walk in, walk out...."

Mr. Good Samaritan.

Uh ... not quite.

At home, preparing to go to the police in Norton, Jim

began to think about his friend, Anthony Calabro. Jim had always viewed Ant as a sort of lost soul, a kid who never really fit in with any specific group. That alternate reality Ant had created out in the woods, Jim realized, was because his own life was such a complete waste. Ant needed a place, Jim realized,, where "he was a God and he had all these minions, yet a place where none of these horrible things had happened. Someplace where he wasn't just some random guy."Jim actually felt sorry for him.

Still, Jim knew that the right thing to do was to go to the police.

Knocking on the glass partition separating him from the Norton cop who was sitting reading a magazine on that late Sunday night when Jim and his dad walked into the stationhouse, Jim said, "I guess I want to … well, like, I don't know, report a murder."

Jim thought bells and whistles would go off after he said it. That the cops would drop everything and roll out the red carpet for him. Come on in. Tell us what happened. You're a hero, son.

But that's not how it went.

The cop looked up from his magazine, handed Jim a slip of paper and said, "Fill that out. Someone will be out to speak with you in a minute."

So Jim sat and wrote down exactly what he had discussed with Jason Weir earlier that day inside the TGIFs.

At the time Jim walked into the police station, he was well known, not in a good way, mind you, by the same cops he was now going to ask to be his allies.

After a while, Jim was walked into an interview suite in the back of the police station.

Two detectives soon came into the room.

Jim was making some fairly strong allegations here, and the detectives were aware that it was entirely possible his true motive was just to protect himself.

"What is it about Sundays," Jim said one of the cops said aloud, mockingly, "that everyone likes to confess on Sundays."

Jim looked at the cop. "What? I didn't do this!" To himself, Jim thought, *What if I actually get blamed for this?* Or, what if, when confronted with Jim's story, Weir, Lally, and Ant each pointed a finger at Jim and said he was there, too?

"They [the detectives] rode me and wouldn't let me leave the police station," Jim said. "For hours."

After answering the same questions repeatedly, Jim felt the interview wasn't going anywhere. He believed he was being backed into a corner by the detectives, and that they didn't want to let him leave unless he confessed.

"I can prove myself," Jim blurted out.

"How?" asked one of the detectives.

"I'll wear a wire. I'll record Jay saying that he did it."

Due to the delay caused by the court order, four days went by before Jim would be able to call his friend and set up a meeting. The phone call from the investigator came, telling Jim it was time, so he went down to the stationhouse, got wired up, and then he returned home and called Jason Weir.

"Jay, can you pick me up? I need to go to the mall to get a sweater."

"Sure. Be right over," Weir said.

Jim was ready. He had several undercover cops ready to follow him and Weir wherever they went. The game was on.

Scared doesn't even begin to describe how Jim felt. One of the main reasons, he explained, turned out to be that, "One, I know that Jay always carries a gun with him, or at least a knife. He's very, very guarded."

The day before the meeting, Jim's dad suggested he carry his grandfather's gun.

Two guns, Jim knew, equaled a showdown.

He wanted no part of the OK Corral.

As Weir was on his way over, Jim sat and thought about the day: *Just get him to admit it again and get back home. Get it over with and get out of there.*

"But after he picked me up," Jim later recalled. "That's when things got really, really crazy."

JASON WEIR PICKED JIM up on schedule. Weir was calm. He seemed okay. As they drove away, Jim said, "You know what, before we go out to the mall, can we stop to get a burger or something … I'm starving."

"Sure." (Jim was thinking, *I'm going to get this done and over with right now, during the first three minutes into our lunch.*)

They sat down.

"Hey, that stuff you told me a few days ago," Jim said, "was pretty disturbing."

Weir thought for a moment. "Oh yeah, you mean about the murder."

"Yeah, Yeah."

"Oh …" Weir said—and, all over again, he proceeded to explain to Jim what happened.

They finished eating. *That was easy enough.* Jim could go get his sweater, go home and be done with it all.

But then the unexpected happened (doesn't it always!). Weir was driving toward the mall. Jim was sitting shotgun thinking he had the entire thing in the bag. Then something went wrong.

Looking in the rearview mirror, "We're being followed," Weir said. "Do you know we're being followed, Jim?"

"What? Shit. No way!" Jim said, looking in the mirror. (To himself: *Those stupid cops. Damn-it-all.*)

"These cops couldn't even stay back far enough so Jay

couldn't see them," Jim recalled. "I warned them that they all watch *Forensic Files* and *CSI* and all those shows. They study this stuff. Stupid cops."

Then the car following behind—because the cops could hear what was being said inside Weir's truck—fell back and disappeared.

The situation got worse, however.

Jason Weir's cell phone rang. "Yeah?" he said. ("This phone call," Jim explained, "haunts my dreams to this day!") Weir started screaming into the phone. "What the fuck! The cops are at my house right now? They think I did *what*?"

What was Weir talking about?

Someone had called to warn Weir that there were cops at his house looking for him.

Jim couldn't believe it. The cops were jumping in *now*?

As Weir continued talking, Jim thought: *I should have grabbed that gun my dad wanted me to.*

Weir sped up. He was cruising now at about 65-70 MPH. *I should bail out. Right now. Jump out of this truck ...*

Weir hung up as he drove.

Jim was worried that Weir, if he knew Jim was wearing a wire, would "kill me and kill himself right there."

After Weir hung up, he looked at Jim with the "most disgusted look" he could muster.

Jim asked, "What happened, man?"

"I don't even want to talk about it."

From there, Weir pulled off the highway and sped toward what Jim called a "really shady looking apartment building."

He parked. Looked at Jim. All business now, Weir said, "Get out. Come with me."

Jim was sweating. He wondered if he should make a run for it or go in. He looked around and didn't see any of his cop friends. Weir had lost the tail.

Shit.

Jim risked it, he said, and went inside with Weir. There were five or six guys in the apartment, Jim recalled, "and they're all, like, tripping and messed up."

"Jim, just go into that bedroom over there," Weir said, pointing, "and wait for me."

Jim walked in and began looking around for anything he could use as a weapon. There were no windows. So he sat on the bed.

Weir entered a few minutes later. He sat down. Flipped his cell phone open and dialed a friend.

Come to find out, Jim was worrying about nothing. Apparently, several cops had gone to Weir's house to question him about another matter entirely—a burglary. It had nothing to do with Marina's death.

"Jim," Weir said, "you gotta help me out, man. I was never there. You gotta tell the cops I was with you. They think I broke into this house."

"Sure, man, whatever you need." Jim was shaking. He couldn't control his body.

"Let's just go get my sweater, Jay. Let's get out of here."

Jim told his friend, as they settled back into Weir's truck and got back on the road, "One last time ... I want you to tell me what happened one last time and I never want to talk about it ever again. If there's ever a problem, I want to know the entire story so I can help you."

Jim's nerves were so frayed, he said later, that when Weir told the story again, adding more "sick details" than he had before, it nearly put Jim over the edge.

After Weir finished and Jim collected himself, he said, "Okay, there's murder weapons hidden in the woods. Let's go find them *right* now."

Weir drove out into the woods where he thought the weapons had been hidden, but they couldn't find anything. It was getting dark.

The next day, Jim took detectives out to the same spot and they found some newspapers from the date Marina had been killed that they believed the weapons had been wrapped in. But the weapons were not there.

Nevertheless, law enforcement had enough to make three arrests; but they couldn't do it right away, Jim was told.

"What?" He wanted it over. He wanted Jason Weir, Thomas Lally, and Anthony Calabro taken into custody immediately. He had just ratted out his three best friends. He needed this to be over.

THE MASSACHUSETTS STATE POLICE put together a case against Thomas Lally first. By October 25, 2002, several detectives headed over to Lally's Taunton Avenue home in Norton to pick Lally up and charge him with Marina Calabro's murder.

Lally gave himself up without as much as a snort.

Sergeant Kevin Shea, from the MSP, and Lieutenant Paul Keenan, from the QPD, brought Lally into an interview room inside the Norton Police Department.

Shea went through procedure and had Lally agree and sign all of his Miranda rights into effect.

"We have information," Shea began, "that leads us to believe you were involved with Anthony Calabro and Jason Weir in conspiring and killing ... Marina Calabro."

Thomas Lally stared.

"Can you tell us how the plot to murder Ms. Calabro began?" Shea asked.

Lally went quiet for a brief moment. Then shrugged. "Sure. It started with Anthony."

"How do you know Anthony?" Shea asked.

"I met him through an old girlfriend. We hung out together. Anthony never had any money. He liked to play that game Dungeons and Dragons. Anthony always thought he was a tough guy. He acted like it. He wanted to be a hit man. ... Anthony was always being bullied, so, you know, I never thought anything about what he said, but he kept persisting to be this tough guy."

The story Lally told seemed to make sense about how a murder plot like this—so vicious, callous and ruthless, a senseless act of violence built around a staple of greed and selfishness—could have taken place over the course of a year. According to Lally, Ant started visiting Marina in Quincy more and more as she handed money over and wrote checks for anything Ant wanted. This seemingly endless flow of cash whet Ant's appetite, however, and made him want *even more*. And then one day, Lally said, "Anthony told me he would inherit a lot of money when she died."

And the seed was planted.

When Ant entered his "hit man" stage, where all he ever talked about was starting his own business and killing people for money, the subject of killing Marina came up, Lally said. "Anthony would joke around, saying, 'I should take out a contract on her [Marina].'" So there was one day when Lally called him on it, "What if, Ant, something just *happened* to her?"

Months went by. Ant and Lally would discuss killing Marina at various times, Lally said. Then, as they were sitting around getting high and Marina was out shopping one afternoon, Lally said Anthony brought it up again: "Well, this needs to be done."

Lally then described the murder in detail.

It was near 3:30 p.m. in the afternoon, on that fateful day when Thomas Lally approached Marina with a frying pan he had placed inside a pillowcase. Ant had left the apartment after learning what Lally was about to do. Ant's job was to act as a lookout outside and make sure no one interrupted the murder.

"What are you doing with that frying pan?" Marina asked Lally.

"I'm doing this!" Lally said, smashing Marina in the head.

As she screamed, Lally grabbed Marina by the head and wrestled with her inside the kitchen.

She fell near the stove.

With Marina on the ground, Lally grabbed a tea pot and bashed her in the head several times. Then he choked her, screaming into her ear, "Just go … just go … Anthony wants it this way."

"Anthony, help me … help me …" Marina had said loud as she could.

Within a few moments of being choked, Marina passed out.

Lally put a pillow case over her head and suffocated the woman to make certain she was dead.

With Marina lying cold on the floor, Lally heard Ant in the hallway outside the door talking to someone. (It was Menz, who had come by while Ant was in the truck sitting with his dog outside.)

When he was done talking to Menz, Ant opened the door, saw Marina, nodded his head, and went back outside to his truck.

Lally figured Marina had caught him on the face with her nails and bit him. He had deep gouges and bite marks. Knowing what he knew from watching all those forensic shows, Lally cleaned underneath all of Marina's fingernails, scraping any DNA off.

Then he and the others cleaned the apartment spotless.

In planning the murder, Lally had placed newspapers over the floor. After collecting the newspapers into a pile, he placed the tea pot, frying pan, pot holders he had used, and anything else with blood on it (from the gash in Marina's head), into a plastic bag and put the bag in the back of his truck.

The deed was done.

LATER THAT NIGHT, OCTOBER 25, 2002, Jason Weir and Anthony Calabro were both arrested. In March 2006, after a short trial, Thomas Lally was convicted of first-degree murder in the slaying of Marina Calabro and is now serving a life sentence without the possibility of parole. June of the same year, Ant pleaded guilty to second-degree murder for his role of acting as a lookout. He will be eligible for parole after serving 15 years.

"I know that no words that I say will ever bring back Marina," Ant said in an apology to his family members present in court for his sentencing. "I'm disgusted with myself. I'm disgusted with my lack of action in attempting to stop it or anything else for that matter."

In exchange for his testimony against Lally, Jason Weir agreed to plead guilty to manslaughter. He received a 10-year sentence.

But then there was Jim Morel—the guy who had turned in his friends. If you recall, my true-crime tale began with Jim being attacked and slashed with a knife as he jogged.

Whatever came of that, you might be asking at this point?

Jim made it home that day after being stabbed by two men who had obviously wanted him dead. Jim's mother walked into the bathroom while he was cleaning himself up.

"Oh my God, Jimmy, what happened?"

"I was attacked …"

Mrs. Morel called the police.

When the police showed up, one of the officers asked Jim what happened. According to Jim, he explained how he had been attacked by two knife-wielding men driving a blue car. They had to be part of Ant's group. This was payback.

Jim had broken one of the golden rules of the street: he had given up his boys.

The cop said, "Oh no, no … we were in that area, we would have seen or heard something."

"I was attacked, man. Can't you see that I'm bleeding?" Jim said.

Jim Morel admitted that he had always had a "kind of touch and go relationship with the police." He was a punk during his youth. But this—to accuse him of slicing up his own skin, as he had felt the cops were suggesting, how could they even *think* such a thing?

The two guys who slashed up Jim's arm were never caught.

The cops told Jim to file a complaint if he wanted to.

Jim never did.

MURDER IN MASSACHUSETTS

TO BEGIN WITH, THERE is no doubt that 42-year-old Patricia Olsen called the seafood restaurant she owned, aptly named "Mrs. O's", first thing in the morning on January 10, 2005, a typically frigid winter day in New England. We know this because, according to the court testimony of Mrs. O's employee Rosa Nicola, Patricia phoned in the same request she had on most other mornings. We are, after all, creatures of habit, if nothing else.

"Rosa," Patricia said in her scratchy, smoker's voice, "can you bring me a breakfast sandwich over to the house for Neil." Neil Olsen, a big man with brown hair and a resolute smile, a forty-eight year old country boy at heart, was Patricia's husband of twelve years.

Everybody liked Neil Olsen.

"Certainly, Mrs. Olsen," Rosa answered.

Mrs. O's was located just down the road from Neil and Patricia Olsen's home on South Main Street, just outside downtown Lanesborough, Massachusetts. It took Rosa only a few minutes to make the sandwich and get it over to the house.

Patricia greeted Rosa at the door and, as usual, invited her in, feeling the need to say (for some strange reason), "I didn't sleep well last night. I took three Tylenol PM pills."

Standard idle chit-chat between an employer and her employee, or so it seemed. Patricia adored Rosa. Most people did. Rosa was a hard worker, one of only a few Patricia had hired in the two years since she'd opened the restaurant.

Rosa nodded. "OK, Mrs. Olsen."

Patricia later told police, "Neil eats breakfast every morning. I don't normally eat breakfast, maybe once a week." Rosa was good about bringing Neil his breakfast *every* morning. It was her routine. Later, in court, Patricia recalled a time when Rosa once went on vacation. "I thought Neil was going to go nuts. I *hate* cooking breakfast."

Upon entering the Olsen household, Rosa wondered where Neil was.

"He's out in the barn," Patricia explained. "I think he's working."

Rosa put the sandwich down on the counter and drove back to the restaurant. It would be the last ordinary, routine situation Rosa and Patricia ever experienced together. Moments after Rosa left, somewhere around 8:00 a.m., Lanesborough Police chief F. Mark Bashara arrived for duty at about the same time as a 911 call came into the Lanesborough Police Department (LPD), a call that rocked this quaint New England town off its axis.

THE 911 CALLER WAS Patricia Olsen. She was frantic. Terribly upset. She said she'd just found Neil dead in the barn, a separate building connected to his sign-making workshop, not too far away from the house he and Patricia lived in. She had no idea what happened. She had gone out to bring him his morning coffee and breakfast sandwich when she saw the most horrible thing.

Bashara had known Neil and Patricia for several years. Neil was a local business owner, a sign maker. For the most part, Neil lettered trucks and cars. He was quite the whiz with a brush and some paint and had an excellent reputation in town. Not a soul in Lanesborough had anything bad to say about old Neil Olsen's work, not to mention his upright character.

Bashara soon heard that Neil had been found dead in his barn, and that Patricia was beside herself. She couldn't tell what happened. Soon after realizing something was terribly wrong ("My goodness, all that blood, Neil just lying there, still as a sack of potatoes."), Patricia explained to Bashara, she ran back into the kitchen to call 911.

"I thought he had fallen," Patricia said later. "I thought maybe he had a heart attack." Bashara and another officer hopped into two separate cruisers and raced out to the Olsen place. In between the time Patricia called 911 and Bashara's arrival, Patricia had called Rosa Nicola again and explained how she had found Neil in the barn, believing Neil was dead.

Startled and quite upset by this, Rosa immediately rushed over to the house.

When she got there, Rosa later recalled, Patricia was "standing over the kitchen sink, vomiting."

When Patricia finished, she and Rosa sat down. Rosa knew Neil well. She liked him. It was indescribable to think he was dead. Impossible to believe. How could it have happened? Neil was one of those guys who was just always there. He never went anywhere far from town.

He was always working around the house, or driving through town in his truck, waving to friends and neighbors.

"That horse killed him!" Patricia blurted out, to Rosa's surprise. Patricia was speaking of Neil's beloved horse, Hannah. Every night, like clockwork, Neil went out to the barn between 11:00 and 11:30 P.M. to feed Hannah. Apparently, Patricia had slept through the night after taking those three Tylenol PMs, unaware that Neil hadn't returned to bed from the routine feeding.

"What?" Rosa asked. She had a hard time swallowing the notion that Neil's own horse had killed him.

"It's my fault," Patricia said. Now the widow was crying. She was almost hysterical. Blaming herself. "I took too many pills. Otherwise I would have been awake."

LOCATED IN THE EASTERN region of Massachusetts, quite close to the border of New York, Lanesborough is part of Berkshire County. The Pittsfield (Massachusetts) metro area is due south. With just under 3,000 residents, Lanesborough median household income comes in at about $46,000, five thousand more than the national average at the time in 2005. Lanesborough is not considered a mecca for crime. Not at all. In fact, the last murder here occurred in 1980, some 23 years before Neil Olsen's suspicious death. Lanesborough residents, we could say without argument, are used to going about their business, without the concern of being accosted or bothered with the kind of crime that has beleaguered other Berkshire towns. Violent crime stats of any sort were so low here between the years 1980 and 2000, that in addition to the one homicide which had taken place in 1983, there were only nine rapes and four robberies were reported during that entire span of time. With numbers like those, most would agree that Lanesborough is one of the safest places on the planet to live.

Still, when the call of a DOA went out, announcing an untimely death had occurred out at the Olsen place, it wasn't that the L.P.D. were unprepared, it's just that murder would have been the last thing on any cop's mind as he or she pulled up and began to look at the scene. Murder just didn't happen in these parts.

Patricia was convinced that Neil had been trampled to death by Hannah, his beloved 31-year-old former trotter race horse. At least that was her initial belief when L.P.D. chief Mark Bashara arrived on that chilly morning just moments after Patricia's 911 call.

"We believed at the time," Bashara said later, describing the crime scene, "that Neil Olsen was actually killed by the horse."

Inside the barn where Neil kept Hannah, Bashara walked into a bloody mess unlike any he had likely ever seen in his decades behind the badge. The horse, undoubtedly spooked, had blood all over her, as she was making snorting sounds and running wild around the inside of the barn.

Patricia was "distraught," Bashara added. She was sitting at the kitchen table inside the house when he first arrived: smoking, speaking in broken sentences, crying, shaking her head. Patricia couldn't believe what had happened. Of all the things, Neil, who had so much adored his beautiful Hannah, had been trampled to death by the same animal he loved so dearly! How could an animal turn on its owner like this—especially a horse?

To Patricia, however, as she sat and thought about it more and more, Hannah's killing Neil, well, it didn't seem all that surprising to her after all. "Hannah is a thirty-one-year-old miserable bitch," was how Patricia described the horse to police. "We've had her for, I think, three years. We got her from one of Neil's friends. I say Hannah is miserable because she doesn't let anyone ride her. Neil bought me a saddle a couple of years ago. I wanted a horse to ride. At night, he always let the horse in because she won't listen to me. The routine is to bring her in and give her a can of grain." Patricia had put the horse in the barn only once, she said. "Even if Neil fell asleep before 11:00, he would get up and bring Hannah in at around 11:30."

After speaking with Patricia, Bashara entered Neil's sign shop, just beyond the breezeway almost connecting the house to the barn, and he re-entered the barn. As he approached Neil's body, he could see there wasn't much left to Neil's head. The scene was horrific. The veteran chief looked down and noticed Neil's face was nearly gone, his head nothing but an unrecognizable slush of blood, tissue, and brain. Neil's face and head had been smashed to bits, as if someone had taken a sledgehammer to a melon. Bashara had once hired Neil to letter some of the police cruisers. Bashara knew and liked Neil Olsen, which made the scene before him all the more horrific.

After Bashara had a look at Neil's remains, he called in one of his coworkers, Officer Jim Rathbun, and radioed the Massachusetts State Police Detective Unit. Before he released the scene and wrote the whole thing off as a terrible accident, it was worth having the big boys come in and take a quick look, see what they thought.

Officer Jim Rathbun was down the road when he took Bashara's call. Arriving at the Olsen house by approximately 8:45 a.m., Rathbun and Bashara "secured" what they were now calling a bona fide crime scene. Whether a horse had committed the act or not, Neil Olsen was dead, that much was a fact, the barn was potentially the scene of a homicide. Detectives would have to investigate. The integrity of the scene needed to be protected.

There was a solid, well-packed coating of snow on the ground around the Olsen property and all about town. It was overcast, thirty-two degrees Fahrenheit. The wind blew in from the southwest at about ten miles per hour. A recent snowstorm had pummeled the region, burying Lanesborough and the surrounding communities. On this morning, however, Bashara, could have looked out on eight miles of visibility, despite the ripening conditions for another major Nor'easter.

Rathbun closed the gate inside the barn to seal off Neil's body from Hannah; this way, the horse couldn't taint the crime scene any more than she already had.

As Rathbun shut the gate, the horse got nervous and restless, and Rathbun had to hurriedly go about his business, "afraid," he later said, "of the horse."

After that, Rathbun walked into the kitchen of the main

house, where Patricia was sitting at the kitchen table, still shaken up and crying, chain-smoking cigarettes. ("She appeared very upset, very distraught," Rathbun recalled.)

"I cannot believe this is happening," Patricia lashed out to no one in particular. Her husband, her confidant, as she later put it, the one man she had loved more than any other, was gone. Just like that. Puff! Here one minute, dead the next.

What the hell happened?

"Please, somebody wake me up!" Patricia said.

Rathbun asked Patricia what she and Neil had done the previous night. He was making idle chit-chat, perhaps, waiting for MSP detectives to arrive and assess the situation. The woman obviously needed someone to sit with and talk— or, rather, to listen to her.

Patricia suffered from Crohn's disease, like three of her four sisters. Crohn's is a debilitating intestinal tract disorder that can knock a person down and keep him or her bedridden for days, in some cases weeks. Some even die from long-term complications.

"Three [of Patricia's sisters] ended up with Crohn's disease," a family member later told me. "One of Pat's sisters died in 2000 of complications from cancer that was so widespread,that when they found it, there was nothing doctors could do. She had just turned forty-three the week she died."

"I took some Tylenol," Patricia told Rathbun. "I went to bed after playing video games with Neil."

"She often took the Tylenol," a family member later explained to me, "routinely, because of her Crohn's disease."

"What about this morning?" Rathbun asked.

"I woke up and found the television still on. I assumed Neil was already in the shop working."

Neil was a workaholic. Having his shop connected to his

home only further contributed to his obsessive work ethic.

Rathbun said later that he asked Patricia about Hannah—and that's when she became annoyed and angry, lashing out, saying, "The horse would sometimes kick us" if poked in a way that wasn't to its liking. "Temperamental, that damn horse. Spoiled rotten. I want that horse gone," Patricia raged to Rathbun, "or I'll kill it myself."

It seemed Patricia couldn't bear to look at the horse again, knowing what it had done to her husband.

At this point Patricia started ranting about "funeral costs" and not having enough insurance to cover Neil's impending funeral expenses. The man hadn't even been lifted from the scene of his death and his wife was worried about spending money she claimed she didn't have.

To say the least, this little ripple in Patricia's story sent up red flags.

After Rathbun finished talking with Patricia, he met with Bashara outside. By then, detectives from the MSP had arrived. State Trooper Jean Thibodeau approached the two local cops and asked them what they had found earlier upon their arrival. Then Thibodeau went into the barn with the medical examiner, who himself had just pulled up to the scene, and began processing the barn, hunting for more information which might lead to answers to this bizarre set of circumstances.

Walking across horse manure and hay, Thibodeau bent down and took a closer look at Neil's head, asking herself, *Could a horse have done this? Was it even possible?*

After assessing the scene, Thibodeau searched around the floor of the barn near Neil's head. She spied several small-caliber, spent shell casings.

It was odd, or maybe just a coincidence, that there were shell casings in the barn. Perhaps Neil had taken target practice from inside the barn? Maybe he pressed his own ammunition?

Was the guy a hunter?

Thibodeau walked out of the barn and combed the immediate area for more evidence that might explain what had happened. There had to be something else. Something they were missing.

Within a few moments, the detective turned a corner in back of the barn and, just beyond the barn doors, there in the snow, she spotted something that was about to turn this investigation on its head.

PATRICIA OLSEN GREW UP in Bennington, Vermont. A family member said she was no different than any other kid. As the youngest of a family of all girls, Patricia was, of course, playing catch up all the time. When she saw that one of her sisters had graduated early from high school under an accelerated program, Patricia wanted to do the same thing. So, at 15 years old, she went to her mother and asked.

Patricia's mother, however, said the only way she'd "approve it" was if Patricia agreed to go to college after graduation.

"Yes," Patricia told her mother. "I'll do that."

But as soon as she graduated, Patricia put college off for a year. During that time, she met James Robinson, a local kid.

"James was the only boyfriend Patricia ever had," that family member told me.

Foregoing college, Patricia chose to marry James a year later, soon after she turned eighteen. The marriage didn't last long. In 1989, after having two kids, Christopher and Amanda, Patricia divorced James. A year after the divorce, Patricia started commuting to Pittsfield, working as a comptroller for Lenco, an armored truck company. Getting away from the town she grew up in, if only to work, was important to Patricia. Although Bennington was home to some 15,000 people, Pittsfield was much larger (45,000). The two towns were only 25 miles away from each other, but worlds apart. Pittsfield offered Patricia a fresh start. A new scene. Different people. Since high school, she had dated one man, become a housewife and mother, and never really had a chance to have a life beyond small-town Bennington. Now she was single for what was effectively the first time, fully prepared to take on life. The kids, Amanda and Christopher, ended up staying with their father in Bennington. Patricia didn't abandon them, she and a family member later said, but due to her suffering so badly from Crohn's, she felt she couldn't work and handle the children at the same time.

By then, Neil had been in the sign-making business for about five years. He did a lot of business with Lenco. One day, while at the office, Neil bumped into Patricia and, after she "openly flirted" with him, they started talking.

"I used to pay him," Patricia told police, "when he got done lettering."

Neil did the work, Patricia cut him a check.

Unbeknownst to her, Neil was in love.

Then, in March 1993, Neil got up the nerve to approach Patricia with an offer. "I need to talk to you," he said one afternoon after she handed him his check.

"Oh," Patricia remarked. "About what?"

Neil didn't say. Instead, he invited her to his house in Lanesborough that night.

Intrigued and, admittedly having a "crush" on Neil, Patricia agreed to dinner.

"I fell in love with you the first time I saw you," Neil told Patricia that night.

She was stunned.

"You know," Neil continued, "we're always busy while at work." He said he'd never had the opportunity to express how he felt. He felt the need to speak out. Patricia was all he thought about. "This may sound strange," Neil said at some point after dinner, "but I want you to move in with me."

Patricia was speechless.

Neil walked over to a desk in his living room. "I have something for you," he said, opening the drawer. In Patricia's words, the rest of the night went like this: "He said he was going to give me a 'get out of this relationship free card,' so if I did move in with him and things didn't work out, I could just leave. He opened his desk drawer and he gave me this stupid plastic skull ring because he said it was all he had for rings."

An otherwise shy and ascetic guy, Neil popped the question, handing Patricia the toy ring. When Patricia left Neil's house, she called a friend and explained what happened. "You're insane," her friend said after Patricia admitted she was thinking about moving in. "You don't even *know* this guy."

Patricia never "even had to think about it," she claimed. She moved in the following Monday.

On May 28, 1994, in a field behind Neil's house, Neil waited beside sixty guests, mostly family and friends, as Patricia drove up the hill to the altar in her Bronco, bridesmaids by her side, cheering her on. A red neck wedding if there ever was one!

After a lovely ceremony amid a perfect New England setting on a beautiful spring afternoon, Neil and Patricia were pronounced husband and wife. According to Patricia, for years things between them went well. They loved, laughed, and enjoyed what was a healthy, uncomplicated relationship.

"It was all fun," she later said, describing those early years.

Neil had graduated from Pittsfield High School in 1974. After that, he studied at Southeastern Massachusetts

University, later completing a degree in business administration at Berkshire Community College. Going into business for himself seemed to fit Neil's nature, friends and family said. After taking a job at several local sign companies—Pittsfield Neon Sign, Industrial Sign, Callahan Sign Company among them—and working toward his full apprenticeship, Neil decided to open up a shop of his own. Almost immediately, Neil's reputation as a master sign-maker worked its way around Berkshire County. Not for painting simple signs, but works of art on fire engines, cars and trucks, along with designing and painting signs for local and national businesses of all types. Neil loved the isolation of retreating to his sign shop and losing himself in his work. There was no mistaking a sign Neil Olsen had made, the craftsmanship alone marked his unique professional signature.

Beyond a love for sign-making, Neil, a member of the United Methodist Church in Lenox, Massachusetts, took great comfort in rebuilding, detailing and refinishing antique cars and trucks —hobbies that fell under the same umbrella of his professional life. It was the meticulous nature of taking something old and making it new again that Neil adored. Yet it was animals that Neil treasured most. His horse Hannah, of course. But also his two dogs, Cletis, a two-year-old Bloodhound, and Bosco, a four-year-old mixed Labrador. Both dogs slept upstairs with Neil and Patricia. Cletis was so big, in fact, Patricia and Neil placed a full-size mattress on the floor next to their bed so he was comfortable at night. It was Bosco who had initially found Neil dead. The dog, obviously confused about what happened, lay down next to Neil in the barn and waited until, Patricia claimed, she walked in with his morning breakfast sandwich and uncovered the ghastly scene. One of the things Neil gave his dogs, family and friends later explained to a local newspaper, was their freedom, essentially. He allowed the dogs to roam the wooded acres around his home. The dogs loved being able to come and go as they pleased.

Neil was a simple man, Patricia insisted, adding that he was never abusive. By June 1998, Patricia had custody of Amanda and Christopher. They were fourteen and sixteen then. Neil thought it was a good husbandly gesture to help Patricia, so they hired an attorney, sued James Robinson for custody, and won. As the kids fell into their new lives in Lanesborough, they started acting out as they both entered high school. Their grades plummeted during their high school years. They became arrogant, wise-ass, and rebellious. Patricia tried her best to control them, but they rarely listened. Christopher, especially, was getting involved in some rather disturbing behavior. What might have seemed to be a misguided youth, disobedient and undirected, Christopher's actions spoke of a dark and menacing seed he harbored, giving the indication that he was mentally unstable. For example, Amanda later said her brother once took a mouse, put it in a jar, filled the jar with lighter fluid, and lit it on fire. More than that, Christopher would go weeks without bathing. He wore all black, painted his hair different colors, and cut himself. He and a friend from school once made a list, Amanda said, that they referred to as a "death list." It consisted of teachers and other kids from school they wanted dead. Christopher downloaded directions from the Internet on how to make a bomb. He called himself an "Anarchist."

"That's when he got in big trouble. He got suspended," Amanda later told police. "That's when Neil pulled him by his hair. Neil yelled at him. I don't remember Neil hitting him though."

Amanda had her own problems. In eighth grade, she was charged with assault after spiking a fellow classmate's drink with Tylenol. The kid was allergic to the over-the-counter medicine and had a terrible reaction.

"My rules weren't working," Patricia said, talking about this period of Christopher and Amanda's lives. "So Neil decided he was going to take over disciplining them. I intervened once in a while," she added, "but tried it and it wasn't working."

Neil took control, indeed, but had little patience. Whereas in most blended families the stress of raising someone else's kids can be detrimental to a marriage, Patricia claimed she and Neil hardly ever had problems because of it, and agreed for the most part on how to punish the kids when they acted out.

"He was my everything," Patricia said. That tension in the house the kids caused hadn't, in any way, she insisted, "affected the marriage."

Christopher became more "distant" and eventually "withdrew" from everyone. He didn't want to be part of the family atmosphere at all. The further along he got into high school, the more despondent he became at home, which didn't sit well with Patricia.

But if the kids had changed since living in Lanesborough, so had Patricia.

"After she married Neil, the first two or three years, well, [she] had a very good relationship [with the family]," a family member later told me. "Then she just stopped associating with everyone, as if she was shut off from us. I don't know if it was by Neil or her. Up until today we have never known why. ... It was so strange." There was no one event, in other words, triggering the disengagement. "One day she was just out of our lives. Which meant that as soon as Patricia and Neil got custody of the kids, [we] stopped seeing them, too."

Patricia later said Neil, in the beginning, wanted to teach the kids the strong work ethic he had displayed before them.

He believed he could, by example, show the kids that hard work paid off. Part of his desire to take the time to teach the kids his ways was rooted, Patricia asserted, in his quest to "relieve" her of "the stress" she was experiencing trying to discipline them herself. However, no sooner had Neil and Patricia put their foot down, that the kids' behavior got worse. During one period, Neil caught Amanda repeatedly smoking cigarettes in her room. So when simply telling her she wasn't allowed to smoke in the house didn't work, Neil grabbed his tool box, unhinged her bedroom door and hid it. Now there was an open portal into Amanda's private world. Part of Neil's concern was that she was leaving ashes all over the place; he worried she'd burn the house down. Then Patricia and Neil found a bag of marijuana in Amanda's room. They discarded the remainder and punished Amanda, after Neil and Patricia rolled a joint and smoked it together, Patricia later admitted.

Another time, when Amanda disobeyed a direct order, Neil brought her outside, put a large aluminum rake in her hands, and told her to "re-grade" the gravel driveway before digging a ditch near the edge of the yard.

This set a precedent with Amanda. She'd act out, get grounded, and then was forced to do some sort of physical labor as punishment. When that stopped being effective, Patricia and Neil grounded her until she was eighteen. Amanda was sixteen at that time, so for two full years.

"Every time we let her off, she would turn around and do something else," Patricia said. "She remained grounded throughout much of her high school years."

By this time, Patricia had opened Mrs. O's. It had been a childhood dream to run her own restaurant. She was a great cook and not afraid of hard work. Besides, being out of the house much of the time didn't seem so bad lately, seeing that she was having so many problems with the kids.

As a comptroller in her past, Patricia supervised the financial affairs of Lenco. She was in control, basically, of how much money went out, how much was left. Now she was doing the same thing with Neil's sign-making business, her restaurant, and the household bills and expenses. Anything having to do with the finances, in effect, was under Patricia's governorship. Insurance. Mortgage. Car payments. Food.

All of it.

If being able to control financial circumstances both at home and professionally satisfied one aspect of Patricia's character, not being able to get a firm hold on the children consumed the other. Christopher wasn't doing any better. By the eleventh grade, Patricia and Neil were disappointed to learn Christopher had only accrued enough credits to be in ninth-grade; he'd have to repeat two full grades and wouldn't graduate until two years after his class.

When the reality of the hard work ahead of him hit Christopher, he decided that going to school wasn't worth the effort any longer and he quit.

"Find yourself a job if you're not going to school," Neil told him, demanding that if Christopher was going to live in the house, he had damned well better have a job. "Either that, or get the hell out."

Meanwhile, by Amanda's own later account, she was getting actively involved in harder drugs. After he moved out of the house, she and Christopher started hanging out together with the same crowd.

A runaway train was in motion—one Patricia later claimed she never saw heading off the tracks.

"One thing I've felt about [Christopher]," a blood relative told me, "was that beyond him being a pathological liar, being near him [later] actually gave me the chills."

BACK AT THE OLSEN house on January 10, 2005, shortly

after the MSP arrived, a discovery was made just beyond the barn doors that sent the investigation into a frenzy: "a bloody metal pipe." For an investigation centered at first on Hannah, the alleged murderous mare, now cops were looking at a dramatic turn of events.

As investigators continued working the scene, Patricia was still inside the house wandering around, reportedly distraught over her husband's untimely death.

While investigators were compiling evidence, talking over the situation, undoubtedly preparing to re-enter the house and question Patricia more pointedly, Christopher Robinson, Patricia's son, called. Since being kicked out of the house by Neil, Christopher had lived at various locations—including in his car and wherever else he could find a place to crash. He had even spent some time with Amanda, who now lived with her boyfriend and his father in New York. Patricia, some of her employees later said, at times had even allowed Christopher to sleep at the restaurant, without telling Neil. Over the past few days, however, Christopher, with no job and certainly no money, had been living at a sleazy motel just up the road from the Olsen house.

"I want to come over and visit," Christopher said. Patricia understood that her son knew what had happened and was offering his support, to be there for her. But, at the same rate, "He just didn't sound sympathetic," she later said.

So she told him no. He wasn't welcome.

Before Patricia had dialed 911 that morning, she said she "ran into the barn and touched Neil's leg and saw flashes of objects" around her, such as "Hannah's face and a coffee can filled with grain." What she didn't see—or so she claimed—was all of the blood pooled around Neil's head—and there was plenty of it.

Now detectives had closed off the scene with yellow CSI tape. There was no doubt a homicide had occurred inside the barn. MSP Trooper Stephen Jones, out on the property with colleagues, spotted "a double set of footprints in snow," which led directly from Patricia's and Neil's house to the street. Then Jones, Trooper Carol Zullo, and a chemist, while searching the Skyline Country Club golf course just to the east of the Olsen property, came upon another set of footprints and traced them from the golf course to the Olsen house. While they were photographing the footprints, one of them spied a shiny item in the snow.

"What is it?" asked a trooper.

"Looks like a machete."

They bagged the weapon and went back to the house.

Patricia had called Nicola Casey, an employee, and asked her to come out to the house. While Nicola was there consoling her boss, an officer stayed in the house with the two of them. At some point, the officer asked, "What about funeral arrangements?"

Patricia covered her ears, as if to say she didn't want to hear about anything related to Neil's death. It was all too much to take, she implied. "We have no insurance," Patricia finally answered. "I don't know what I'm going to do."

It was an odd statement. Although Mrs. O's wasn't doing all that well financially, it was still an active business, as was Neil's sign-making enterprise. Not to have insurance through either business—or both—seemed strange. The only way the insurance could have been dropped was if the Olsens had failed to keep up with the premiums.

Nicola went back to work. When she returned to the restaurant, she explained to Christopher, who had been hanging around there most of the morning, what had happened to Neil. He said he had heard the news already. "Go to your mother, Chris," Nicola suggested. "She needs you." Christopher didn't seem to care. He shrugged it off, saying instead, "I'm going to the mall with a friend."

ON JANUARY 11, 2005, the Office of the State Medical Examiner in Holyoke, Massachusetts, released its findings regarding Neil Olsen's death. As the shell casings found near Neil's body had suggested, it was confirmed by the M.E.'s office that Neil had been killed by gunshot wounds—a total of seven. More than that, the M.E. found out Neil had been beaten in the head with a blunt object, likely the metal pipe and/or the machete which state troopers had found outside the barn. The likely scenario seemed to be that Neil Olsen's murderer killed him with a shotgun, but then tried to cover it up by bludgeoning his head into a mess of tissue to make it appear as though he had been trampled to death by his horse.

With that information, detectives headed back over to the Olsen house to give Patricia the bad news that someone had murdered her husband.

Detective Lieutenant Richard Smith, a 27-year veteran of the MSP, was first to tell Patricia they had changed the focus of their investigation. "We no longer believe Neil's horse killed him," Smith stated.

"I'm in shock," Patricia said. "I don't want to accept that Neil is gone."

Considering the circumstances, detectives had an entire new set of questions for the grieving widow. Number one, who might have wanted Neil dead? On the surface, the guy had no enemies. Why would someone kill him? The person responsible for Neil's death obviously hated Neil—that much was clear from the viciousness of the attack. It was no random murder. Nothing was missing from the barn or house. Neil's pockets had been turned inside out and his killer had taken any cash Neil had. But other than that, nothing appeared to be out of place. No tools were missing. No one had broken into the house. Patricia was even home, upstairs, according to her, sleeping off three Tylenol PMs, when seven shots interrupted an otherwise peaceful Berkshire night. She said she had not heard a peep.

In looking at the house, a family member later suggested, Patricia's and Neil's bedroom was upstairs on the south side, almost as far away from the barn as possible. It was late. There was no way she could have heard the shots, this source insisted. In fact, Patricia told detectives she fell asleep after playing a video game with Neil and then having sex while *Desperate Housewives* and the beginning of *Boston Legal* played on television in the background. Neil must have gone out to the barn after Patricia had fallen asleep. On top of that, Patricia had a bad habit of falling asleep with the television on and claimed she needed to have the television on all night in order to sleep. In addition to the Tylenol, she'd had "three or four" glasses of white wine.

The officers asked Patricia if she was willing to head down to the LPD to give a statement.

She thought about it momentarily. "Sure."

At 12:35 p.m., after cops read Patricia her rights as a procedure, she talked about her last day with Neil. There was not an attorney present and Patricia freely offered all the information she could—with the hope, one would assume, of helping to find Neil's killer.

After talking about her life in Bennington and how she met Neil, Patricia went through the entire day. The detail she recalled was remarkable—as if she had written it all down and studied it. She said she "spent most of the day lying on the couch. I didn't feel well." After Neil ate French toast, he kept himself busy sheet-rocking one of the bathrooms. Then one of her employees from the restaurant brought Neil's breakfast by the house after stopping at the local Getty gas station, under orders from Patricia, to pick her up a pack of cigarettes and the *National Enquirer* magazine.

A man's man, Neil was a big fan of Spike Television

programming. He loved the shows about cars and trucks. Spike was running a marathon of car shows on that day. By 10:30 a.m., Neil had taken a break from sheet-rocking and settled down in the living room next to Patricia to watch a few of "his car shows."

At some point, Neil's parents, Ruth and Harold Olsen, stopped by. Patricia, who spent some time cleaning the house before they showed up, greeted the couple outside when they arrived.

"Ruthy," Patricia recalled to police, "went to hug me but I told her not to because I hadn't been feeling well."

"Where's Neil?" Ruth asked.

By then Neil had gone upstairs to play video games.

"I love his parents," Patricia recalled, "they have been good parents to me, but they never call before they come over. Neil and I get pissed off sometimes because we [like] our privacy."

Why would Patricia say she had cleaned the house if she hadn't known Ruth and Harold Olsen were stopping by, since both Christopher and Amanda later told police their mother had gotten extremely lazy the past few years and rarely cleaned anything. According to them, the house was filthy all the time. Rabbit and dog excrement was everywhere, Amanda said, claiming that Patricia just left it there, besides allowing many of the pets to roam freely around the house and even sleep in her room on her bed. Cleaning was something Patricia had given up long ago.

Part of that privacy she and Neil enjoyed so much, Patricia said, included sex. Lots of it. Since Amanda had moved out, Patricia and Neil had the house all to themselves. "[We] had a *lot* of sex at different times of the day. When [Amanda] moved out last year, Neil said it was great because we could run around the house naked."

Ruth and Harold didn't stay long that Sunday. Patricia

was in no mood to entertain. She wanted to do nothing more than rest, drink some wine, and spend time with her husband.

When Ruth and Harold left, Patricia made her and Neil a "roast beef and cheese" sandwich. While Neil ate, he worked on a crossword puzzle. After they finished eating, Patricia sat down on the couch and turned on a movie. Neil went off and did a few chores, but ended up watching the end of the movie with her.

After the movie, Neil painted the dining room wall and put sheetrock compound on the walls in the bathroom. Near 3:30 p.m., he finished working and went upstairs to play video games again.

That's when Patricia phoned Amanda, who was living in New York with her boyfriend, although at that time he was incarcerated. Patricia wanted to know where the Play Station games were. Neil was looking all over the house for a specific game and really upset because he couldn't find it.

While they were on the phone, Amanda's boyfriend called from prison.

"I have to take the call, mother."

Patricia called back ten minutes later. They talked about several of Amanda's friends who were, according to Amanda, worried about getting AIDS. Drugs and unsafe sex between large groups of people is a good recipe for the spread of HIV. It was happening all around Amanda. She didn't know what to do. She was worried about a few of her girlfriends; each had slept with one or more of the guys who were thought to have been infected.

"We also talked about her work and how Amanda," Patricia said, "was demoted because she doesn't have a driver's license and how her hours were being cut back."

Both Amanda and Patricia described the conversation in similar ways. Patricia was worried about her daughter. She felt Amanda was running with a group of people who were not good for her. She was concerned that with all the drugs floating around, Amanda might get caught up again. Ever since she'd had a problem with cocaine some time ago, which she had admitted to police and testified to in court, Amanda had been a good girl. But Patricia knew how tough peer pressure could be and worried about her.

Throughout the day, Patricia drank several glasses of wine. She liked wine in the box, she said. It helped her relax. At 7:15 p.m., she poured a fresh glass of boxed *vino* and went upstairs to spend time with Neil. He had found his Play Station game by then.

"You want to race me?" Neil asked.

Patricia sat on the bed. "As long as we use separate controllers."

Neil often teased Patricia about having sweaty palms. He called called her "Sweaty Betty" because of it.

"We played for a while ... maybe fifteen minutes," Patricia said. "He kicked my ass."

Next, Patricia went downstairs to call Christopher's ex-girlfriend, the mother of her grandchild. Christopher and his girlfriend were estranged, but Patricia kept in touch with the girl. She worried about the baby. She and Neil would often slip $50 or $100 bills into the ex-girlfriend's diaper bag whenever she stopped by the house with the child, mainly because they knew Christopher never helped.

While they were talking, Patricia mentioned *Desperate Housewives* and said she had to get off the phone because she didn't want to miss the show. She and Neil loved to watch it together.

After Patricia and Neil watched *Housewives*, Neil got undressed and sat on the bed, saying with raised eyebrows, "I'm all ready."

"Neil sleeps in the nude and doesn't wear pajamas," Patricia commented.

With Neil in bed waiting for sex, Patricia went into the bathroom, undressed, and walked into the room naked.

"Neil was watching a law show [*Boston Legal*] with Captain Kirk in it, William Shatner," Patricia recalled. "We watched the show together."

At some point during the show, Patricia explained, they "made love—had intercourse. I couldn't really tell you what happened on the show."

As they started, Neil asked, "You OK?"

"Yeah," Patricia answered.

"Are you sure I'm not hurting you?"

"Yeah, I'm fine."

About fifteen minutes later, Patricia got up and went into the bathroom.

"I lied to Neil," she recalled. "It did kind of hurt. I was just really tired and wanted to have a good night's sleep."

After swallowing three Tylenol PMs, washing them down with a gulp of white wine, Patricia crawled into bed next to Neil and fell asleep—knowing, of course, that Neil was going out to the barn to feed Hannah at some point.

The remainder of Patricia's first statement to police details, primarily, the moments after she found Neil in the barn. Still, it wasn't the last time Patricia would sit with police and talk about the events leading up to her husband's murder. At the same time law enforcement interviewed Patricia, Troopers Brian Berkel and Michael Hill were up the road speaking to Christopher Robinson—which would send the investigation into a new direction entirely.

ABOUT A HALF-MILE DOWN the road from the Olsen house, the Mountain View Motel stood across the street from Pontoosuc Lake, a massive body of water bordering North Main Street (Route 7) on the eastern side. A rather tiny, cabin-like dwelling, with a total of six or seven rooms, the motel houses travelers, visitors to the lake region, but mainly those who have nowhere to live and need a room by the night. Christopher had been evicted from the Olsen house by Patricia and Neil since the fall of 2004. In October of that year, Patricia wrote Christopher a "no trespass order," stating, "You are hereby notified to leave and remain away from the [restaurant] ... as well as from the premises owned and occupied by Neil Olsen and his wife ..." Further, Patricia explained that she had notified law enforcement in Pittsfield and Lanesboro[ugh] that if Christopher were to appear at either of these premises in violation of this notice, he would be subject to arrest."

The letter was copied to the Lanesborough and Pittsfield police departments. Patricia signed it, but, for some reason, Neil hadn't. According to her statement later, Patricia never gave it to Christopher or sent it to the police.

Christopher found himself without a residence. Yet several of Patricia's employees later told police that Patricia allowed Christopher, without Neil's knowledge, to sleep at the restaurant if he didn't have a place to stay; and some later claimed, she routinely gave her son money to rent a room at Mountain View. There were times, too, Christopher later admitted, when he dipped into the cash register at Mrs. O's.

When detectives arrived at the motel, Christopher was more than willing to accompany them to Pittsfield for questioning. Several things weren't adding up. For one, when detectives found out Christopher and Neil were at odds with each other, before they could write Christopher off as a suspect, they had to find out just how much animosity and hatred there was between them. Hatred was a definite motive for murder. Christopher had a baby with his girlfriend. He rarely took care of the child. Patricia and Neil, a family member said, were thinking of allowing the mother of the child and the baby to move into the house. Christopher, however, wasn't welcome. Neil loved his step grandchild. He had never had children of his own, and to watch him with the baby, you would think it was his own.

This, coupled with Neil's strong-arm disciplinary tactics earlier in Christopher's life, riled Patricia's son, making him very angry.

Was it, however, enough to turn Christopher from an irritated young kid, a dark, jobless, ambitionless, homeless roamer and substance abuser, into a cold-blooded murderer?

When detectives looked at Christopher standing in the doorway to his motel room, there appeared to be dried blood droplets and blood spatter on his pants.

Detectives looked at each other, then at Christopher.

At the MSP Detective Unit in Pittsfield, detectives read Christopher his rights and asked him about his life at home with Neil and his mother.

"Living with Neil was good," Christopher responded. Shabbily dressed, donning a tar-black goatee, earrings and tattoos, Christopher appeared dishelveled. Friends said he used to be into what was known as the "Goth" movement, sporting black nail polish and face make-up to accentuate the look. There was definitely a sinister side to Christopher Robinson, at least one that spoke of his wild youth. Continuing, the boy added, "[Neil] always provided us with what we needed, but I kinda grew up with the tough love kinda thing."

During high school, Christopher said, Amanda called Child Services one day and reported that Neil had hit them. When the social worker showed up to conduct an interview, Christopher explained, "I strongly believe in the family thing, [so] I lied [to them] and said nothing had happened. I didn't want to break up my mother's family."

Christopher claimed Patricia started "to have a nervous breakdown" somewhere around 2002. He gave no reason why, other than her problems with Crohn's disease. Regarding Neil, he said, "The last time I saw [him was] on Merrill Road. He was going to Home Depot. My mother told me they were rebuilding the house, so I guess he was going to buy stuff. I didn't wave or anything. He saw me."

Christopher came across fidgety, nervous. Something was bothering him. As he talked, detectives asked when he last saw his mother.

"Last night," Christopher said, "because I heard what happened and I wanted to see if she was all right."

After being asked, he then talked about what he did on the day and night Neil was murdered. At one point, Christopher said he went down to Mrs. O's. The feeling he got when he walked in was that something terrible had happened. "They were looking all glum."

"Smile," Christopher told Rosa and Casey Nicola, hoping, he claimed, to cheer them up.

"Neil's dead!"

"You're fucking kidding me," Christopher said.

"Hannah crushed his head."

Next, Christopher explained what he did the reminder of that day.

Then detectives asked: "Did you have anything to do with Neil Olsen's murder?"

"I had nothing to do with Neil's death," Christopher said defiantly. "We would get into a fight, but I would disappear until he cooled off. Then we would get along again. The only thing I know about how Neil died is that Hannah stomped on his head. I've known her and she is old. All I know is what they told me about Hannah and how they found him."

They cut Christopher loose, until later that same day, when at 4:10 p.m., detectives caught up with him again. Christopher was even more disheveled and jumpy. He claimed to have more information he wanted to include in his original statement. Investigators knew he had lied to them earlier. After a quick look around as Christopher was being led to a patrol car, detectives had seen blood all over Christopher's motel room, in his car, all over his clothes.

"Come on, Chris," said one of the detectives, encouraging him to fess up.

Christopher looked around the tiny interrogation room. "OK," he said just like that, without any rejection. Then, without warning or fanfare, Christopher Robison proceeded to explain what had happened.

He said he took $50 from the restaurant cash drawer, got a motel room on Sunday evening, and left his room at about 10:30 p.m.

"I drove up to Skyline" (the golf course next to Neil's house).

He parked his car at the top of the driveway, on the edge of the golf course. He walked across the driving range and hopped the fence near the horse field.

Then he snuck into Hannah's stall.

"I went in through the open garage door [and] stood by the second door. ... I waited until I heard the breezeway door open." That sound was Neil coming into the barn to feed Hannah. "I put the butt of the gun on my right shoulder and waited to hear the door open. Then I heard the door open and I closed my eyes and pulled. He couldn't see me because it was dark back there but he was looking right at me. I heard a loud bang and then a thud and then I came to and I was walking toward the black truck and down the hill. That truck is Neil's truck. All I remember is pulling the trigger once."

Pressing further, detectives learned Christopher "bought the rifle at a Wal-Mart in New York more than a couple of months ago."

For the next hour or more, Christopher described the events leading up to (and shortly after) Neil's murder. In pointed detail, he remembered times and places, even the exact amount of money—"I thought I must have got it from Neil"—he had taken from Neil's pocket: "$186.00." Christopher continued to tell detectives he had "blacked out"—"I do that sometimes"—for much of the night. He couldn't recall, for example, going into Neil's pocket and taking the cash; but said he must have, because he didn't know where else the money could have come from. Then, "at 12:00 … [on] Monday, I called my mom. … She said that she thought I should get out of here and leave. She assumed that I had done it. I didn't say anything about that. That was it. I said, 'I'll just talk to you later.'"

Since Christopher had indicated his mother knew he had murdered Neil, detectives were curious: Was Patricia simply trying to protect her son; or was she saying, in not so many words, she was relieved her son had finally done the job?

"When I went to the garage [to kill Neil]," Christopher said, "I went there because I wanted to help protect my mother. I was first asked about it after my daughter was born, so it would have been towards the end of May [2004]. My mother was saying how she was so upset and wished that things were better and that she wishes me and my sister were back in her life. He wasn't violent with her until recently. She never really told me that he hit her, but she portrayed it as if it happened. This last time, beginning on Friday afternoon, he did hit her repeatedly on the back of the head. She told me this."

After claiming that his mother was the mastermind behind Neil's murder, Christopher Robinson went on to describe how he had tried to murder Neil on numerous occasions, but couldn't muster the "nerve" or "courage" to go through with it. He claimed his mother kept pushing him to get it done, but that he had continually backed out. He painted quite a picture of mind manipulation on Patricia's part, saying that, over a period of months, she convinced him that Neil was a brutish, abusive husband, and once he was gone, Christopher claimed, his mother promised that Amanda, Christopher and his child could live happily ever after in Neil's house with her.

Interestingly enough, after describing a conversation he had with his mother about the bloody metal pipe found the day after Neil's murder, Christopher said, "My sister was there last night [when we talked]. She did not hear our conversation. She's kinda got a big mouth so my mother didn't want her to know."

According to Christopher, this manipulation by Patricia picked up serious steam during the summer of 2004. Christopher said he bought an eighteen-inch machete to chop wood and take on camping trips and then decided to use it to kill Neil. He waited outside the house several times, prepared to attack Neil from behind with the machete. Every time he felt he could go through with it, however, he backed down when the moment came. When he failed to complete the job, he said his mother became angry and pressured him to go through with it.

When January 9, 2005, came, Christopher said he had made up his mind. In a second statement, taken by Trooper Michael Hill, Christopher explained the night of the murder yet again, adding new details. He said he left his motel room around 10:30 p.m. and, a few minutes later, parked near the Skyline Country Club close to the driving range, which was only separated from the Olsen house by a large culvert.

Quietly, Christopher said, he walked across the driving range, in through a small area of trees and brush, and made it into Neil's barn without anyone hearing or seeing him. Once inside, he found a cozy place by the entryway to hide, and waited for Neil to walk in. Hannah was outside the barn in her pen. Christopher knew Neil fed the horse every night at around eleven o'clock.

Neil Olsen was large man, big-boned, barrel-chested. Strong as rebar. He had worked with his hands all his life. Considering Christopher's small frame and frail body, Neil could have likely snapped Christopher in two with one hand tied behind his back. Hiding, ambushing Neil, Christopher knew, was the only way to get the job done. So, as soon as Neil walked into the barn and prepared Hannah for her nightly feeding, Christopher stepped out behind his stepfather and, standing about "a foot-and-a-half away" with his "eyes closed," pulled the trigger.

After the first shot, Neil fell to the ground—but Christopher couldn't remember what happened next. He "blacked out." Still, the evidence proves he fired nine more rounds, seven of which ended up in Neil's head, and then beat Neil with a forty-inch metal pipe, hoping to cover up the crime. Moreover, Christopher said he left the barn door open so Hannah could find her way into the barn—and that he ran into his mother's house to hide the gun in a closet and explain to her what he had done. Both decisions would have taken calculated thought. It's hardly conceivable that he could have blacked out through it all. Killers—especially when extreme violence is present—have been known to describe a period during a murder as "hazy" or somewhat difficult to recall in full, much like a drunk trying to remember portions of a bender. Yet during those brief periods of blacking out, if you will, most killers don't remember much of anything, more or less just snapshots of recall.

"Robinson stayed up until about four in the morning," Trooper Hill's report stated, detailing the hours following the murder, "because he couldn't get that sound out of his head. That thud sound, the sound of Neil Olsen getting shot in the head." Christopher said he felt "really dirty and took two showers and kept washing his hands" over and over.

The next day, apparently now over the guilt of having murdered Neil, Christopher went to the Berkshire Mall, saw a movie, *White Noise*, ate lunch at McDonald's, and even did some shopping.

Asked why he committed the murder, Christopher told police he wanted to "help and protect his mother."

In addition to the detail Christopher provided police during those two interviews which took place within a few days of the murder, he had even more to offer. In the coming weeks, Christopher Robison would change his story yet again, offering additional, specific elements of murder that would further incriminate Neil's wife, Patricia Olsen.

POLICE HAD THEIR MAN under a confession. Even better was that he had given up the crime's true motivator, Patricia. This did not mean, however, that she was guilty. Detectives had to build a case against the alleged Black Widow and, most importantly, try to back up what Christopher had told them. After all, without corroboration, Christopher's statement was nothing more than hearsay.

When detectives caught up with Amanda Robinson, it was clear that the young girl had fallen on hard times, but had also been trying to rebuild her life. It wasn't only alcohol and weed that had dragged Amanda down. According to Amanda's court testimony, she'd had a serious problem with cocaine, which Neil and Patricia had discovered a year before Neil was murdered.

Born on Valentine's Day 1986, Amanda was Patricia's youngest child. Quite stunning, with long blonde hair and, as one family member later admired, "puppy dog eyes," Amanda now appeared weathered and drawn. She was 19, but looked much older. When detectives found her, Amanda was living in New York with her boyfriend at his father's house.

Amanda admitted that, after she'd tried cocaine for the second time, in the bathroom of her mother's restaurant, she soon "developed more of a coke habit …" Her favorite places to snort the drug, she said, were at home in her room, inside the restaurant, and outside in "the horse's stall."

As she explained to Trooper Jean Thibodeau and Sergeant David Bell, her drug dealer would come by the Olsen house and swap cocaine out for the money she left in the mailbox. She would wait anxiously, staring out her room window, facing the mailbox, and then run out and grab her drugs as soon as he dropped them off. This went on for quite some time.

"My mom usually slept upstairs," Amanda said, "and Neil would be passed out on the couch."

Working at Mrs. O's for her mother, Amanda said, was more of a chore than a job.

"I was working … like every night. I wasn't getting paid. I would go in my mom's wallet. She didn't call me on the money. I stopped getting coke … after my [last] birthday. I got caught by my mom." Patricia had walked into the restaurant one morning and threw a "rolled up dollar bill on the counter" in front of her, asking sternly, "What's that?" She didn't appear angry, though, Amanda remembered, just "disappointed."

"Why didn't you come to *me* about this?" Patricia wondered when Amanda didn't respond. Neil had found the coke, along with empty bottles of liquor Amanda said she used to come down off the coke. Neil knew it was coke, Patricia told her that day, because he had "tasted" the residue left in her room and it had made his lips "go numb."

"You need to get out of the house now," Patricia told her, "or you'll be grounded until you leave."

In her first statement to police, Amanda Robinson confirmed the telephone calls between her and Patricia on

Sunday afternoon, down to the details Patricia had described during questioning. But Amanda remembered her mother calling back later that night (something Patricia had maybe chosen to forget) around 10:30 p.m.

She said her mother asked about her boyfriend, and then mentioned how Neil had been pulled over by the Lanesborough police because his truck was uninsured and unregistered.

"Oh, does he have to go to court for that?" Amanda asked.

"Yeah."

"That sucks."

Patricia said nothing else. They hung up.

A day or two later, Amanda couldn't recall exactly when, Patricia called back and they talked about what Christopher had apparently reported to police.

"Chris said that Neil hit me and that he was trying to protect me. Neil wouldn't do that," Patricia told her daughter.

In her statement, Amanda said, "She never told me that Neil hit her. She said *that* never happened."

For the next thirty minutes, Amanda told police stories about her life with Neil and her mother. How Neil's disciplinary tactics bothered her and Christopher, but yet, looking back, they were disobedient kids and perhaps deserved to be punished. She also described her mother's reaction to Neil's death as "distraught," saying Patricia was crying and drinking wine, blaming Hannah. "That fucking horse. That fucking horse."

By the end of the statement, one of two things became clear: Either Amanda and Patricia had gotten together and discussed what they would tell police (because their descriptions of that Sunday and the days following were just about identical), or they were both telling the truth to the best of their knowledge.

Concluding her statement, Amanda said, "My mom never said she didn't want Neil around. She mentioned to me a while ago that they argued, but it was nothing out of the ordinary. She never mentioned to me that she wanted to leave Neil or she wanted him to leave. She never mentioned that she wanted Chris to kill Neil. I don't know why Chris did it. Something had to happen to make him snap. That's *not* my brother. That's *not* the Chris I know that did that."

As police would soon find out, much of the information Amanda had given them in her original statement was, according to Amanda herself, spun into a very neat package of lies.

IT WAS THE FIRST HOMICIDE in Berkshire County in years. Christopher Robinson was arrested on January 11, 2005, for the murder of his stepfather, and was held on a $1 million bond, pending a later arraignment. Residents in and around Lanesborough were astonished by the news of Christopher's arrest, and more so by the gruesome details of the crime being released. Berkshire County is known for its remarkable aesthetics, fall foliage, breathtaking views of the Berkshire Mountains, the Norman Rockwell Museum, and the immense and sacred National Shrine of the Divine Mercy in nearby Stockbridge. Murder was perhaps the last thing on the minds of Berkshire residents as the 2005 holiday season wound down and everyone started looking toward the New Year.

When detectives returned to Patricia's house after interviewing Christopher, she gave them consent to search the house and, without so much as a breath, handed over Neil's dental and medical records. One of the detectives later said he felt Patricia didn't seem too concerned, and actually acted "sharp and direct" as they collected evidence. Patricia, whether she knew it or not, was on notice. Detectives were watching her every move.

"She was upset, not thinking straight," a family member later said. "They made a big deal out of what she was wearing on the night Neil was killed. Patricia couldn't remember. She called them pajamas one day and a nightgown the next—and *suddenly* that made her a suspect."

In all fairness to police, it was a hell of a lot more than a pair of pajamas.

Patricia's own son had sold her out.

At the foot of Patricia's property line, cops located the rifle Christopher had used to murder Neil. He told detectives he and Patricia put it in the house, in one of the closets, but he had gone back a day later and thrown it into the woods.

"They made a big deal out of Christopher saying that he went into the house after killing Neil," that same family member told me. "They claimed he hugged Patricia, and she helped him hide the gun in the house."

Why would Patricia, one might ask, hide the murder weapon inside her own house if she was involved? Furthermore, if Christopher hugged his mother, wouldn't her night clothes be covered in fresh blood? Christopher had Neil's blood all over him. Wouldn't there have been blood in the house: on the doorknob, upstairs in the hallway, in the closet, the kitchen, anywhere Christopher had been *after* the murder?

Very little blood had been found in the Olsen house.

Claiming Patricia Olsen was involved in her husband's murder was one thing, proving it would turn out to be another matter entirely. Detectives would have to come up with a motive. Since Christopher's arrest, detectives had figured out that Patricia was the beneficiary of Neil's $175,000 life insurance policy, Neil's retirement savings, the home they shared together, and a half-dozen or so vehicles. With the enormous financial debt Patricia had run up between the two businesses, not to mention her total disregard for the household bills, state police felt they had a solid case against her. Berkshire County District Attorney David Capeless knew he could easily explain to a jury why it was that Patricia wanted her husband dead. The oldest motive on record.

Neil Olsen was worth more dead than alive.

If Patricia seemed able to handle the stress of her husband's death as detectives and crime scene investigators combed through her house, it was only because she was hiding it pretty well. That would all end quickly. Three days after Neil's murder, on January 14, Patricia was admitted to the psyche ward of the local hospital under observation (where she remained for several days).

According to detectives and David Capeless, Patricia hadn't just forgotten to pay the cable television bill for a few months, or simply blown off the light and phone bills, as most people short on cash do from time to time. Not even close.

By the first of the year 2005, Capeless said in court, Patricia had "more than $10,000 in utility bills and taxes ... [and had] borrowed $45,000" from one of Neil's brothers "to prevent the bank from foreclosing on their home."

She and Neil were in deep financial trouble.

Patricia admitted becoming "sloppy" with their money throughout the years, but vehemently denounced allegations that she kept her inept bookkeeping and money handling skills from Neil. Instead, she and Neil were "extremely busy," mainly because they ran two businesses and didn't communicate all that well. Apparently, Patricia felt there just wasn't enough time in their busy lives to tell her husband that everything he had ever worked for during most of his adult life was about to be stripped from him because his wife hadn't paid their bills.

IT JUST SO HAPPENED, that on January 7, 2005, two days before Neil was murdered, a police officer had pulled him over and ordered Neil's vehicle towed after figuring out that Neil had no insurance and no registration. As shocking as this was to Neil, a routine traffic stop had opened up a Pandora's box, police believed, of mounting financial debt, revealing it to Neil for the first time. Having found out that Patricia had failed to pay those bills, it wasn't such a stretch to think Neil went home and laid into his wife, demanding answers, probably asking to look at the household finances more closely. Once Patricia realized Neil was getting curious, it was only a matter of time before Neil would uncover the fact that she hadn't paid *any* of the bills.

By February 2, 2005, law enforcement believed they had enough evidence to arrest Patricia Olsen. At 12:05 p.m., police caught up with Amanda Robinson once again and confronted her with the notion that she knew more than she had admitted in her original statement. Amanda was brought to the state police barracks in New Scotland, New York, and asked her if she was willing to add anything to her previous statement.

After discussing it with her boyfriend, Amanda told police she didn't need a lawyer. "I want to [talk] about my mother's involvement in Neil Olsen's death," she stated, understanding clearly that this was her one chance to come clean.

Amanda claimed her mother's obsession with having Neil murdered began as far back as her sophomore year in high school, quoting Patricia as saying, "Life would be so much better without him." Patricia was "evasive" at first, Amanda added, but soon came out with it: "Is there someone you know that would kill him?" she came out and asked Amanda one day. "I'll pay them."

Further, she explained how Patricia's desire to have Neil killed grew "aggressive." As the years passed, said a report of this interview, she would bring it up and "make [Amanda] feel bad about [her] life" with Neil, so Amanda would become comfortable with helping her "make all of her troubles go away."

Amanda said she "ran into Christopher" one day at Wal-Mart while he was purchasing a gun, which he eventually used in the murder. "He told me that my mom gave him the money to buy it."

Christopher couldn't recall having said this to Amanda.

During the last part of the interview, Amanda went into great detail about her mother's after-the-murder plan, describing how Patricia believed she was going to "get away" with the crime. "You're not going to get away with this," Amanda told her mother. "Yes, we are, as long as we stick together it will just come back to your brother," Patricia had said. "We should tell the police that Chris wasn't there." But after she thought about it, Patricia added, "They're going to catch him. But hell, it wouldn't be that bad a thing, because he would have a place to live. Do you think I did the right thing?"

"I'm a terrible liar, mother."

"Come on, you used to put on plays in high school."

"She thought it was a big fucking joke," Amanda admitted. "She'd fake crying and call Fred [Neil's brother], and I'd look at her [while she was on the phone] and she'd turn around and smile at me."

During her arraignment on February 3, inside the Berkshire District Court, Patricia entered a plea of not guilty. Looking quite withdrawn, her dirty blonde hair wildly frayed and unwashed, she wept during most of the proceeding. She was dressed in a bright red prison jumpsuit, with both her hands and legs shackled. Her appointed counsel, Pittsfield's

Leonard Cohen, a rather well known trial attorney, and later, Lori Levinson, spoke on her behalf. Quite interestingly, several members of Neil's family were in court supporting Patricia. They couldn't believe what had happened. They felt they knew Patricia and that Christopher must have made up this terrible story about her to cut a deal with prosecutors.

Prosecutor David Capeless told the court that Patricia Olsen "cajoled and prodded her twenty-year-old son to kill her husband." Capeless was adamant about his conviction that Patricia was the mastermind. "She provided him [Christopher] with money to stay at motels nearby her house," Capeless explained. "... Patricia Olsen provided [her son] with money, in fact, to purchase the rifle, which was ultimately used to murder Neil Olsen."

Cohen, meanwhile, reminded the judge that members of Neil's family were in the courtroom, and said, "I think that it's a factor the court should perhaps take into consideration— that the family of Mr. Neil Olsen, the victim in this case, would like to see her released."

Undeterred by the presence of Neil's mother, Ruth Olsen, the judge ordered Patricia held without bail.

The following day, Christopher Robinson was indicted and held without bail.

ON FEBRUARY 9, TROOPER Stephen Jones and Lieutenant Patricia Driscoll brought in the father of Amanda's boyfriend. Word was that he had spoken to Patricia on numerous occasions.

Amanda's boyfriend's father had run into some hard times recently, admitting in his statement he had been a "recovering drug addict ... [who had fallen] off the wagon." He said he returned from Bike Week a while back only to find Amanda staying at his house. At that time, Christopher was also living there. "He owed my son a bunch of money, so I told my son to throw him out. I came home one day and found him packing a bunch of stuff."

When he saw Christopher, the father told him to put his stuff back into the house to leave there as collateral. Christopher could come and get the stuff as soon as he paid his debt. He even walked Christopher out to his car to be sure he didn't take anything with him.

"One of the things he had in his car," the father noticed, "was the gun, a .22 [caliber] rifle."

Christopher, thinking the guy was going to ask him for it, said, "Can I keep the gun?"

The father was a convicted felon. He couldn't have guns in the house. "Keep it," he said.

When police asked him about Patricia, he said she "upset Amanda a lot." He often saw Amanda crying after she'd had a conversation with her mother. On a few occasions, he had spoken to Patricia himself on the telephone. "She was kind of flirty with me on the phone." One time, Patricia said Neil "was abusive and beat [her]."

"Why don't you just leave him then?" the father asked.

"I can't because of our businesses," Patricia responded.

The day before detectives questioned the boyfriend's dad, he said Amanda was in her room crying. So he asked what the problem was; he hated seeing her like that. Amanda was always so depressed. He knew it was Patricia causing it and felt helpless to do anything to fix it.

In a tearful reply, Amanda looked at him and said, "I think my mom pressured Chris into killing Neil."

"Well," the dad told her, "you should do whatever you can live with. If Patricia had something to do with it, then it did not seem fair to let Chris take the full brunt of it."

According to Amanda's boyfriend's father, Christopher had severe "mental issues." But, at the same time, he claimed Christopher "seemed like a nice kid." Still, it was Patricia causing all the problems. "Amanda kind of hinted once that her mother wanted to find someone to get rid of her stepfather. ... I got the impression her mother was looking for someone to kill [Neil]." When he spoke to Patricia himself, she gave him the impression she wanted Neil dead.

"Just the way she was talking about Neil," the dad told police. "That she could not get away from him and that she couldn't leave him."

Christopher seemed like the perfect hit man. "I can tell you that he was a little weird," the father said. "You could tell he was *out* there. The books he had: like black magic shit."

Under further questioning, Amanda later opened up about her mother's desire to have Neil murdered. There was one time at Mrs. O's, Amanda recalled, when she claimed her mom had asked if she "would either help kill Neil or find a gun. She wanted him killed with a gun," Amanda recalled. "She would tell us [Amanda and her friend] that [my friend] could do it and we would have anything we would ever want."

"No, mother!" Amanda said she snapped that day. "My friend is *not* going to kill anyone. I'm *not* going to help you."

"Well," Patricia answered, "can you at least help me get a gun?"

"No!"

Faced with growing evidence that she knew more than she had originally told police, on December 6, 2005, Amanda came forward and gave police a third statement. She now wanted to set the record straight. There was a phone call between Amanda and her imprisoned boyfriend recorded by prison officials—which made it clear to law enforcement that Amanda knew even more. The phone call explained, in part, that Patricia may have been involved. During that call, which took place on the night of January 10, 2005, Amanda told her boyfriend, "That thing [went down] that my brother said, 'It was going to happen tonight,' and my mother said if it doesn't happen, 'She's gone.' ..."

Further, Amanda explained how "shocked" she was that the murder had actually taken place. She never thought they would go through with it. "I told [my boyfriend]," Amanda said after being confronted with the recorded call by police, "that my mother was asking me to find someone to murder Neil. I can't give a timeline as to when my mom started talking about wanting to have Neil murdered. After a while, that became the main topic of my mom's conversations with me. It's not that *I* wanted him dead like my mother did. I felt that I was being pressured by my mother to help her. My mother would talk to me about it morning, noon, and night. It wasn't easy living in that house. It was the only thing she seemed to want to talk about."

Someone close to Amanda, Christopher, and Patricia, told me later that Amanda "lied about a lot of things" to protect herself from prosecution. That same source said Amanda denied her entire statement to police and "feels guilty" about it. The source said Amanda and Christopher had dredged up this terrible lie about Patricia to "get back at her" mother for the way Neil treated them. They were upset, this source was certain, because their mother allowed Neil's disciplinary tactics to incapacitate their lives and she never stood up for them.

Nevertheless, during the early part of 2005, days after her husband's murder, the pieces of a conspiracy to kill Neil Olsen fit together. The more police spoke to Amanda, the more she remembered—and the more those words made it appear that Patricia Olsen had not only sanctioned the murder of her husband, but financed, planned and initiated it, as well.

STATE TROOPER JEAN THIBODEAU said Patricia's "initial account of her activities the night before" Neil's murder "did not check out." Patricia had told Thibodeau, for example, that she went to bed after watching *Desperate Housewives* and the brief opening portion of the show *Boston Legal*. But Thibodeau soon discovered that Patricia recovered two voicemail messages on her cell phone on the night of January 9: the first at 11:56 p.m.; the second at 11:58 p.m. How could she be awake to retrieve those messages? And who would be calling at that time of night, anyway?

Christopher.

As detectives interviewed other sources close to Amanda and Christopher, people who could back up what the kids were saying, a rather sobering account of the last days of Neil Olsen's life came into focus.

During the months leading up to Neil's murder, Patricia racked up a litany of bills she couldn't pay. There was even word that, at one time, a foreclosure notice for Neil's house was going to appear in the local newspaper. Amanda said she started looking for a hired killer through her drug dealer, but realized after a time that her drug dealer wasn't as "connected" as he claimed, and the offer was subsequently taken off the table. Even after that, Patricia never let up, Amanda said. "I told my mother that I talked to a person about finding someone to kill Neil. She said she didn't want to know his name, but when I told her, she would say, 'Really!'" as if she were excited the plan was moving forward once again.

Christopher visited his mother one day before the murder and explained that he needed tires for his car. He had no money and refused to hold down a job.

So Patricia began funneling him cash.

When Christopher returned to New York later that afternoon, Amanda's boyfriend claimed he saw a box for a

.22 caliber rifle in the backseat of Christopher's car. ("No gun, just the box.") So he asked Christopher were he got the money for the weapon.

"My mother gave me some money for new tires. I bought a gun and radar detector instead."

Amanda's boyfriend was on probation at the time. He went to Christopher and told him, "Get rid of the gun, or get out of the house."

"I'll put it in my trunk," Christopher said. Amanda's boyfriend asked him why he bought a gun to begin with.

"I am going to take target practice."

"That was his only explanation for owning the gun," Amanda's boyfriend recalled.

Before Christopher was asked to leave Amanda's boyfriend's father's house, he and Amanda's boyfriend had several discussions about Neil. Same as Amanda, Christopher hated Neil. But it seemed Christopher was confused about his association with his mother.

"I love my mom," Christopher said. Then, in another breath, "She's a manipulative bitch."

THE CONVERSATION TOOK PLACE over the telephone. Amanda's boyfriend was standing by Amanda as she and Patricia talked.

"I want Neil dead," Patricia told Amanda, "and [I'll] pay money to see it happen."

From that first moment Patricia mentioned a desire to have Neil killed, Amanda went to her boyfriend and told him about it. She grew tired and worried. She didn't want any part of it, she claimed. "I don't want to hear this," Amanda said after she got off the telephone. "I don't want anything to do with it." Amanda cried. It bothered her. "That's all she talks about," Amanda said one night. "She's so [screwed] up in the head."

It bothered Amanda so much, she once contemplated suicide. Soon, she stopped talking to her mother all together.

"Leave him, mother," Amanda yelled over the telephone.

"I can't do that," Patricia said. "I'd be broke."

"Wouldn't that be better?"

"No!"

The last time they spoke about Neil's murder over the telephone, Patricia told her daughter: "I am going to kill myself right now." No one would help her, she claimed, was the reason for suicide. She was upset the kids couldn't find someone to do the job on Neil.

Amanda started crying. "I do not want to talk to you anymore." She hung up.

It was at that time when Patricia, according to Amanda, started "working on" Christopher.

AFTER SEVERAL DELAYS, ABOUT eighteen months after Neil's murder, Patricia Olsen—who had been telling friends, relatives, and Neil's family that all she wanted was her day in court to explain the truth—finally got that chance. On May 3, 2006, David Capeless began presenting witnesses in what was presumed to be a month-long trial.

Patricia Olsen's defense that had their work cut out for them. In theory, they had to prove the state's case was built on the false testimony of two liars; two kids looking to get back at a mother they felt had abandoned them. After a strong case presented by the prosecution, by May 18, Patricia's lawyers called Lynn Reilly, a Smith Barney employee, who tried to explain away Patricia's financial situation. Later that day, Patricia took the stand.

Here she was, prepared to step up and defend herself. How dare these children cut her throat? A jury shouldn't believe any of it.

Patricia had gained some weight while in jail. Completely

disheveled, she looked ten years older, and was clearly nervous. An outright wreck.

For the most part, Patricia's direct testimony focused on her love for Neil and their relationship over the past decade. At one point, she said the relationship between Neil and Christopher was volatile: "I didn't believe it. I mean, I knew they hated each other, but I wouldn't imagine Chris doing this."

Finding Neil dead was the worst thing she had ever experienced, Patricia intimated. "I thought he had fallen. I really thought he had a heart attack, just that something was wrong."

David Capeless felt differently, of course. When he got a crack at Patricia, the prosecuting attorney never let up, centering most of his questioning on the financial debt she had sunk the family into during the year 2004. It all sounded good on paper. Classic black widow behavior. Patricia claimed she never "kept" their finances from Neil. She said they were "extremely busy" with both businesses and that the subject rarely came up—that it didn't seem like a big deal to her or them.

Money—of lack thereof, actually—was a motive for murder, at least from where David Capeless argued. Thus, he made a point to let jurors know that Patricia failed to pay more than $10,000 in utility bills and taxes, along with a reported $45,000 she borrowed from Neil's brother to stop the bank from foreclosing on their home. These were extremely important factors, and certainly proved that a motive for murder *existed*.

For hours, Capeless hammered his points at the witness, saying once, "Neil was going to find out that *you* had disrespected him—and *that* would have enraged him, wouldn't it have, Mrs. Olsen?"

"You're wrong, Mr. Capeless. You are absolutely wrong,"

Patricia denied.

Regarding the explanation for running into the barn only to find Neil dead after touching his leg and seeing "flashes," as she put it, of Hannah and the horse's grain bucket, Capeless didn't buy any of it. So he decided to show Patricia—and the jury—what she claimed she never saw: the murder scene via autopsy photographs. Capeless insinuated that there was no reason for her to go into the barn in the first place, simply because she knew damn well her son had murdered Neil the previous night. The fact that there was no blood found on Patricia's person indicated clearly that she never went into the barn.

"You don't want to visualize it, do you, Mrs. Olsen?" Capeless asked.

Patricia pleaded with the prosecutor not to show her the photographs of the graphic crime scene.

"You don't want to see what you never saw because you were never there, were you, Mrs. Olsen?"

"You're lying," she lashed out, "it's *not* true. I *didn't* want Neil to be dead."

"You knew clearly what was in that barn stall that morning, didn't you?"

"No, I *didn't*."

After several more questions, Capeless concluded his questioning.

Shocking mostly everyone in the courtroom, after Patricia stepped down from the witness stand, co-counsel Lori Levinson and her partner, Leonard Cohen, rested their case. Apparently, Levinson and Cohen believed the state had not done its job and the jury would see through what they believed to be a transparent case of two liars (Patricia's own children) trying to frame their mother.

ON MAY 23, 2006, twelve jurors and four alternates began deliberations. The jury must have paid close attention to the case as it was tried, because within a day they were able to find Patricia guilty of, believe it or not, first-degree murder.

Patricia looked on in total disbelief as Lori Levinson cried.

What had gone wrong? How could a jury find a woman guilty of first-degree murder on the testimony of an admitted murderer, his disgruntled, former drug-using sister, and her convict boyfriend?

Immediately after she was found guilty, Patricia was sentenced to serve life at the Massachusetts Correctional Institution (for women) in Framingham, Massachusetts.

In June 2006, Christopher Robinson pleaded guilty to second-degree murder. The man who fired seven gunshot wounds into Neil Olsen's head, beat him to a pulp with a metal pipe, stole his money, went to see a movie, and shopped at the local mall afterward, had managed to get the Berkshire County District Attorney's office to agree that a second-degree murder charge was a clean swap for his testimony against his mother.

Some argued that Christopher cut a sweet deal. Prosecutor David Capeless defended his position, saying he offered Christopher no such thing.

Regardless, Christopher was given a life sentence, which, by Massachusetts standards for second-degree murder, entitles him to a coveted spot in front of the parole board within fifteen years.

Patricia Olsen awaits word on her appeals in prison.

BLOOD ON SESEAME STREET

AT 7:36 P.M., ON Monday, December 12, 2005, the Connecticut State Police (CSP), in Danielson (Troop D) received a telephone call that seemed completely out of character for the area of the state in which it originated. For one, Monday nights, especially during the winter months, were not the most active part of the week for criminals. Sure, maybe a break-in, a domestic dispute, drunk driver, or bar room brawl.

But this ... well, this was quite different.

The call was from a man named Jon Baker. He wanted to report that his wife, 44-year-old Judith Nilan, was missing. Judy had left their home in North Woodstock, Connecticut, at about 4:30 p.m. that afternoon for what Jon described as her "daily run," but had failed to return home some three hours later. It was unlike Judy to be gone so long. It was as dark as ink out on the streets of Woodstock, where street lights were as hard to come by as office space or a corporate chain restaurant or retail store. There's no way Judy would be out running at this hour of the night. Jon was worried.

In talking to the police, Jon said he had driven the normal route Judy had taken during her jog. He knew it by heart. Still, driving slowly up and down those roads, Jon said, he saw nothing. "We'll send out a few troopers," the cop said nonchalantly.

This was the beginning of a nightmare for Jon Baker.

IT'S THE COZY IDLENESS of Woodstock—Connecticut's

second largest town by area—that makes it so likeable and pleasant to pass through. The rolling hills of what seem like dark green carpet during spring and summer juxtapose nicely with what become during winter fresh blankets of snow that appear so pure and perfect you have to wonder if you're not standing inside a snow globe.

The roads of Woodstock are twisting and winding. There are general and hardware stores, café's, taverns, pizza parlors and even a winery or two. People smile at one another and wave. The 7,800 residents here go about their daily business and head home at night to settle into the privacy they cherish so much, snuggled up alongside a sense of security living in what is a remote piece of suburban bliss on the border of Massachusetts.

Woodstock is a town not famous for much, but ask anyone in Connecticut about Woodstock and you'll likely hear about the Woodstock Fair, which overtakes the center of town every fall. An annual event for more than 150 years, the fair, according to the Agriculture Society, is "a harvest celebration ... a homecoming. It's fun, educational, and entertaining. An Institution of its very own."

Up on a rise, heading toward the center of Pomfret, one of Woodstock's neighboring towns, on Route 169, the Woodstock Middle School sits near a town green dotted with century-old homes, antique shops and oak trees older than the town itself. Jon Baker's wife, Judy Nilan, had worked at the middle school for many years. Judy was a social worker, one of those adults whom students admired.

"She was always so happy," one student wrote in her essay about Judy, "she made everyone else happy."

The middle school once received a stipend from the town to fund a program that was eventually tagged PEERS (Prevention & Education for Early Resistance of Substance Use). Teachers, of course, wanted to do everything they could to promote sobriety, instructing kids on the dangers of making such unhealthy, life-changing choices as using drugs and alcohol. As the program was integrated into the curriculum, it seemed to be working. To this measure, Judy Nilan, who had seen the effects of drugs and booze on students on a firsthand basis, later told a newspaper reporter, "I found it to be extremely successful because it focuses on the substances that adolescents are most likely to use: alcohol, tobacco, marijuana and inhalants."

To Judy, these kids she interacted with everyday were everything to her: her life, her enjoyment, her quest.

STATE TROOPER GREGORY TRAHAN arrived at Jon Baker's and Judy Nilan's home in North Woodstock on the night of December 12, 2005, shortly after Jon called 911 to report Judy had gone out for a run and seemingly disappeared. English Neighborhood Road, where Judy and Jon shared their home, is exactly what the name implies: a winding, curvy rural road that connects to Brickyard Road North toward the east, and Rawson Road heading west. There's an ink blot of a pond not too far from Jon and Judy's country home.

Jon Baker said he last spoke to Judy at 3:00 p.m. "I believe she went for a run on area roads near our home."

"What was she wearing?" Trahan asked.

Jon said, "A yellow-colored windbreaker with a reflective stripe, dark colored spandex type pants, black colored fleece type gloves, gray or white sneakers and ear warmers."

Those were great, exact details.

With that, the CSP opened an official missing person investigation. They first searched the immediate area around Jon and Judy's house. Maybe Judy had gone out in the back, slipped on the snow, hit her head, and for all anybody knew, she may have been passed out somewhere, freezing to death in a snow bank.

English Neighborhood Road and the surrounding region is a desolate and thickly wooded forest.

Judy Nilan could have been anywhere.

Meanwhile, as additional troopers arrived on scene, they retraced the route Judy usually took on her run. Initially, troopers didn't find much and frustration quickly built.

Where in the heck could she have gone?

Jon knew his wife. According to what he later said, they'd had a storybook marriage for 20 years. They spent all of their free time together: working on their home, raising a few dogs, and bringing up Jon's children. They had been talking lately about opening their own business, a day care for children. Jon had spent time working in the business world, he knew it well, and believed nothing could be better than spending the latter days of your life with the woman you love, working together?

Still, Jon needed to answer some questions. After all, he was the last person to talk to Judy andhe was the one who had reported her missing. *Was it all part of a ruse?* Cops needed to consider everything. The most common suspect in any missing persons case involving a spouse is the other spouse.

As the night progressed, the state police brought in the K-9 team, additional manpower to assist in the search, as well as the blue and gold Trooper-1 helicopter. It was getting colder as the night sky darkened. By midnight, temps were set to fall into the teens and single digits. What *if* Judy had tripped, hurt her ankle, and was lying in a ditch somewhere?

Someone needed to find Judy before she froze to death.

JUDY NILAN HAD AN insatiable appetite for sports. She loved being outdoors, riding her bike, running, or just working around the house. "Judy was a champion body builder," Jon later said, "a long distance cyclist, runner, wonderful cook, avid gardener, and enthusiastically jumped into designing and building with her own hands ..."

Jon and Judy had purchased their Woodstock property when it was, according to Jon, "a shell of a home ..." Judy had never worked on a house before,but, like "most everything else she took on," Jon said, she had grabbed a hammer and started banging sheet rock against the walls "as well as any contractor." All of it, insisted Jon, brought out a spirited shade of Judy's lovable character.In whatever she did, Judy Nilan gave one hundred percent and wasn't afraid to take on new responsibilities. "I can't tell you," Jon added, "the number of times she would stand in the middle of our unfinished house and say, 'I love our home.'"

Beyond being a sounding board for students as a social worker, caring deeply about every kid she worked with at Woodstock Middle School, Judy was an exceptional mother to Jon's children. "It would be a mistake," Jon later wrote, "not to mention what a great mother Judy was ... always there for the children and [she] never missed an academic, musical, or athletic event—and there were many over the years."

One aspect of Judy's life that the CSP did not yet know as they began searching for her was that Judy had recently been involved with the State's Attorney's Office in Danielson, working with state's attorney Patricia Froehlich in particular. There was a problem at the school, a sexual abuse case involving a child. Judy was a witness. She was helping the State Attorney's Office build its case.

"I remember that discussion over the dinner table," Jon explained later, "and how furious Judy was at what had happened to the child." What inflamed Judy most was that within it all, "this child," Jon commented, "was somehow being blamed for what happened to her."

For Judy, here was "bureaucracy" at its highest level, at work. She had "no tolerance for abuse," or a system that the media portrayed as seeming to fail children over and over.

A TELETYPE WENT OUT on the night Judy went missing to all the local police departments and other law enforcement agencies. It was sent from the CSP's Troop D Barracks:

The missing person is identified as JUDITH NILAN DOB: 6/7/61. She is described as a white female 5'2" 100lbs, brown hair, brown eyes last seen wearing brown ear warmers, yellow windbreaker with dark stripe, dark running pants, and white sneakers. Anyone who may have seen this female jogging in Woodstock about 4:30 p.m. on Monday 12/12/05 is asked to contact Connecticut State Police.

As 8:00 p.m. became 9:00 p.m., there was still no sign of Judy.

An hour later, still nothing.

It was as if she had run away, which Jon Baker knew could not have been the case. Something had happened. Judy would never be gone this long without calling, without telling someone where she was or what she was doing.

And then a clue—one very important piece of evidence that gave investigators a foreboding feeling that this missing persons case wasn't going to turn out the way everyone had hoped. At 10:25 p.m., Trooper Michael Robinson, doing a sweep of the neighborhood, searching the streets with a spotlight, came across a piece of clothing. As Robinson was traveling west on Redhead Hill Road, which connected English Neighborhood Road where Judy and Jon lived, to Brickyard Road, in a semi-triangular-shaped tract of land, the trooper spied something off to the south side. It was a black and gray colored headband. Jon Baker had not reported that

Judy was wearing a headband, but it wasn't so much to think that she had left the house wearing it. It was cold out. She had ear muffs on. The headband made sense. Moreover, the road where it was found was part of Judy's running path.

The headband wasn't what piqued the state police's interest the most, however. When Robinson got out of his cruiser and combed the immediate area near the headband, he found a receipt from a local sales and service store that sold heavy equipment and tools. Among the items on the receipt was a chainsaw. The date of the purchase: December 10, 2005.

Two days ago.

A man named Scott Deojay had signed for the receipt on the account of Carroll Spinney, who had an enormous estate up on Brickyard Road, not too far away.

Carroll Spinney is better known as Big Bird, the tall, yellow-feathered creature on Public Television's hit show "Sesame Street." Spinney, a puppeteer, had played Big Bird for decades.

Even more than the headband and receipt, though, Trooper Robinson found something else. There were "several spots of a bloodlike substance" quite visible on the receipt.

Bad sign.

Upon further inspection, Robinson noted that minute bloodlike spots were on the snow next to where the headband and receipt had been located. What's more, the receipt, Robinson observed, had not shown any signs of "weathering."

Turning around, heading back to his cruiser, Robinson found yet another clue—which, added to everything else, made investigators assume something terribly violent had taken place on the road where these items had been discovered.

SEVENTY-TWO-YEAR-OLD Carroll Spinney's estate is set back a ways from Brickyard Road. Looking at the property from the street, it's hard to comprehend how enormous the house and the property it is situated on are.

"Nice grounds," said one man, "almost like a retreat with ponds."

The one image that comes through, however, as you stare into the property is that Big Bird cares about his terrain,as the landscaping and gardening throughout is immaculate and aesthetically appealing, no doubt an expensive endeavor. Carroll Spinney was born in Waltham, Massachusetts, and made his name in show business as a puppeteer, mainly playing the roles of Big Bird and Oscar the Grouch on "Sesame Street," an experience he once humorously described to a newspaper reporter as, "A lot like growing up to be Mickey Mouse—only taller."

The Spinney estate, which he shared with his wife and three children, is situated on a sect of land so far into North Woodstock that part of the property actually resides in Southbridge, Massachusetts. Scott Deojay, whose name was on the receipt the CSP had found, was a thirty-six-year-old convicted felon from Plainfield, Connecticut (about a forty-five-minute drive south of Woodstock). Deojay had been employed by Spinney for a quite a while, and was a hard worker with a solid build. One man, who interviewed Deojay later, reported that he "was one of the best stone masons I have ever seen." Beyond building fountains and steps and patios, Deojay took care of Spinney's property and kept up with the pruning and weeding and grass cutting, or all those things a landscaper/caretaker might do. He kept to himself for the most part, and did his work. Save for a few local merchants, no one in Woodstock knew Scott Deojay or could claim they had seen him around town. Deojay didn't live in town; he traveled into Woodstock each morning, worked, and generally left that evening. During the week of December 12, when Judy Nilan went missing, the Spinneys were in Europe on vacation. Besides another of Big Bird's employees, Deojay was alone on the estate.

LOOKING MORE CLOSELY AROUND the area where he had parked his cruiser, CSP Trooper Michael Robinson noticed "skid marks" leading up to where he found the bloody receipt and blood droplets in the snow. After a quick measurement, it was clear that the skid marks were forty feet long. They were definitive and fresh: just made on the road. Whatever happened had occurred within the past 24 hours, Robinson, an experienced accident investigator, knew for certain.

In such a densely populated area, with herds of deer and other animals wandering about freely, it wasn't out of the question to think that the person who had caused those skid marks could have come upon a deer and struck it. However, an analysis of the blood would have to determine whether it was human or animal.

Still, the headband, if it belonged to Judy Nilan, most certainly did not belong to an animal.

By 11:33 p.m., the first witness came forward after police canvassed the neighborhood. A man said he had seen Judy earlier that day. The guy was a local who lived on English Neighborhood Road. He said between that between 4:20 and 4:30 p.m., while he was returning to his residence, traveling north on Redhead Hill Road, he had seen a woman who he recognized as Judy Nilan, heading south, jogging towards him.

If Judy left her house and jogged south on English Neighborhood Road, she would have taken a *right* onto Redhead Hill Road, traveled a short distance west, then headed north up Brickyard Road, where she would have taken another *right* back onto English Neighborhood Road to complete the full circle of her run.

The neighbor told police, when they asked him how he could be certain it was Judy, that he and Judy "exchanged waves," adding, "she was wearing a yellow nylon type wind suit, black gloves, and possibly a black colored hat." If indeed he was correct about Judy having been wearing something black on her head, it may have been the previously discovered headband, which bore an ominous sign to her safety and well-being.

Moreover, off-duty CSP Trooper Todd Stevens, who was driving in the area of English Neighborhood Road that afternoon near 4:30 p.m., filed a report that corroborated the interview state police had conducted with Judy's neighbor. When he approached the intersection of English Neighborhood Road and Cherry Tree Corner, a road that led into the eastern part of Woodstock toward Route 169, a popular main road running through town, Stevens said he saw Judy Nilan. Stevens recognized Judy due to "various professional contacts" he'd had with her throughout the years.

After Trooper Stevens passed Judy and continued north onto English Neighborhood Road, he saw a vehicle, which had been traveling east, past him, heading in Judy's direction. He later described it as a Ford Escort or Mercury Tracer, a station wagon, which was beat up, shabbily painted with a dull, black primer. Stevens further reported that a white male was driving the vehicle, and that he couldn't see anybody else occupying the vehicle.

Thus, with the evidence the state police now had, it appeared Judy had taken a right onto Redhead Hill Road with this black car on her tail. After gathering all of this new information, Connecticut State Police grew increasingly concerned that the skid marks and blood droplets were also on Redhead Hill Road, alongside a headband that was, sadly, confirmed later on that night by Jon to belong to Judy.

CONNECTICUT STATE POLICE HAD a receipt with a few drops of blood on it. They had names: Carroll Spinney and Scott Deojay. They knew the name of the store from which the receipt originated. They had a headband. Two credible witnesses had seen Judy. Still, could they tie all of it, including that one small slip of paper containing blood, to Judy's disappearance? Sometimes the most obvious set of circumstances fail to add up to enough in the end. Nonetheless, it all had to be checked out before CSP could move further into another direction.

At 4:10 a.m., early in the morning following the night Judy disappeared, CSP detectives Michael Contre and Richard Bedard dragged the owner of the sales and service equipment center, where the receipt with blood on it had been obtained, out of bed. The man lived in Putnam, a solid thirty-minute drive from Woodstock.

The area of Redhead Hill Road where Judy's headband and the bloody receipt had been located was now considered a crime scene and had been taped off. Investigators continued sweeping the road and nearby woods for potential evidence.

"Carroll Spinney is a good customer," the owner of the sales and service center said, noting that purchase for the receipt in question had been charged to Spinney's account.

They asked him about the name on the slip: Scott Deojay.

The man thought about it. "I recall Deojay and a heavyset female with blonde hair coming in on December 8." His records verified the visit by Deojay. "He wanted to purchase a chainsaw and bar oil and he wanted to put them on Carroll Spinney's account." The man said he asked Deojay who he was and how he had access to Spinney's account. Deojay said, "I'm the outside caretaker. I work for Spinney."

The guy wasn't buying Deojay's story; he told him to hit the door and don't let it hit him in the ass on the way out.

Deojay became agitated. He said he needed the tool and oil to perform some work on Spinney's property. Then he became visibly angry. So, to calm him down, the female with him wrote a check for the items.

"You have that check?" one of the detectives asked.

The man said he did.

The woman was from Central Village, Connecticut, a small town outside Plainfield, Deojay's hometown.

"Did he ever return?" asked one of the detectives.

Deojay had indeed returned, just recently, a few days ago, on December 10. He bought a "splitting maul and several other items," the store owner recalled, looking at an invoice of the transaction. This time he was allowed to put the items on Spinney's account.

Detectives had a photograph of Scott Deojay. He was a rather plain looking man with a thick, Tony Orlando-Saddam Hussein style mustache that fell down below his lip line. He had the brown, beady eyes of a crow, a round face, and two-day's worth of five-o'clock-shadow stubble. He appeared dirty and unkempt, perhaps due to working on the landscaping. He came across in the image as a loner.. As evidenced by his darkly tanned complexion and crow's feet in the corner of his eyes, Deojay had worked many a day in the sun.

"That's him all right," said the owner of the store. "He was dressed in an orange rain type suit when he came in that day."

"Any idea what he was driving?"

"A small station wagon," said the owner of the store "... dark forest green in color ..."

The detectives looked at each other. They had a feeling where this was going.

FEW COULD CLAIM THEY led a life like that of Judy Nilan. Her smile alone was enough to make you feel comfortable and alive. Most of her family came from Oxford, Massachusetts. She was one of five children, having four brothers and two sisters. Judy had graduated in 1979 from Oxford High School. From there, she went on to attend college at the University of Connecticut, where she eventually earned her master's in social work. Judy's true passion in life was teaching and caring for children, which was evident in the respectful way people talked about her and her chosen vocation. Her first love was her family. In 1979, Judy wrote what would become an endearing and timeless phrase which family members later printed in the newspaper: "As the years pass by, we'll glance at faded photographs recalling memories shared with special friends and family, never wanting it to end. Memories are the only thing left within the end."

Judy Nilan's adult life was dedicated to education. Woodstock Middle School once posted a tribute to her on its website, saying, in part, "Judy Nilan was a social worker at the Woodstock Middle School who had a tremendous impact on the lives of the people around her. Her positive energy influenced the students and staff in the middle school."

If there was ever a person who fit into the lexicon of the age-old cliché, *one in a million*, Judy Nilan was that woman.

THAT BLOODY RECEIPT TROOPER Michael Robinson found on Redhead Hill Road was a turning point in the investigation. It told investigators that something violent had occurred on that road. The question became: *Did it involve Judy Nilan?* Finding a headband near the receipt, an accessory that was now also confirmed to belong to Judy, certainly added to the gravity of the discovery, but it still didn't mean much.

In light of the evidence (and the name on that receipt), it seemed the state police needed to find Scott Deojay and have a few words with Big Bird's gardener.

Detective Marty Graham had been with the CSP for nearly two-and-a-half decades. He had worked several of the state's most high-profile murder cases during the past twenty years. On the morning of December 13, 2007, Detective Graham and his partner, David Lamoureux, were called into the investigation.

"We were mobilized," Graham said, "to go up to Woodstock ... and while en route, one of our guys found that receipt. We had an off-duty trooper who had seen her. We had several addresses for Mr. Deojay. It seemed he lived everywhere. We went to one address where he had lived with a woman who had three of his kids."

No one was home.

So they went to the next address on the list connected to Deojay.

Again, no sign of their man.

Then they found Deojay's brother, who said, "I think he's living with this girl in Plainfield."

By now, it was close to six in the morning. The sun was about to come up, a new day was dawning.

"So we knocked on the door," Graham recalled.

Deojay's girlfriend, a heavyset blonde, was half-naked, still- half asleep, when she answered the knock. "Give me a minute," the woman said before walking back into the bedroom to change.

Deojay was in bed. He spoke up when his girl walked back in: "Who is it?"

"The state police," the blonde answered.

Hearing that, butt-naked Scott Deojay jumped out of bed and took off as fast as he could, not even stopping to get dressed.

AS DETECTIVES TRACKED DOWN Scott Deojay, several CSP troopers obtained maps and land records from the Town of Woodstock, as well as GPS readings they had taken themselves. It was important to get a clear picture of Big Bird's estate and its relation to Redhead Hill Road. Carroll Spinney's name was also on that receipt. It wasn't much of a lead, but checking out the Spinney property was certainly a starting point. Maybe more importantly, knowing Deojay worked for Spinney, it wasn't a stretch to think that perhaps Scott Deojay had accidentally hit Judy with his vehicle. He might have even driven back to the Spinney property, located about 1.5 miles from the crime scene on Redhead Hill Road; and if he had, the potential was there for evidence to be found on Big Bird's property.

Even though he was in another country, Carroll Spinney had no problem allowing the state police onto his property. The CSP had cleared Spinney entirely from any involvement. It was impossible, in fact, that he (or anyone living in his household) could have had anything to do with Judy's disappearance. They had all been on vacation at the time.

As the state police went through the Spinney grounds, one of the troopers noticed something strange. There was an "access road" on the property, set off by an immaculate and immense stone archway, which led to a right-hand turn off the main driveway leading *into* the property—a fork in the road, if you will.

"We believe," one investigator later said, "Scott Deojay built the archway—he was *that* good at what he did."

The road led to the far west end (rear) of the property, heading toward a thickly settled wooded area. For investigators, it was a challenge just to get around the property without falling; the frozen snow on the grounds made the estate as slick as an ice skating rink.

Near the end of the access road was a "picnic" area with a large Chinese pagoda-like structure built up on posts in an A-frame. It had no ground flooring. Two paddleboats were stored underneath the structure. A pagoda is generally a term given to "a temple or sacred building, usually a pyramid-like tower and typically having upward-curving roofs over the individual stories." It is a place to relax, a structure separate from a main living space, where one can retreat and disconnect from the world. To the Chinese, a pagoda is a spiritual den—a temple, as its description clearly states, to contemplate those moments in life when one is trying to unite with a higher power or an inner peace.

What was strange about this particular access road was that there was also a trail of blood leading directly to the pagoda, yet it stopped once you got inside, as if disappearing underneath the structure. The paddle boats, investigators noticed as they approached, had blood spatter and smudge marks on them. How could a trail of blood just stop abruptly?

As the CSP continued to search the property, troopers looked up inside the pagoda and spied a set of pull-down stairs, which were obviously connected to an attic or storage area of some sort on the first built floor of the pagoda.

That blood trail had stopped directly underneath the pull down stairs.

DETECTIVE MARTY GRAHAM AND his partner waited patiently at the door for Scott Deojay's girlfriend to fetch the gardener. They needed to speak to Deojay about the receipt stained with what appeared to be fresh blood droplets. It was too early for any lab results to have returned, so there was no definitive answer as to whose blood was on the receipt or in the snow. Still, maybe Deojay could clear the matter up and point the state police's investigation in a different direction.

The key was to be able to talk to him to find that out.

Deojay's girlfriend returned to the door and let Graham and Lamoureux in. "Where is he? We want to talk to him," Graham asked respectfully.

"In the bedroom," the blonde said. ("She was very helpful," Graham recalled later. "Ready and willing to help us.")

But Deojay had run from the bedroom into a garage attached to the house. He was naked as a jaybird and nowhere to be found. His clothes were still sitting on a chair by the bed.

"When we got into the bedroom," Graham explained, "we were all surprised because Deojay was no longer in bed, where his girlfriend had said he was."

"This is odd," the girlfriend said to Graham and his partner. "We were just sleeping. He asked me casually who was at the door."

Realizing Deojay had bolted, Graham walked into the garage and looked around. Lamoureux went out to the cruiser to call for backup. With snow on the ground outside, Graham quickly determined that Deojay could not have taken off, or there would have been fresh footprints in the snow. Even so, Graham and his partner had to be careful here on a another level entirely. They were there, inside this house, without a warrant. All they wanted to do was talk to Big Bird's gardener, to ask Scott Deojay a few questions and, with the right answers, be on their way. They weren't accusing Deojay of anything; they were simply trying to locate a missing person and the evidence up until that point had led them to need to question Scott Deojay.

As they entered the garage a second time, Graham and Lamoureux heard some movement near one of the walls. The sounds were coming from, it seemed, *inside* the wall.

Scott Deojay, they soon figured out, was hiding *underneath* the house in what Graham described later as a "three foot high crawl space."

Graham and Lamoureux stripped off their coats so they could fit into the small crawlspace and have a look underneath the house.

"Hey," Graham said, his chest to the ground, "what are you doing?" He could barely see Deojay. Yet, shining a flashlight underneath, Graham could tell that Deojay was "bare-ass naked," and was also now shivering.

Even so, Deojay wouldn't respond.

Then a thought occurred to both detectives: *Why is this clown hiding if he didn't do anything?*

"Scott, we just want to *talk* to you," Graham said. Sizing up the situation, being well over six feet tall, Graham decided *he* wasn't going in to fetch Deojay.

Graham and Lamoureux were in a rough position. They had a woman who was still missing. With any luck, she was still alive. They needed any information Deojay could provide. They also needed to consider whether or not Deojay had a weapon? What was he planning to do? So, Graham said, he and Lamoureux, who was the smaller of the two troopers, decided Lamoureux would go in underneath the house after Big Bird's gardener.

That didn't work too well.

So they regrouped and decided, you know, why not flush Deojay out from underneath the house the old-school way.

By using pepper spray.

What helped was that Deojay's girlfriend was standing there during the entire ordeal. In effect, she was the CSP's witness. They were still on "touchy ground," Graham explained later. "They weren't there to arrest Deojay; just question him."

"What's going on, Scott?" Graham asked. "Why didn't

you come out? Why'd you run?" Deojay rubbed his eyes as he brushed himself off.

Deojay mumbled something about how he always "fled" the cops. It was just habit, he said. He was scared. What did they want, anyway?

"Get him some clothes," Graham told Deojay's girlfriend.

Graham and Lamoureux never told Scott Deojay what they wanted to talk to him about after he pulled himself out from underneath the house. They asked him, however, if he was willing to go down to the local Plainfield Police Department and answer some questions.

Deojay, teary-eyed and shaken up from the pepper spray, said he had no problem with that request.

Strangely enough, Deojay never asked why they wanted to speak with him.

"We did the usual: timelines, history, trying to reason with Deojay," Graham said. "We were hoping that Judy Nilan might still be alive and we needed to find her." The investigators considered the possibility that Deojay had hit her with his vehicle and panicked, so he hid her somewhere.

"I had no involvement with the missing woman," Deojay said immediately after the detectives asked him about Judy Nilan.

Graham asked about the bloody receipt. Deojay's name was on it. Why would blood be on a receipt he had signed?

Deojay said he frequently purchased items for the Spinney estate. He had no idea how the receipt ended up on that road, or how blood got on it.

"Where is she, Scott?" Graham took a stab.

"I *don't* know."

The interview went on for three hours. They got nowhere. "Obviously, our angle was, 'Where is she?'" Graham recalled. "We had nothing to hold him or arrest him on. We believed she might be alive. The interview went on and on and on … and we eventually got to the point where we let him go."

Graham and Lamoureux gave Deojay a ride home; he lived near the Plainfield PD. In the interim, however, they learned an important fact about Scott Deojay.

Deojay had been questioned about a rape in Plainfield years ago, which put an additional spin on how he looked as a possible suspect in Judy Nilan's disappearance.

After their arrival back at Deojay's apartment, Graham and Lamoureux observed a 1997 Ford Escort station wagon parked in the driveway, the same type of vehicle reportedly seen heading toward Judy Nilan as she jogged past off-duty Trooper Stevens on the day of her disappearance. The vehicle in Deojay's driveway was black.

"This yours?" Graham asked.

Deojay nodded his head yes.

Graham and Lamoureux took a closer look at the car. As it turned out, it was registered to Scott Deojay's former girlfriend. Along the passenger's side rear door and quarter-panel was a smearing of an ample amount of blood, as well as a "pattern impression [of blood] on the rear passenger's side of the vehicle."

This constituted probable cause and was enough to seize the car pending the issuance of a search warrant.

They asked Deojay about the blood. He denied knowing anything about it.

Graham called a tow truck service and had the vehicle removed to Troop D, which is what? An impound lot? Please identify for the reader.

"We interviewed his girlfriend, and she had a timeline for him going to work and coming home around his usual time, with nothing unusual about him from what she saw." Deojay, on the day Judy Nilan disappeared, sat down with his girlfriend and her teenage daughter and ate dinner, the girlfriend said, and then he watched television and "did their usual stuff."

He wasn't acting unusual, she told Graham.

They interviewed the girlfriend's daughter to see if Deojay had ever assaulted her. They were looking to grab him on anything until they could find out what was going on.

She said he had never touched her.

AN OMINOUS CLOUD OF suspicion continued to hover over Scott Deojay. The CSP had his car, which had blood on it. Lab reports would soon return confirming the presence of Judy Nilan's DNA inside Deojay's vehicle, as well as the presence of human blood DNA matching Judy's type, which was located smeared liberally all over one side of it. With each passing hour, evidence increased which pointed to the likelihood that Scott Deojay knew where Judy Nilan was, and yet he still refused to talk about it.

Deojay's girlfriend was not happy with the circumstances she now found herself in. Here was Deojay at her house, a man she thought she *knew,* being accused of heinous crimes. That morning, after police left, she approached Deojay, saying, "We need to talk."

Deojay knew what she was about to say: *Get the hell out of my house.*

He looked at her, "I need ten minutes alone."

As Deojay went into the garage, his girlfriend followed him. "Leave me alone," he said. "I need some time."

So she went back into the apartment.

Several minutes later, when Deojay still hadn't returned, his girlfriend walked into the garage to find out what was keeping him. When she entered, she saw Deojay standing with a "blue strap around his neck." The other end was attached to a rafter in the garage.

Scott Deojay was trying to hang himself.

She looked up at him and gasped.

"Say good-bye," Deojay said.

The woman ran toward Deojay in an effort to help him down. Hurriedly, she picked up the phone and called 911. When dispatch answered, she screamed, "I need help at [my apartment] …"

As the girlfriend spoke to the dispatcher, Deojay kicked the phone out of her hand, screaming, "Give me that knife!" referring to a knife lying nearby on the tool bench. "I'm not going to stab myself," he pleaded, "I just want to cut myself down." The strap was still attached to the rafter and around his neck.

Scared, the girlfriend reached over and handed Deojay the knife.

BACK AT BIG BIRD'S estate, the investigators, who had already located the bloody trail leading up to what they now believed were pull- down stairs heading into a storage room located inside a pagoda-like structure, found something else.

At the edge of the pagoda, around the corner, was a wooden bench, perhaps another sacred place to sit and contemplate the true meaning of life, while gazing upon the beauty of the landscape. In front of the bench was a "large area of blood-like substance." Furthermore, on one of the "support posts of the pagoda near the wooden bench" was a second smearing of what appeared to also be blood, which appeared to be somewhat fresh because it was still tacky.

It seemed rather obvious that something terribly brutal had taken place in or around the pagoda. With this evidence in mind, troopers pulled the stairs down and proceeded to search the upper storage area.

As soon as the first trooper reached the top of the stairs, the reality of what had happened to Judy Nilan became sadly clear. There before him was "the deceased body of a white female, who was wearing a yellow windbreaker, gloves, and black colored spandex type running pants which were pulled down to her knees."

Judy Nilan was dead.

By studying the crime scene, detectives were able to determine that Judy had been viciously murdered. This wasn't just a case of a potential car accident gone horribly wrong. Looking at the way in which her body was positioned, investigators reported that she had been "beaten about the head, her hands were tied behind her back and the rope was also wrapped around her neck and tied around her ankles ... [with] black tape." Essentially, Judy's killer had hog-tied her.

"There appeared to be no rhyme or reason why her killer had tied her up the way he did," one investigator later noted.

In light of locating Judy Nilan's body tied as it was, investigators asked themselves questions: Was she too bloody to carry up the stairs? Was her killer afraid to get blood on himself? It made no sense, really, in the scope of what they knew. If it had been an accident (if Judy had been accidentally stuck by a car), and someone was trying conceal her body, why would he go to the trouble of tying her up and taping her body? The scene was horrific. There was blood all over the place.

"She was beaten really, *really* badly," one investigator said.

Another problem soon emerged within the investigation. GPS readings indicated that the pagoda was located so far from the main Spinney house that it was actually in another town, not to mention another state: Southbridge, Massachusetts. Thus, the CSP was obligated, under the laws of jurisdiction, to hand Judy Nilan's body and the crime scene over to the Massachusetts State Police (MSP).

A review of the evidence up to this point indicated that

it appeared Scott Deojay struck Judy with his car, maybe even by accident, and then, in trying to cover up *that* crime, had hidden her body. The apparent sign of of sexual assault, investigators believed, due to how she was found with her pants pulled down to her ankles, caused investigators to suspect that perhaps Deojay had stalked Judy for a period of time and carried out a plan to attack her.

"We don't believe," one detective said, "that Deojay struck her with any force with his car. There were tire marks left on the road. Sometimes, tire marks are tough to gauge. One theory was that Deojay knew Judy's route. Perhaps he had seen her jogging before. Most people are creatures of habit. Could he have come racing up to her, locking up his brakes and stopped her on the road? She probably stopped running, at which point Deojay may have jumped out of his car and punched her indicated by the small amount of blood at the primary scene (Brickyard Road). He then would have somehow gotten her into his car. Now, remember, we later found a small amount of blood on the *rear* passenger's side door of his car. After he got her in the car, we believe, he drove her to the Spinney estate, where he knew no one was home because the Spinneys were away traveling. He then drives through the gate and there the driveway splits. There was an outbuilding which was half bathroom-changing room and the other half storage. There were stains there that came back to Deojay after DNA testing. One theory was that he assaulted or attempted to sexually assault her in this building and then brought her up to the bench that was under the pagoda and just beat her and then dragged her up those stairs. It looked like he just left her there for dead. Horrific. Truly upsetting."

Even though Deojay would ultimately never be charged with sexual assault, a source involved in the investigation later told me, "We knew that Miss Nilan was sexually assaulted. We found Mr. Deojay's DNA inside a [separate location] on the Spinney property. We also found his DNA on the rope he used to tie her up."

Judy's body was transported from the crime scene to the medical examiner's office in Boston where a complete autopsy was conducted. According to the M.E., Judy Nilan died from "blunt force trauma to the head and neck." These injuries, said the report, "caused multiple fractures, subarachnoid hemorrhage and brain contusion by manner of homicide."

BACK IN 2004, SCOTT Deojay was a suspect in a home invasion and rape of a woman in his hometown, Plainfield. Because of Deojay's possible role in the death of Judy Nilan, he was nabbed for the 2004 rape, which had gone unsolved for two years. Addressing those new charges in court, State's Attorney Patricia Froehlich said, "This man is an incredible danger to the community."

At one time, Plainfield was best known for its Dog Track off Interstate 395. It is a small town. The rape Deojay committed took place on the night of June 19, 2004, when a local woman was attacked in the safety of her home by an "armed man" who, after disabling the woman's telephone, "sexually assaulted" her, and then went through the house and took what he wanted. The description the woman gave Plainfield Police at the time fit Scott Deojay to a "T."

Deojay had lived in the same neighborhood where the rape occurred. It was the type of neighborhood where doors were left unlocked. On that same night, after the rape was reported, Plainfield Police set up roadblocks in the region and stopped people and asked questions to see if there was someone in town who knew about the crime.

Years later, it was dogged gumshoe police work, and the courage of the victim who was willing to come forward, and the solid evidence of forensic science which finally led police to Scott Deojay. When Judy Nilan was found dead and DNA became part of that case, lab results matched the DNA from the Judy Nilan case with Scott Deojay for the rape and burglary in Plainfield. The system, you could say, eventually worked in these two cases.

Scott Deojay was a repeat sexual offender whose behavior had escalated from rape and burglary to murder.

After his girlfriend talked him down from the strap in her garage, Deojay jumped inside his girlfriend's car. Meanwhile, the Plainfield Police Department had dispatched a few officers to the scene after receiving the 911 call from Deojay's girlfriend.

Deojay's girlfriend ran after him, grabbed the knife which Deojay had dropped on the ground and, just before Deojay was about to pull out of the driveway, the courageous woman managed to slash three of the four tires on her own car so he couldn't leave.

Deojay tried to take off in another car in the same driveway, belonging to X, but didn't have the keys.

By then the Plainfield Police had pulled up.

THERE WAS NOW ENOUGH evidence to arrest Scott Deojay on suspicion of murder. Since the case originated in Woodstock, where Judy Nilan had been "kidnapped," it fell on State's Attorney Patricia Froehlich to prosecute Deojay, who was now being held on a $10,000 cash bond at the Plainfield Police Department, pending a court date for what type of hearing? Indictment hearing? at Windham County Superior Court the following morning, December 14, 2005.

It appeared that State's Attorney Froehlich had a slam dunk case against Scott Deojay. The major problem, at least from the onset, was that a truly lovely woman, adored by her community, who had simply gone out for a jog one evening in a safe community, feeling securely guarded by her surroundings, ended up being brutally murdered and, state police now believed, savagely beaten and raped.

"I often think that it was especially tragic that a strong and courageous woman who just went out for a run, to make herself stronger by conquering the country roads near her home," Froehlich said, " died such a violent death."

Scott Deojay was transported to Day Kimball Hospital in Putnam for a mental   evaluation. Detectives David Lamoureux and Pricilla Vining arrived at Day Kimball to speak with Deojay. The state police had heard about his so-called suicide attempt and wanted to ask him about his possible role in Judy's death. In truth, they knew Deojay was involved because the evidence was outstanding. They just needed him to admit it.

The detectives read Deojay his Miranda rights. Deojay quickly declined speaking to a lawyer and signed a waiver, which allowed the state police to photograph several injuries he had on his hands and ask him questions.

Detective Vining, at Deojay's request, left the room. When she exited, Plainfield Police Department Sergeant Bart Ramos, who had been waiting with Deojay for the detectives to arrive, sat in on the interview. Detective Lamoureux began by letting Deojay know that they had found Judy's body on the Spinney property. Then Lamoureux said the state police were well aware that he had been working at the property as an employee of Carroll Spinney for some time. During this time, as Lamoureux talked about the discovery of Judy's body, Deojay began to sob, folding into himself, weeping like an infant.

Lamoureux wondered aloud if there was something Deojay wanted to talk about. What was weighing on his conscious?

"While I was driving on Redhead Hill Road, I struck

her," Deojay explained. He implied that he didn't mean to hit Judy. It just happened. "It was an accident. I believe she died at the scene."

Nonsense.

If that was true, the obvious question had to be: Why not call police and report the accident? Why try to cover up the crime? It's no secret that ninety-five percent of these types of hit and run "accidents" involve a driver leaving the scene, getting out of the location as fast as he or she can. It was almost unheard of that a hit and run driver would actually leave the scene *with* the victim's body.

"I panicked," Deojay said, trying to explain why he removed Judy's body from the scene.

Still, why was she hog-tied? What was the purpose of tying her up?

"I tried unsuccessfully to carry her up the folding ladder staircase, after carrying her from my car to the pagoda," he said. Apparently, he couldn't get her up the stairs without tying her up. "So I went back to my car to retrieve a rope and tied it around her," adding that he used the rope to hoist Judy up the staircase.

It seemed awfully strange to Lamoureux that Deojay would go through all that trouble, tying the body in such a way, taping her up, placing the rope around her body—her neck!—in such a methodical manner, to simply carry Judy up those stairs. Why not just dump her body in the woods somewhere nearby? Did Deojay actually assume that no one in the Spinney household would ever go up into that pagoda storage area again?

Deojay couldn't give an answer.

"On the way out of the driveway," Deojay continued, "I found one of her shoes in my car and threw it behind a tree in the snow near the end of the driveway." (The sneaker was later recovered exactly where Deojay had said he tossed it.)

Deojay was released that night from the hospital and immediately arrested on kidnapping charges—the only crime the state police could prove at the moment—and held on $1 million bond. The medical examiner, it turned out, disputed Deojay's account of the injuries that had killed Judy Nilan, saying they were "inconsistent with being struck with a motor vehicle." Later, one of the investigators said, "I saw the woman. She was beaten severely. No way a vehicle did that. It's impossible."

On top of that, Judy's pants had been pulled down to her ankles. Deojay's DNA had been found in two locations connected to Judy Nilan's body. His explanation that he had to drop her pants in order to tie her up and hoist her up the stairs made no sense.

The state attorney's office believed Deojay stalked Judy Nilan, struck her down with his car, viciously beat her into submission and continued to beat her until she died. It would be a tough case, especially on the victim's family. State's Attorney Patricia Froehlich later said, approaching this case was no different from any one of her other murder cases: "The same way I try to prosecute each of them, by looking at the crime scene, the evidence, the defendant's history and by treating the victim's family with dignity and respect, which means being honest with them, whether it's good news or bad."

At first, it seemed like an ideal case for the death penalty. Froehlich took a deep breath, studied the law, and realized it was going to be a tough sell. "As in each of the capital felonies I have handled," she added, "I agonized over whether or not the facts fit our very strictly limited death penalty law. There are two possible penalties for capital felony: life without the possibility of release (not parole, release!) or death. Our Supreme Court has very strictly interpreted our death penalty statute. The information from the experts in this case, the medical examiners who conducted the autopsy, led me to conclude that the facts did not fit our death penalty law."

In short, the medical examiner would have to agree that Judy Nilan went through a period of torture and extreme cruelty *while* she was alive.

Looking at Deojay, sizing him up, Froehlich later explained, "Scott Deojay committed at least two very violent crimes against women. He savagely murdered Judy Nilan and approximately two years earlier brutally and repeatedly sexually assaulted another woman in what was supposed to have been the privacy and safety of her own home. I can only characterize him as a serious threat to society. I would rather not give any additional attention to a convicted murderer and rapist but would instead like to pay tribute to the memory of the courageous women he victimized."

AS MARCH 2007 ARRIVED, with a little more than a year to think about it, Scott Deojay decided it was in his best interests to accept a plea agreement. After all, juries have little use for a two-time rapist. It would not have been a hard sell for State's Attorney Patricia Froehlich to prove that Deojay had raped, beaten and murdered Judy Nilan.

During his sentencing hearing on March 9, 2007, before a courtroom packed to capacity with friends and family of Judy Nilan, along with state troopers and police officers from all over Windham County, Deojay stood before the court, appearing disheveled and dirty. He wore a banana yellow state-issued jump suit, three days' worth of stubble, and a strange look of despair over his puffy face.

Deojay's defense attorney, Ramon Canning, addressed the court on Deojay's behalf, offering, for the first time, Deojay's "defense"for the two rapes and murder he committed. In short, Canning suggested Deojay couldn't help himself because he had been wired when he was sixteen years old to become a rapist, and therefore it *wasn't* his fault.

Many in the room were taken aback. "What the heck is this guy getting at?" one person asked. "It was appalling."

Canning said it was theState of Connecticut's fault, essentially, that Scott Deojay had turned out the way he did. "What?"

On probation as a teenager, Deojay had to visit Richard Straub, his probation officer. Deojay was now claiming that Straub had sexually assaulted him repeatedly for three years.

As Canning spoke, Judy Nilan's brother stood up and walked out of the room in tears.

In 1999, Richard Straub had indeed been convicted of more than thirty counts of sexual assault, kidnapping, and unlawful restraint pursuant to sexual abuse allegations from more than a dozen of his clients. Scott Deojay, however, had *never,* before this day in court, reported any such abuse by Straub, nor been included as a victim in any such allegations or legal prodeedings. "The state had a great impact on him because of this probation officer's actions," Canning explained. "It went on for *three* years. The aftereffects tormented his mind and caused an outpouring of rage."

"Previously undisclosed abuse is a tired, worn out excuse for a defense," Patricia Froehlich said, "that many people who finally face the consequences of their actions try to assert. I wouldn't have expected anything different from someone who committed the crimes to which he entered guilty pleas." Scoot Deojay was a gutless, coward looking for a way out of his animalistic, evil behavior. How outrageous and humiliating to the memory of Judy Nilan.

Superior Court Judge Antonio Robaina, clearly upset by the notion that Deojay had used such an underhanded tactic to try to lessen the impact of such a ghastly crime, explained that sexual abuse was *no* excuse for these offenses. These victims were so remote from the violence. Judy Nilan was a person who personified kindness and caring for others. She was clearly not in the defendant's circle of violence."

Picking up on that point, Judy's husband, Jon Baker let it all out during his impact statement, saying, "Judy was clearly no victim. She was a strong woman who accomplished more in her forty-four years than most others do in their lifetime."

When Jon Baker was nearly finished, he paused for a moment to collect himself before addressing Judy personally, saying, "Come on, kid. Let's go and leave what we can here. We have a future elsewhere, and maybe another song to sing together in the garden. I love you."

The gallery was in tears.

The judge piled on another twenty years for the sexual assault Deojay had committed in Plainfield, and sent Deojay on his way to a lifetime behind bars.[1]

---

1   *I do not want to sound as though I am in any way blaming Judy Nilan for what happened to her, but I want to say something here to any female reading this book. If you are a jogger/walker, I beg of you to take a different route each time you head out for a run, even if you change it up just a little bit. No matter where you live, no matter how safe you think you are, there could be a psychopath like Scott Deojay lurking in the shadows, watching you run/walk by his house or place of employment every single day, and as each day passes, he might become more and more obsessed with you to the point where he needs to act out on the twisted fantasies flowing through his mind. Don't give him that satisfaction. Take a different route. And also, please check the sex offender's registry in your area with a quick Google search and find out where the sex offenders in your neighborhood live. Believe me, no matter where you live, there are sex offenders near you. Again, I am in no way blaming Judy Nilan for what happened to her by saying this, but let us learn something from Judy's brutal murder.*

NOTHING THIS EVIL EVER DIES
THE LOST LETTERS OF SON OF SAM

INTRODUCTION

Son of Sam, David Berkowitz, has found God and claimed to be remorseful for his crimes. He's come out recently and talked about how Jesus has saved him. As recently as August

2011, Sam has written to the press. In a two-page letter to FoxNews.com, Sam claimed to have "no interest" in parole thanks to, being totally forgiven by Jesus Christ.

Sam is 58.* He has been, by the most recent tally, denied parole five times.

"I have no interest in parole and no plans to seek release," he wrote FoxNews.com. "If you could understand this, I am already a 'free man.' I am not saying this jokingly. I really am. Jesus Christ has already forgiven and pardoned me, and I believe this."

Dare I say, God bless him.

On Sam's official home page, the convicted serial killer once explained how he locked up for the past two decades has weighed on him. "My criminal case," he writes, "is well-known and was called the Son of Sam shootings."

Eleven years prior to penning these opening Web page lines, this vicious killer went on to say, while he was "living in a cold and lonely prison cell," God grabbed hold of his life and set him on the righteous path. He said his story—or, rather, his path toward righteousness—has become an example of "hope."

This letter to his readers was written in 1999. The date is important to what you are about to read, because my book, *Every Move You Make*, where I first published excerpts from the lost Son of Sam letters, was published five years later, in 2005. Now, here, in this exclusive ebook, I am going deeper into those letters to give readers another layer of understanding into the mind to this serial killer.

As he has written in the letter to Fox News, Son of Sam claims to be "free" from the confines of prison. He claims Jesus Christ has led him to the light of a new way. He calls his Web page "Forgiven for Life."

This story is about the real Son of Sam, not the façade Mr.

Berkowitz wishes to display in his letters to news agencies and Web writings. It is about the person who murdered six people, and tormented and terrorized a city. As for prison life, Berkowitz says his days and nights behind bars are a constant "struggle," and that he's had his "share of problems, hassles and fights." He claims another inmate cut his throat once and he almost died.

Ah, the life of a serial killer on the inside. One rather high profile serial killer just recently told me during a phone interview, "In prison, you're either someone other inmates fear or want to kill."

"Yet all through this," Sam says, "and I did not realize it until later, God had His loving hands on me."

Further along into his Website writings, Berkowitz writes that while he was "reading Psalm 34" one night, he "began to pour out [his] heart to God." He says this moment of clarity, when God entered his soul, took place in the year 1987; he gives no specific date, just the year. "Everything seemed to hit me at once," he claims. "The guilt from what I did ... the disgust at what I had become ..." And then, he says, he "got down on his knees and began to cry out to Jesus Christ."

This revelation, a word I hesitate to use here, by a sadistic killer is a complete fabrication. Pay close attention to the year he has given us of his conversion, 1987, as you read this. When you get to the lost Son of Sam letter excerpts I quote, you'll have a hard time believing God's hands were resting on the shoulders of Mr. Berkowitz as he wrote those letters. Personally, I do not believe it is possible for a serial killer to experience remorse or sorrow. Forgiveness by God, absolutely. I am a man of faith. But that, I also believe, is between Sam and his maker—and not for the local press. In this story, you'll see the real mind of this serial killer at work, then you can decide for yourself if you believe Sam's current redemptive and colloquial conversion and dedication to Christ is legit.

Serial killers have become my life these days. That obsession, if you'll allow me the term, began with my first book, *Perfect Poison*. It went into overdrive while I was working on and finishing a second serial killer book, and was introduced to an aspect of Son of Sam's character I thought I'd never, for the life of me, run into inside a cardboard box which had been left collecting dust for many years.

It happened on one of those cold New England winter mornings when you feel as if your bones will snap if you stay outside too long. I was at my desk working on a new book, *Every Move You Make*. I received what I presumed to be then was a mildly irritating telephone call. *Every Move You Make*, which is an important part of this story you are reading, chronicles the life of serial killer Gary Charles Evans, and a relationship, friendship is perhaps a more fair word, which Evans had with the investigator who eventually caught him, James Horton. Think a real-life version of *Silence of the Lambs* meets *Catch Me If You Can*. That's *Every Move You Make*.

As I picked up the phone, I had no idea this seemingly annoying call would change the entire scope of my book. Or better yet, introduce me to a side of David "Son of Sam" Berkowitz no researcher or writer had ever explored.

Why had this call come across as such an annoyance at the time? For one, I was ten months into the writing process of my book; I felt I had finished the research. In a few months, my editors were expecting a manuscript. In addition to that, I get calls all the time from people who want to be included in one of my books, but when push comes to shove, they generally have nothing of substance to offer or add to the background of the book.

"Mr. Phelps, my husband would like to speak to you about Gary Evans," said this gentle sounding woman's voice. She seemed kind, sincere. I was taken right away by her affect.

"Oh … in what context?" I asked, believing then that I had uncovered all there was to know about Gary Evans. Knowing now (after writing 23 books) what I didn't know then, it always happens: someone, somewhere, as soon as you're ready to hand in a manuscript, comes up with what they feel is groundbreaking information about your subject. You're obligated, if you have any journalistic integrity, to at least listen to this person and hear them out.

"Bill went to grammar school with Gary Evans," the woman explained.

My interest was at first piqued, but then fizzled out. Rolling my eyes, I'm thinking, *Grammar school? What in the world could this guy tell me about my serial killer that happened to them in grammar school?*

"Okay, put him on the phone," I said.

As Bill and I talked, I realized I'd heard of this man before, but believed he was one more in a long list of "friends" my serial killer had early in life that knew very little about him personally. You know, one of those casual acquaintances we all have in life. Yeah, I went to school with him … didn't know him that well, though.

We spoke for a minute.

"Well," Bill said when I started to ask pointed questions, "I would rather you come up here and talk to me in person."

This can sometimes be a hassle—especially at the end of the book writing process.

"Where do you live?" I asked Bill.

Come to find out, his house was in upstate New York.

Great, I told myself. I live outside Hartford, Connecticut. Bill's house was a five-hour drive on a good day.

I spoke to his wife again a few days later. She told me that a friend of the family wanted to meet me. This person had read one of my books. She was a fan.

I wanted to tell her no. I just don't have the time. I have to finish the Gary Evans book. I'm on a deadline. My publisher was expecting it. A trip like that, interviews, meet 'n greets. It's all good. I love doing that stuff. But time was my enemy here. I didn't have much left.

Before I could nicely articulate that thought, however, Bill's kind wife mentioned something about having chocolate and gourmet coffee, sandwiches, "all sorts of goodies," I believe she said. Damn, this woman must have known my vulnerabilities. My weaknesses. Robust, dark coffee and expensive chocolate—the right kind—are like kryptonite to me. I rarely refuse.

"Would you mind, Mr. Phelps, snapping a few photographs with everyone and signing some of your books?"

For a week I agonized over this trip, desperately wanting to call them back and say no. I just couldn't do it, but they still had not told me one thing about Gary Evans I thought I could use.

Yet something beyond the chocolate and coffee dancing in my head nagged at me; my gut was telling me to go. Plus there's always the possibility of a problem later to consider: When the book comes out, they could step forward and say, "We wanted to talk to him but he wouldn't interview us."

In the end, the truth—and my quest for it—is what matters to me most. These people had something to say. I needed to be there to hear it.

So I headed up to northern New York, stressing over every mile, traffic light, and stop sign, pounding on my steering wheel in frustration.

Part of me repeated this mantra: *This is a waste of time. A damn waste of precious time which I need to finish my book.*

Heading to Bill's house, I got lost for about an hour,

but finally found the street and soon rolled up the driveway to his house, pulling into a parking spot near a set of horse barns. The house was quite beautiful, nicely built, rustic, country. This was soccer-mom territory. The Waltons. Beaver Cleaver. You know, suburban bliss.

Stepping out of my car, an interesting and jarring blend of aromas hit me: pine tree and horse manure.. What a juxtaposition of smells. These days, I live in a farming community, so I have become quite aware of the dynamic of a place where animals are raised and worked. You either accept it or move away. But up there in New York it was different. The air was fresh and crisp. It was going to be a good day, I could feel it.

As I stood for a moment, collecting my coat and brief case, I couldn't help but recall a trip I had taken for the same book a few months before this. It had been a bit longer of a ride, but in the same general region of the state. A woman had called me after receiving a letter I had written her asking for an interview. She was the wife of one of Gary Evans' victims. As we spoke on the phone, she cried. I felt bad. Talking to victims' family members is tough stuff. You're pillaging their memories, asking them to open up a portion of their lives they may not have thought about for years— and may not want to. Years later, conducting these same interviews on my TV series, DARK MINDS, had taught me that murder affects a family in a myriad of ways. There's a ripple effect that lasts forever. The pain stays fresh no matter how long it's been.

Anyway, this woman, through tears, agreed to speak to me, but again, "I will only do it in person. I have photos of 'my Timmy,' " she said (the victim's name was Timothy), and she wanted to share them with me. "Please come up here."

"Timmy," I thought. This is going to be a tough interview

with a woman in a tremendous amount of emotional pain.

Knocking at her door after a long, tiring trip, this old man, very frail, with wrinkled, leathery skin, like a baked potato, and lots of sun spots, greeted me. He was wearing black slacks, a button-up dress shirt, and, strangely enough, tan socks and no shoes.

I thought, *This is strange.* An old man with no shoes on; he must be the dad. Timmy's father.

"I'm [the boy's] mentor," the old man said, inviting me in. I stood for a moment on the stoop, slightly puzzled.

Timothy had a teenage son. The old man that let me in claimed he was mentoring the boy. For what, exactly, I had no idea, but he was providing a stable role model for a boy who had lost his father to a serial murderer. Who was I to question what he was doing?

Ok, great, I thought to myself, let's do this.

The wife I spoke to on the telephone was sitting on the couch, wailing, with a box of Kleenex on her lap. One leg crossed over the other, arms folded at her chest, her craned leg moving a mile a minute. I felt uncomfortable, like a voyeur, as if I was peering in through her window and she didn't know it. This woman had lost her husband, she was clearly devastated by that loss, and uncomfortable with me writing about it. But she had agreed to help. So here I was.

This is very important. I should explain that her husband, Timmy, wasn't only shot in the head by Gary Evans; but Evans dismembered Timmy's body with a chainsaw into several pieces and buried his remains throughout an area north of Albany, New York. I had viewed the crime scene photos, studied the reports, and understood what this woman had gone through in identifying her husband, not to mention dealing with his gruesome death. This was a horror show. This man wasn't just murdered. His body was defiled in ways one cannot imagine.

I sat at the dining room table. She sat next to me. The old man in tan socks sat directly in front of me, staring and smiling, his arms cradled under his chin as if he had a crush on me. He gave me the creeps, to be perfectly honest. It gave off this very strange vibe.

The wife started weeping loudly, in a very dramatic fashion. "My poor Timmy," she said several times through a Niagara of tears. "I cannot believe what Gary did to him."

I couldn't either, even though I'd seen the crime scene photos. I read the autopsy reports with my mouth agape.

Admittedly, I felt small and incredibly intrusive at this point. However, I understood her pain. Years ago, my brother's wife was murdered by a serial killer. She was five months pregnant. Reports said her assailant put a pillowcase over her head and strangled her with a telephone cord. If some journalist had come and asked my niece and nephews and brother about it, I'm not sure they would have wanted to go into detail.

"I'm so sorry I have to do this," I said. "But I want to portray Timmy with absolute care and gentleness." Timmy, I should note, was not such an upstanding citizen, but that was not my interest in writing about him. Instead, I wanted to also talk about who he was as a father and husband.

"I know ... I know ... but my poor Timmy," she said, accompanied by more tears, more sniffling, and more body trembling.

The old man just continued to stare at me. Remember that kid in "A Christmas Story" wearing the goggles, standing in line with Ralphie waiting for Santa, the weird kid who randomly said, "I like the *Wizard of Oz*." That's what this felt like.

I considered leaving, and would have, if my office wasn't so far away. I had even thought about getting a room for the night and returning the next day. But, after blowing her nose,

Timmy's wife turned to me with a straight face, shutting off the tears completely, as if she could at will, and said, "Before I begin talking, I want to know how much money you're going to pay me?"

Ah-hah! Here we go. That's the vibe I was feeling. Ulterior motives. Here they were now front and center.

As she waited for my answer, I looked over at the old man in tan socks. He smiled. Then said: "I'm her lawyer."

Bingo! It was starting to make sense.

"I'm not a tabloid journalist," I said defiantly. "I do not work for the *National Inquirer*—and I certainly do not pay sources."

She got up, saying, "Then I don't talk about Tim."

It was funny how, at that moment, he wasn't "Timmy" to her anymore; he was Tim, a commodity, a memory to barter with, something she thought she could spin into a few dollars. Most people think because you've written a few books, you're living in a McMansion, driving a BMW and vacationing with the likes of the Kardashians and Hiltons in Hawaii and Paris and Prague. The truth is far different, of course.

"How 'bout we come to a deal," the lawyer suggested. As he said this, I realized who he had reminded of. It had been bothering me. One of those tip-of-the-tongue things. Hume Cronyn. The old guy from the film *Cocoon*. This lawyer was a dead ringer for Hume. I could see him and his actress wife, Jessica Tandy, being whisked up to space while standing aboard that boat at the end of the movie. Hume and the lawyer were identical twins.

A deal? I thought. What *deal,* dude?

"Can she co-author the book or something? Maybe you can give her a percentage? She's a wonderful writer and has a unique perspective on this story."

I dropped my head. "Look, if she doesn't want to talk to

me, I'm leaving."

"You can't really tell this story without her," he said, trying his best to sound threatening.

Timmy's wife started pacing in the kitchen. Then, I think after gathering up the nerve, she spoke, saying, "If you"— and now she was pointing at me— "print anything bad about Tim, I will sue you. He wasn't a thief, as everyone says. And if you say that in your book, you'll be sued."

Timmy had been committing burglaries with Gary Evans. They had known each other for many years. I had a photograph of Tim planting a kiss on the barrel of sub-machine gun. Evans had taken the photo. These two guys together were expert thieves.

"I'm tired of people talking about Tim like that and I will sue you, Mr. Phelps!"

"You can't really write your book without my client's help," Hume Cronyn added.

I ignored him and asked her to take a breath and sit down. She did.

I waited a few beats. Allowed her to settle down. Hume went back to staring at me. Now I realized the look in his eye wasn't a crush, but he saw me as a cash cow. Hume saw dollar signs.

"Your husband was a convicted burglar, ma'am," I explained. "That's why I'm here. I want the complete story, not just the side of Tim that was a thief. I want to know who he was as a father, a husband. You know, the *good* times."

"Tim was no thief. He was a good man. And if you print that he was a thief, I'm just warning you that you will be sued."

I reached inside my briefcase and pulled out Timmy's mug shot. "You see that," I said, sliding it toward her, "that qualifies your husband as a convicted thief. Would you like to see the police reports and arrest record I have on Tim?"

She ran out of the room. I got up and left. Hume Cronyn stopped me on the way out and said he'd call me if she changed her mind.

"She just wants a little bit of money," he said, doing that thing with his fingers—you missed it by that much!—to make a point of what he meant by "a little bit."

I left my card with him and took off.

Weeks later, he called. "She's not going to talk to you unless you pay her."

"Tell her I said good luck."

Bill and his family were waiting in the foyer for me. Cameras. Chocolates. Cookies. Just as promised. I signed several copies of my books, gave a few copies away that I had brought with me, talked a bit about my career, and sat down. My previous experience with Tim's wife convinced me that Bill and his family also wanted money—that the chocolates and photo ops were a precursor to the inevitable.

Ugh.

As I would come to find out later, they had all met at the house hours before my arrival to discuss "things." Turns out Bill invited me to his house to size me up, check me out, make sure I was responsible enough to leave with the significant information I was about to be given. One person there that day later told me, "I remember being very eager as we drove up to [the house that day]. Neither one of us chatted too much on the ride up as it seemed we were both deep in our own thoughts. Once we arrived, we went right into the house to go through Gary [Evans's] things and determine what could and could not be exposed. There are many possessions and secrets that are held dear to Uncle Bill."

I had landed on a treasure trove of information without realizing it.

Uncle Bill was the man my serial killer, Gary Evans, had

gone to grammar school with; but, as I soon found out, Bill had also remained friends with Evans up until Evans's final arrest.

Continuing, the family member explained what was said before I arrived: "We discussed how you may just be some guy out to tell a story and we were afraid you would tell only the bad stuff, not knowing any of the good things, or any of Gary's background."

As I talked with everyone briefly after my entrance, I got a sense that they were your average, wholesome, good-natured people, one of whom was excited to meet me because of my work. I felt comfortable. These were standup citizens. They were honest and honorable. I was flattered by the attention they gave. They sincerely felt they had important information for me to include in my book about Gary Evans. They were proud to be part of it.

I had been overreacting.

Before I get back into the meeting, let me give you a bit of context for what will soon happen.

In *Every Move You Make*, I describe serial killer Gary Evans this way: "[Evans] was, when it came down to it, a twisted sociopath who had burglarized dozens of antique shops around New York, Vermont, Massachusetts and Connecticut. New York State Police Investigator James Horton had been playing a game of cat and mouse with Evans for the past 12 years, using him as an informant and arresting him for various crimes. Evans, a master escape and disguise artist, had helped the state police on a number of unsolved crimes in the area. Horton had developed a personal relationship with Evans throughout the years, and some cops didn't like it.

"Evans, at just under five foot six, 185 pounds, had built his body into a machine, carving it like Greek statue through years of lifting weights. He never drank alcohol, didn't use tobacco or drugs, and hated anyone who did. He lived on a very simple, yet disciplined diet of cereal, bread, pasta, rice and sweets. He despised meat of any kind. Even when he was in prison, Evans would trade meat for bread. As a criminal, he took pride in his work and tried desperately to outdo himself with each crime. It was a game. Every part of his day was spent detailing and thinking about his next job and how he was going to avoid being caught. He had never worked a full-time job in his life and had told Horton numerous times he never would. Horton had pulled some strings for Evans once and found him jobs, but Evans always ended up quitting after a few days.

"Horton's last encounter with Evans was the final blow to their relationship. In 1995, Horton needed Evans to testify in a rape-murder case against a known rapist and alleged serial murderer. Evans had even befriended the guy, under the direction of Horton, after being put in a jail cell next to him, and eventually got him to admit to murdering a local college student. All Horton wanted Evans to do was stay out of trouble until the rapists' trial.

"But Evans ended up stealing a rare book from a Vermont museum and Horton, in his words, later told Evans that he 'fucked' him on the murder case.

"They hadn't spoken since."

It was important to Uncle Bill and his posse that they explain their connection to Gary Evans. They shared a profound loyalty to Evans, regardless of the crimes he had committed. The killer that Evans had become wasn't the tender, caring individual they had known. This was important. One of them later told me, "Not that Gary's actions were condoned by us in any way, but think of it as if your best friend slowly became a different person ... you'd still have that love of friendship toward him. Gary had a very troubled childhood and everyone seemed to look past that [once he admitted to killing five people]. Not that all children from abusive families turn out to be serial killers, but once you feel no one cares for you and you are constantly told you are worthless, you begin to believe it and care less about yourself."

All this was true about Evans. He was viciously sexually abused, according to him, by his father. He had been treated, by both parents, like an animal, starved, beaten, and so on. According to sources for my book, Evans' mother had taught him how to steal. He never really had a chance in life. I got scores of letters after the book was published. Readers felt guilty that at some points in the book they felt sorry for Evans. None of this excuses Evans' behavior later on in life, but it does explain it and put it all into some sort of psychological context. It somewhat answers that "why" question we all ask after hearing about the crimes of a malicious, brutal killer.

"We discussed in depth the things we would *not* tell or show you," a source at Bill's that day told me later. "We put some things away and began to lay out the items Uncle Bill wanted to show you. We sat around and shared stories about Gary, both fond and not so fond. You have to remember that Uncle Bill knew Gary for many, many years, and most of his memories are that of a friend."

To me, this was new information. I had thought Evans and Uncle Bill lost touch throughout the years. I never knew Evans had stayed in contact (right up until the end) with this man.

When they heard my car enter the driveway, I was told later, they all ran toward the window.

"We were nervous and anticipating what you had to share with us as well." I had been researching Evans for about a year by then. They knew I had uncovered a lot of new information about him.

"Once you began to talk and ask questions and share

information with us, Uncle Bill reciprocated. I distinctly remember at one point, as I sat at the table, I noticed him and [my fiancé] make eye contact. [My fiancé] was the most pessimistic about meeting you, and with his eyes, he seemed to 'tell' Uncle Bill you were trust worthy."

It was then when Uncle Bill began to "let his guard down," my source explained later, and make a decision to allow me to see the additional items they had hidden before my arrival.

Enter Son of Sam.

AMERICAN FAMILY

As we talked, I learned that they were hardworking, middleclass people. I enjoyed their company from the moment I arrived. It was just the thought of having to drive ten hours to and fro in order to hear a few stories of what I assumed was a guy who knew a now-famous serial killer and wanted his voice in my book. I understood it. But it pained me to think that I may have come all this way for nothing.

"Don't turn on your tape recorder yet," Bill told me as I took it out and placed it on the dining table.

That's when things took an interesting turn.

"Oh," I said. "What's up? I record everyone."

"Yeah, I understand. But I want to tell you something first."

The man I had traveled all this way to interview then bellied up to the table he was sitting at opposite me, leaned in, and said, "Gary was a thief in school! He stole records [LPs] for us and we paid him." He was whispering. Sort of smiling.

I nodded my head. "Wow. That's fascinating."

"Before we get started," he said next, "I was wondering if you'd be interested in looking at something I have?"

"Sure. Why not."
He disappeared into the house.

CLOSET LIFE

Leaving my grieving, money-hungry widow and the old man .
in the tan socks, I kept going over what had taken place inside
her house: The woman's husband had been dismembered
with a chainsaw, his body stuffed in plastic bags, and she
was worried about money for his story. I had seen and heard
many things throughout my book writing career. I had been
asked for money by at least one or two people per book. I
always refused. But until this time, I had never before felt so
disgusted, so dirty.

Throughout the process of researching *Every Move You
Make*, I had developed this "feeling" that Gary Evans was
a closet homosexual. I had even asked Investigator James
Horton, a cop who knew Evans better than Evans knew
himself, but he disagreed.

"Gary? No way! Look at all of the girlfriends he had.
They all talked about how good a lover he was."

"That's my point. Gary always went above and beyond the
norm to talk—even brag—about his sexual performances."

Horton couldn't agree. And who was I to question a
senior investigator with the New York State Police? One
who had been on the job for twenty-plus years no less.

For months I wrote off my theory as just that—
speculation. I had no evidence, nor did I have a reliable
source claiming Evans was gay. I had a hunch. It wasn't that
it mattered one way or another. All it did was make my serial
killer that much more of an interesting subject to explore in
the book. But I couldn't put hunches and speculation into
print.

I also knew Evans was mesmerized, if not obsessed, with

celebrity and stardom. In the hundreds of letters I studied as part of my research for the book, there were several times when Evans talked candidly about a celebrity he thought he saw on the street, or some film company shooting on location in his neighborhood. Hollywood excited him. Bruce Lee was one of his favorites. He had even visited Lee's grave—as I would, too, while doing research for the book—while on his final run from Investigator Horton. Hiding out in the Pacific Northwest, while Horton was back in New York, trying to find Evans, and interviewing people who knew him, Evans mocked Horton by sending him a photograph of himself at Lee's gravesite, ingeniously insinuating, *See, I'm right here ... you can't catch me!* He also sent photos of himself in the wilderness of Washington state, one inside a fresh grave Evans was lying in, and several of him just out and about.

Still, as I wrote the book and continued researching Evans's life, I didn't know what it was exactly, but something about the tone of the Evans letters struck me. As I got closer to finishing the book, I forgot about it, not thinking for one minute that I'd find some of the answers to my questions at the end of the process in a stack of papers one of Evans's grammar school chums had stored away in a box somewhere in his house.

THE HANDCUFF KEY

As Bill disappeared into his house, his wife said, "You wait until you see what he's bringing back."

"No kidding."

I expected to be shown a grainy photograph of Bill, Gary and the rest of their fifth grade class. Horned-rimmed glasses, high waters, Converse sneakers, and pocket protectors. Maybe a note Evans had written to Bill, and perhaps an old school paper Evans had written about a love he had as a child for psychotic killers.

After a few minutes, Bill walked into the dining room area where I was sitting. He held two boxes.

"Before Gary went to jail that last time," he said, coming back into the room, "he stopped by here to drop off some of his personal possessions. Would you be interested in any of it?"

I thought I had heard him wrong. "Uh ... yeah," I said, barely getting the words out, "I'd like to see that stuff, if I could."

He smiled and opened the first box.

Before I continue, I should say that Gary Evans was not only a serial killer, but probably one of the most prolific antique thieves New England has seen in the past twenty years. The guy could steal a wallet from a cop at a policemen's convention. He once wanted an antique piece of jewelry so bad that, after realizing there was no way into the building without tripping the alarm, he spent several days tunneling underneath the building so he could come up inside, beyond any of the alarm system's tripping devices. Once inside, he took the antique and left a note in its place: "Thank you, the Mole."

Evans was able to get into any jewelry store he wanted, and antique shops throughout New England feared him. He would go so far as to scope out a shop for weeks, set up a tent in the woods in back of the property, gain the trust of the shop owner and then, when he felt he knew enough about the shop and its security, burgle the owner blind. He had even burned down an antique barn he burgled in order to cover up his crimes. The guy had escaped from prison twice and was able to get out of any situation. After Horton finally caught him, Evans was suspected then of killing three people. Yet he somehow managed to hide a handcuff key in his right nostril, a razorblade underneath his gums, and escape from two armed U.S. Marshals.

Knowing all of this and writing about it, by the time I sat down with Bill I believed there wasn't much left in Evans's life that could shock me. Evans had become one of the more interesting murderers I have ever studied and written about. I thought there was nothing in his criminal life of twenty-five years he had *not* done.

But that was before Bill opened those boxes.

NOTHING NEW

I walked over to where Bill stood by the boxes and stared down at them for a moment. Here, in front of me, was the entire life—from his point of view—of my serial killer. Anything important to him was inside these boxes: photographs, letters, little trinkets he had stolen and kept, drawings, paintings, stained glass windows he made while in prison.

"Can I start with one of his photo albums?" I asked.

"Sure," Bill said.

I picked up the book and sat down at the table. Flipping through the pages I started to see scores of photographs I had in my possession already. In fact, they were already on my editor's desk, typeset with captions, ready for the photo layout of the book.

I remember thinking as I went through page after page of photographs I had seen before, *Damn, I have all this stuff already. Where is something new?*

I put the album down for a moment, took out a package of letters Evans had stored in the box, and started reading.

Again, I recognized the letters. Evans's sister had sent me over one hundred letters he had written to her throughout a twenty-year period. Here, in front of me, were copies of some of those same letters. What at first seemed like a great journalistic discovery was turning into photocopies of things I had already uncovered.

Exactly what I feared most: a wasted trip.

But then Bill, perhaps sensing my disappointment, looked at me and smiled.

"Keep looking."

SON OF SAM

Bill moved a bit in his seat and, after taking a moment, said, "Did you know Gary and Son of Sam were friends?"

I had heard this throughout my research. Investigator Horton had mentioned it to me, saying Evans had bragged about knowing Son of Sam, but Horton could never prove it—and Evans was in no position to talk about his life anymore. Horton believed Evans was lying about Son of Sam, just another one of his fantasies of having been close to someone he viewed as a celebrity.

"I've heard that," I said to Bill. "But I don't think it's true."

Bill, his wife, and those standing by watching us, laughed. It turned into a joke, actually, which I believed at that moment was directed at me. I felt confused. Like I didn't know what I was talking about and they knew more. It seemed as if they were having fun with me.

"Oh, it's true all right," Bill said after a moment.

"How so?" I quipped. "How do you mean?"

"Let me show you."

He reached into the second box and pulled out a photograph of Evans standing beside Son of Sam. They were in front of a paneled wall.

"No kidding," I said, startled by the photograph. Here was proof, indeed, that Evans had at least met Son of Sam. But it still didn't prove they were friends. Maybe Son of Sam, like a retired baseball player forced to show up at trading card shows and hock himself, charged for photographs. It was a stretch, but knowing Evans the way I did I had to consider it.

Again, the laughter came. I felt like the joke was on me—as if they were pointing and laughing (which they weren't) in my face. *Sucker. You fell for it all, didn't you! You drove all the way up here for nothing.*

"Wait a minute," I said, "what else do you have?"

Bill bent down and took out another photo album. He slid it slowly across the table. "Open that up and take a look. I think you'll like what's inside."

I must admit, I was hesitant. I believed in them as people, sure, but at this point I was questioning everything I knew about Gary Evans. Was there a second life he had that no one except my new friends knew about?

CLINTON STATE PRISON

There comes a point when you're working on a book that you have to decide you've covered every base, turned over every rock, and it's time to end your search and be happy that you've managed to cover at least eighty-five percent of the story. No reporter or book author can ever get the *entire* story. It's just not possible. With *Every Move You Make*, I had reached that point somewhere around the day Bill's wife called and told me her husband wanted to meet me. I had interviewed scores of people, some dozens of times. Near the end, I was starting to hear the same stories, which is the point when you know you've covered everything you're going to get.

Or so I thought.

As I opened the photo album, I couldn't have imagined the story could get any better. I mean, I already had, as I wrote in the author's note of the book, what I believed was the most "incredible true story, which, in my opinion, includes the most shocking and surprising ending in the history of true crime" at my disposal. The book had turned into a cat and mouse game between a serial killer and a cop, who had befriended, arrested and chased his prey for twelve-plus years. My goodness, Evans had broken into Horton's home at times and wandered through it while Horton was not at home. He'd followed Horton and his wife. Horton had gotten Evans jobs. Evans had set up drug dealers for him. They were polar opposites, but appreciated the idea of interacting on a professional level. For ten years, Horton never knew Evans was a serial killer; he thought he was a burglar and wanted to help him. Catching Evans, realizing he was a serial killer, was the apex of the story. What Evans did *after* he was captured became the story of legend.

What more could I ask for in a crime story?

Inside the album were scores of letters between Son of Sam and Gary Evans. They had "done time" together at Clinton State Prison in Dannemora, New York, through which they had developed a close personal relationship.

"Are you kidding me?" I said out of excitement and fear. Excited for obvious reasons, fearful because I now had this new vein to my story that hadn't existed before that day. I would have to rewrite much of my book, which wouldn't be a problem under normal circumstances. But with a 500-page book already in my hard drive, a daunting task, nonetheless, to have to reshape and keep the book somewhat in the neighborhood of its original page-count, flow and narrative.

"Can I take these back to my office?"

To my surprise and delight, Bill said, "Of course. That's why you're here."

THE CHOSEN ONE

Sitting in Bill's kitchen, grateful I had been called by his wife, I understood why it had been so important for me to drive up to the house to meet with everyone. They couldn't have told me any of this over the telephone. They had to meet me in person to see if I was worthy of such exclusive information. They had studied my work and believed I was thorough, but they read people—God bless them—by the way they interacted and communicated. They knew the difference between a hack looking for an easy story and a journalist digging and scratching his way to the bottom.

"Wow," I said, "I feel honored." They probably realized the sheer enthusiasm I had written all over my face. I had a tough time containing it.

"But there's more ...," Bill said.

I dropped my head for a moment, thinking, *This guy likes saying stuff like that ...*

"What do you mean, there's more?" I wanted to get back to my office immediately, brew a large pot of coffee, break out the Son of Sam letters, and get to work.

"Take a look at this photo album," he said, sliding it across the table.

As I said, Evans had gone out of his way to tell people he despised homosexuals. To call him a homophobe was beyond an understatement. But as I heard this from several different sources, I kept telling myself that he who screams the loudest is at once someone who has skeletons regarding the same issue.

I opened the album.

A TRUE LADY'S MAN

For practical purposes, homosexuality and Gary Evans were

an important part of my story, only because Evans had such strong opinions throughout his life regarding his hatred for any relationship that wasn't between a man and a woman. So, to find out that this same man was in fact experimenting with his own sexuality (at the least) was not only shocking to me as a researcher, but was going to throw my book into a second tailspin. If true, I would have to go back and re-read the letters Evans had written, re-interview several of my sources, and look at Evans under an entirely new light. This revelation would also change Evans's victim pool. For the most part, Evans had killed people he believed had victimized him in some way. He was staunchly against killing women and/or children. But there was always the feeling that he had killed others—several others.

As I sat and opened the album Bill had slid across the table, there in front of me was Evans dressed as a female. Beyond that, there were photographs of transsexuals. This was amazing for several reasons. First, no one knew about this side of Evans, at least no one I had spoken to for the book. Not cops, girlfriends, or family.

Nobody. Except, of course, Bill and his posse.

Secondly, this changed the dynamic of the relationship Evans had with Son of Sam. I was now more eager to crack open those letters to see what Son of Sam and Evans had talked about.

In this excerpt from *Every Move You Make*, I explain how those photographs Bill shared with me played into Evans's life:

To further bolster the theory that Evans was perhaps confused about his sexuality, the Polaroids depicted a man who was experimenting with his sexuality. For one, Evans liked to dress in women's clothes on occasion. Wearing a blonde wig, make-up and lipstick, he embodied the persona of a female rather affably. Although many might have thought it was nothing more than a Halloween costume, there is evidence he had a penchant for transsexuals and may have dated one while in prison. Not only had he taken Polaroids of a man he had met while in prison that lived life as a female, but later, when she got out of prison and completed her transition to a female, Evans visited her and took more photos. One might ask, why would he visit a transsexual, if, in his prison writings [to his sister and others], he ridiculed those same types of people and carried on about how much he hated them?

"If it is true," Investigator Horton said later, "he certainly had me and every other cop he had contact with fooled. I had no idea. I would have viewed our relationship entirely differently if I would have known then what I know now. He acted like a tough guy and gave me no hint whatsoever that he was bisexual."

Could Evans have been bisexual?

"I can definitely believe it," Horton concluded. "Gary worked so hard to keep it from me that it's most likely true."

LIPSTICK AND CANDY

While in Clinton State, Evans wrote a letter to Investigator Horton describing the "most famous person" he had met while incarcerated. Evans told Horton he and Son of Sam had become friends, but Horton didn't believe Evans. When Evans wrote to Horton, he said, "I lifted weights with [Son of Sam] for about a year. I never used to go near him because that's fucked up, killing innocent [people]." Evans, who had killed two people himself by that point, had justified his killings, writing them off as people "who needed (and deserved) to die." So, when he said he didn't understand Son of Sam choosing random people to murder, he meant it, in his own sick and twisted way of thinking.

Yet as quick as Evans tagged Son of Sam a psychopath, in that same letter to Horton he changed his opinion and described him as "a likeable guy, really. . . . He never talked about the killings. I used to kid him that he should've shot ... rapists instead and he'd laugh. I had a brief look at that new book about him, *The Ultimate Evil*, by Maury Terry, and the author was claiming Son of Sam was with a satanic cult and he had proof. I asked Dave about it and he laughed it off."

By the end of the letter, Evans promised to send copies of his Son of Sam letters to Horton, who eagerly waited, but never received them.

Instead, Evans tucked them away and placed them inside plastic sleeves and bound them together in a notebook. And there they were, about two dozen letters between Evans and Son of Sam, showing a side of the famous serial killer no one, in some thirty years of studying him, had ever seen.

As soon as I got home from my trip to Bill's, I sat down at my desk and started reading.

CRYPTIC LANGUAGE

I was amazed by the sheer immaturity displayed in the letters. Some of them seemed to be written by a child. Or, rather, an adult with the mind of a child.

Evans's relationship with Son of Sam was far more personal—not to mention bizarre—than he had explained to Horton. Throughout their friendship, when Son of Sam was sent to solitary confinement, he wrote letters to Evans, passed through the hands of another inmate. The language was cryptic. At times, they wrote in a medieval dialect — "Take care, White Knight of the Dunes," Son of Sam would sign off, or "Dear, The Barbarian . . . Sir Gary," or "Sir Lancelot Evans." It was as if they had their own language.

For the most part, Son of Sam thanked Evans for sending him magazines, books, tapes—he favored Bob Dylan over Logins and Messina, for example—and food. Other times, they discussed weight lifting and general life behind bars.

As one might imagine, Son of Sam was a target in prison. Because of his celebrity status among criminals, other inmates gunned for him, and he often described to Evans the notes and threats he would routinely receive.

Interestingly enough, in one letter, Son of Sam wrote that he had ran into "two Puerto Rican friends" of Evans and was "sending them over" . . . "a gift from Big Dave." What he meant by this is unknown.

Some of the letters were typed, others handwritten.

One of Evans's favorite books, he explained to Son of Sam, was *Red Dragon*, by Thomas Harris, the prequel to Harris's blockbuster bestseller *The Silence of the Lambs.* Evans insisted Son of Sam read the book. He did, he said, but didn't much care for it. It was "fair," Son of Sam said. Ironically, Sam said he didn't "like psycho stories."

The AIDS crisis had been major news the year the letter was written. Son of Sam said AIDS was "a lot of shit." He called it "media hype." Evans, though, was worried about it affecting the world, while Son of Sam said it would stay confined to the "inner cities, prostitutes, and junkies." He then went on to list which states had reported cases, along with how many cases were in each state.

A FRIENDSHIP BLOSSOMS

In one letter, Gary Evans told Son of Sam how much he missed seeing him. "I miss visiting you, too," Son of Sam wrote back. In the same letter, Sam thanked Evans for supplying him with what was an endless array of fruit cocktail, juice and other snacks.

One note somebody had slipped into Sam's cell and frightened him, and he expressed to Evans that he was afraid to "go to sleep at night." The guy had called him a "cheap cocksucker" for not having snacks in his cell to steal, then went on to say that if Sam didn't fill his cell with donuts, oatmeal pies, or nutty bars, and "chocolate, he was going "rip the veins" out of his neck while he was sleeping.

Evans was totally absorbed by these stories. It was important that *the* Son of Sam was sharing his life with him. He could hardly believe it. Sam, on the other hand, continually fed Evans's ego, complimenting him on his muscles and addressing him in a way he must have known would cater to Evans's grandiose thoughts of himself.

In his final few letters, before getting out of solitary during one stint, Sam talked about collecting "mouse droppings" on his "cell floor." He'd shoot the "shit pellets," he explained, using a homemade slingshot, at people who walked by his cell. He promised to bring a "bag" of "shit pellets" with him so he could show Evans how to do it. "You'll be impressed," Sam promised.

Son of Sam had sent Evans a copy of *Muscle & Fitness* magazine one day, but Evans sent it right back. To Evans's sheer horror, the editors had chosen to use an African-American bodybuilder in an article, which totally turned Evans off to the entire magazine.

"I forgot," wrote Sam, "how prejudiced you are."

BODY IMAGE

These lost Son of Sam letters, as I call them, show a different side of the infamous killer that has escaped researchers and writers for decades. For the most part, they are not dated; however, the few that are suggest they were written between June and December, 1987, a period during which Sam claims to have been touched by the hand of God and born again.

Son of Sam referred to himself as "Big Dave," "little Dave," "Berko," "The Great Berko," "The Great Mouse-kit-eer," "Master B," "D," "White Knight," "Torch," "The Missing Link," "M. Mouse," and "Dave." A familiar way for him to sign off was, "Your nasty friend," and "Keep swinging your royal sword."

Sam liked to draw Evans pictures and cut out photos from magazines and photocopy, or embed, them into different sections of the letters. In one, Sam cut out a photograph of a German Shepherd. There's a caption—"Hi, Gary"—draw in, and a note from Sam on the bottom of the page, "There are lots of little Garys, but only one Big Gary."

In some of the letters, Sam's mind wanders. He goes from one subject to the next and has a hard time staying focused, almost always referring back to Evan's body. Here's an excerpt:

Wayne [a fellow inmate they both knew very well] tells me you still take your showers under the faucet in the yard. I'm surprised. You're so big, Gary, my goodness, I don't see how you fit. I can tell when you walk past my cell. The sun always shines in my windows, but when you go by, suddenly the sun gets blocked out and everything gets dark. It's like a big truck passing through.

Sam was forever giving Evans a list of things he wanted, hoping Evans could somehow come up with the items (which he always did).

I'll write more tomorrow. Here's my new tape request:
1.) The Band – Last Waltz
2.) Streets of Fire – Soundtrack
How's that?
Cruel Might Warrior, remain steadfast against all OBSTACLES! True Brother – Great Tricep King – Carry

on, IRON Torch.

Dave

LOVERS OR FRIENDS?

One of Sam's letters begins with the line, "How's my favorite Popcorn Eaten criminal? This morning I awoke to find two shiny apples on my cell bars and a little note from the Big 'GARY EVANS.' "

Some have suggested that Evans and Sam were lovers. I am not so sure they were lovers and cannot make that leap, but I know for certain that there was a mutual respect between them and that they remained great friends until Evans said one word that made Sam never speak to him again (I'll get to that in a minute).

Further along on page one of the letter, Sam lists several rules he had developed for the inmates who hung around his cell area.

"I fined [a fellow inmate] ten dollars payable to Dave Town," he writes, "... and wrote him up for breaking the following Dave Town rules: 1) Parking a smelly, stinky mop in front of my house and leaving it there, 2) No smoking in front of Dave's house, 3) No loitering in front of Dave's house without an invitation, 4) No 'retards' in front of Dave's house, 5) No talking 'shit' in front of Dave's house."

It is amazing, really, when you read these letters and think this was how a world famous serial killer spent his days. Reading Sam's Web page today, one has to wonder, is this how a born again Christian acted when the light of God supposedly touched him?

In the second part of the letter, Sam goes on to speak of an inmate who "broke every one of those rules." Then he tells Evans about a "jerk who fell off a six floor roof and lived to tell about it, due to his fabulous training." Using his natural charm, Sam wrote, "Listen, if you send me a few munchies—fine, great. But don't send me cash." When Sam was shipped off to another part of the prison, he missed Evans, that much is clear. "See you on Oak Island," he ended, "with your moles ... there's popcorn buried in those treasure chests. ... yours truly, The Great Mouse-kit-eer." As a postscript, "Don't forget to visit Dave Town, Exit 1 on the Thruway ... more directions later."

What is Sam actually saying here? Is there some sort of hidden affection in his words?

THE GREAT BERKO

Much of the communication between Evans and Sam was rooted in fantasy. Sam generally wrote to Evans when he was put in what he described as "Keep lock." It was Sam's way of keeping in contact with what was going on inside the small section of the prison of which he liked to believe he was the master and commander.

"My brother," he wrote to Evans one afternoon, "I will ... be out of KL [soon] ... then I will try to get into ARCHITECTUAL DRAFTING to obtain a degree in Lighthouse Structualization [sic] and Interior Design. Then I will build a lighthouse! Goodbye cruel world. There will be No Trespassers near my Lighthouse."

At the time, Evans had been thinking about getting into drafting after his prison term ended. He was an exceptional artist in some respects; he made stained glass window pictures, paintings and drawings, and was fairly good with a pencil. He felt drafting could set him on the right track. Although, as soon as he was released, he always went right back to thieving (and killing), justifying it by saying it was too easy (and lucrative).

Sam had a strange sense of humor, and in just about

every letter he wrote to Evans, he tended to throw in at least one joke of some sort. Evans would often choose various books and music tapes for Sam and send them to him when they were apart. Fleetwood Mac was a Son of Sam favorite. Evans had sent him some organ music once, about which Sam wrote back, that it was "zzzzzzz … play this music for someone on their death bed—they'll go quicker. See you before Christmas, I think. The Great Berko."

SIR EVANS AND THE WHITE KNIGHT

"Sir Lancelot Evans, My Fellow Viking," Sam wrote. "The gods have been most favorable and kind to me today. The Voodoo Queen, my number one Tormentor, has been driven off by the forces of Good to another pasture where she can work her evil upon other unfortunate pasture where I have been freed of her spells …"

This was the type of cryptic language Sam and Evans liked to use more often than not. They had written about past lives, in which they both were knights. Because of Evans's massive body-builder physique and enormous, almost freakish triceps, Sam often called him "The Great Tricep King."

In that same letter, Sam went on to say, "Upon completion of said 'punishment' I shall again return. Please be patient with me; it won't be long now. … A fellow Viking is worth more than all the gold of Oak Island."

DEATHWORK

After Evans sent Sam a copy of *Red Dragon* and encouraged him to read it, no doubt thinking it was right up Sam's alley, Sam rejected the book.

"I finished the book," Sam said of *Red Dragon*. "The book was fair—very overrated. Now I'm on *Deathwork*."

Published in 1977, *Deathwork* basically follows the stories of four murderers on death row, three males and one female.

Son of Sam related to *Deathwork* on a psychological level, this was obvious. He could feel the pain of these condemned inmates, as he had similarly felt the world was against him and the deeds he had done.

"Listen," he told Evans, "this book is GREAT! A look inside the Florida prison system. I can't put this book down. In fact, I'm reading it with my left hand and typing with my right. I also slept with it last night."

SAM THE PROPHET

Sam began one letter to Evans by saying, "I've got some really bad news for you. I just received a revelation that the world is going to end on June 22, 1987, at about 1:30 PM. Take care, man. See you later. You'll probably be in your cell when it happens, or maybe in the gym if you have a gym."

This was Sam's way of lightening the mood between he and Evans. In the next paragraph, he went on to add, "Man, I had a terrible nightmare last night. I had a dream that two peppermint patties were flying all around my cell chasing me and bouncing off my head."

Sam had an incredible skill for manipulating people into doing what he wanted. There's no doubt he sensed Evans envied him, even looked up to him, and he used that to his advantage. He fed Evan's enormous ego and often wrote letters to Evans as if he were a fan of his body. "Sir, Hello, my name is Donald Jones and I am writing to you, Mister Evans, because I seen [sic] a picture of you in Muscle & Fitness Magazine and I seen [sic] you on the front cover. Sir, I hope one day my triceps are as big as yours. You are my idol and I have a big poster of you on my bedroom wall."

Evans supplied Sam with an endless supply of food and magazines. "Thanks for the granola bars," Sam wrote. Of course I still eat them. Heck, in keeplock I'll eat anything. No smut for now—not enough strength."

Evans often talked about his penchant for breaking out of prison, and even once catered to the idea of buying a small flying machine. In light of that, Sam wrote, "Listen, I have a hideaway in the woods in case, in the glorious future Gary Evans, AKA 'The Man With Wings,' needs a place to lay low. I'll send you instructions in my next letter."

In none of the letters does Sam mention or even allude to God or Jesus Christ, as one might imagine a born again Christian might.

BACK AT THE OFFICE

After I returned to my office and had a chance to read all of the letters, I was faced with having to sit down and think about how I would incorporate them into my book. Thank goodness, it was easy, only because I had a foundation of a book already written. Getting the letters, at least some of them, into the narrative turned out to be pretty effortless. Understanding Evans and Son of Sam's relationship would be an on-going dilemma.

As for Bill and his wonderful family, who greeted me with kindness and trusted me with these treasures, I am forever grateful to them.

"Once you left," someone there that day later told me, "we took a moment to clean up the items and we all discussed how confident we were that you would portray all facets of Gary's life and childhood. We also were confident you'd return the pictures etc. you had taken with you. [My fiancée] and I discussed many of the stories again and anxiously spoke about reading *Every Move You Make* and wondering what it would actually contain. Everyone had a sense of relief that Gary's story would be told from a non- judgmental point of view and nothing would be one-sided."

All Bill ever wanted, he told me later, was for Evans's complete story to be told. He saw Evans's criminal life as a byproduct of the sexual, emotional, and psychical abuse Evans suffered during his formative years. Bill doesn't want people to think that it excuses Evan's five murders, but it does explain how and why he ended up the way he did. Taken in full context, Bill believes that Evans's story can help people understand.

As for the cache of Evans's materials that Bill once had, today they're all gone.

"I have no idea where everything is," Bill said, "just the way I like it. I gave it all to [the authorities] and never saw any of it again."

A FRIENDSHIP ENDS

According to Evans, the relationship between he and Sam ended when he called Sam "David Bezerk-o-witz" one day while they were lifting weights. "He got really pissed," Evans said, "and we never spoke again."

Evans came up with a rather bizarre theory regarding Sam's pedigree. He claimed a news article he'd read said Sam was "really adopted, and his name at birth was . . . are you ready? Richard Falco, son of [Michael Falco's parents]! I almost shit reading that! I haven't said anything to him because that's personal and I don't want him catching an attitude at me."

Michael Falco was Gary Evans's first victim. He shot Falco in the head and buried his body in Florida. Investigators wouldn't find it for fifteen years.

Asked later about the connection between David

Berkowitz and the Falcos, Investigator Horton said, "I do remember [Evans] telling me that. But I didn't take it any further. I really had no reason to at the time. It was meaningless to what I was doing with Gary. And, to be honest, it was one of those Gary statements that just seemed to be so far out there, I didn't put much credence into it."

The moment Evans and Sam stopped being friends shows how fragile the mind of Son of Sam actually is. He could take a lot of things and, one could argue, used Evans for food, friendship, reading materials, protection, and Lord knows what else. But when it came to insulting his intellect, thus perhaps holding up a mirror and forcing Sam to think about what he had done, it was too much. As a researcher, a guy who has studied murderers for many years, I can say that the insult was a strike to the character that Sam had built up over the years while incarcerated. He had pushed the killer he was out of his mind and perhaps believed, like a lot of convicted murderers, that the person who committed those crimes was someone else. He was a new man by the time he met Evans—not the evil killer America had branded him.

DANCE WITH THE DEVIL
BEHIND THE SCENES OF INVESTIGATION DISCOVERY'S "DARK MINDS"

INTRODUCTION

This story is designed as a behind-the-scenes look at the investigation and production process involved in filming my Investigation Discovery series, "Dark Minds." My hope in writing these shorts is to give the viewer of the series a deeper understanding of what I do, how I go about choosing cases, and why my involvement in these unsolved murders is, of course, for the purposes of entertaining an audience on television. But more importantly, it's my hope to shed new light on cold cases, some of which have gone unsolved for nearly 40 years, and, with any luck, unearth new information. With the public's help, serial murder cases are solvable. That is the model we work under on "Dark Minds."

Each case I chose for this series was chosen with the help of my production company, Beyond Productions, along with what is the best group of people in television at Investigation Discovery. Each eisode focuses on a series of murders that I believed needed the careful and renewed attention of a hungry investigator willing to bang on doors, ask tough questions, reach out to the people who didn't want to talk to police, and uncover information that could further the investigation along.

Our hope is to reignite a stagnant investigation, not

to walk into town and point fingers. I didn't want to play in the same box as had other journalists, and even some investigators, before me, as a particular case evolved. What purpose would questioning the work of others serve? My aim was to rattle the cage of the case with the hope that, along with the assistance of the public and my expertise and experience, a little bird might fly out and lead police in the right *direction.*

In some of these cases, I worked closely with police; in others, I walked a fine line between talking to the family members of victims, interviewing witnesses (and even suspects), and being led astray by knuckleheads. I did so knowing all the while that I would hand over anything of significance I found to law enforcement. My goal, always, is to help law enforcement, never to get in the way, or mock and make enemies of those people. Any cop I have ever interviewed can attest to my integrity and personal belief that murder cases are about the victims, their families, and the justice both deserve. My intention is to help families and victims of crime heal by providing answers, and, as a bonus, to hopefully help put scumbag killers in prison, where they belong.

The idea of involving an actual serial killer in this hunt was something I had wanted to do for a long time. The information and insight only a (convicted and imprisoned) serial killer can add is so important when hunting these predators, simply because non-sociopaths like you or me do not *think* like a serial killer (sociopath/psychopath). I don't feel people in general give that idea enough credence. A sociopath absolutely views the world differently. In order to understand that dark mind, and to hopefully gain some insight into it (obtaining information that can help solve cases—yes, like Clarice Starling in *The Silence of the Lambs*), who better to ask than someone who has walked in those same evil footsteps?

His code name on "Dark Minds" is "13," and he is a unique individual in this regard. It took John Kelly, the expert profiler I return to in every episode, ten years of conversations to understand how this killer could help. Not through a television show, mind you, but in Kelly's work (the TV show came later). I don't want to get too far into this thread of "Dark Minds" here in my e-book, because I believe Kelly does the best job, during the series, of explaining 13's role. Obviously, "13" speaks for himself quite emphatically and chillingly.

All that said, please enjoy this brief exclusive look at the series from my perspective as I go out and hunt these psychos. Please understand that what you are about to read is my own opinion. It is not the opinion of Investigation Discovery, Beyond Productions, John Kelly, or anyone else involved in "Dark Minds." The e-book shorts accompanying the series are my own creation, the content is based solely on my own findings and the interviews which I conducted behind the scenes for the show as I got to know my sources. I took extensive notes every day while on the road. I collected thousands of pages of documents. My intention is not to claim superiority over anyone, to speak for anyone, or to undermine other opinions on the same cases. I am merely writing about my personal experiences, feelings, and recollections as I recall them.

Any mistakes, errors, misquotes, etc., are on me. I accept responsibility. I simply want viewers of "Dark Minds" to be able to enjoy a deeper experience within the context of my work on the series. I hope these e-book shorts can accomplish that.

If you want more information about the series, please go to the Investigation Discovery website: *http:// investigation.discovery.com/* or visit the "Dark Minds"

Facebook page at: *http://www.facebook.com/pages/Dark-Minds/192493800815468?skip_nax_wizard=true*

PROLOGUE

It was the look on her face and the unmistakable pain present in her scratchy voice. The sheer need this woman harbored deep down to have an answer. It is a recurring theme serial killers leave in their wake, and they enjoy this part of it. Locked away in prison, their lives wasting away on death row in a small, dingy, and smelly cell, some of their evil still has a hold on victims' families.

"Just find out who killed my daughter." she said to me.

My heart sunk. It was one of the first things Aletta Goodwin said to me as we spoke. She had asked me this on the telephone a few months before. "Can you prove that he did it?"

"He." Indeed, neither of us had to say his name.

I thought I knew the answer to Aletta's question. In fact, not only did I believe I knew who had killed Aletta's 30-year-old daughter—Jane Goodwin, a name that has haunted me since 2007—but he was serving a life sentence in a Cheshire, Connecticut, prison. That sentence was for murdering a Hartford, Connecticut woman, Carmen Rodriguez, after strangling and stabbing a second victim he had once dated, Karen Osman, in 1983, a beautiful and young Rutgers graduate who aspired to one day become a veterinarian,and nearly killing a third after choking her to the point of unconsciousness and stabbing her multiple times in the chest during a brutal sexual assault. With a résumé like that, it was hard for me to exclude this monster from Jane's murder. Plus, I had uncovered several pieces of information that connected him directly to Jane.

The road to these conclusions, and my "dance" with Edwin "Ned" Snelgrove, the devil in the title of this final episode of DARK MINDS (season one), actually began after I wrote a letter to him. Ned is a two-time murderer who served eleven years in a New Jersey prison (but was paroled with good time served) for killing Karen Osman at Rutgers University, where Karen and Ned went to college together, and for later sexually assaulting and stabbing another woman, Mary Ellen Renard. I embarked on the journey of writing a book, "I'll Be Watching You," about Ned Snelgrove in early 2007. I had followed his case for many years. What follows in this e-book is the continuation of that story and how I came to the conclusion, that Snelgrove in my opinion, could have had something to do with Jane Goodwin's murder and why I turned that into an episode of DARK MINDS. For the first time, I am publishing original documents connected to Ned Snelgrove, including the chilling letters he wrote to me and a judge. Ned is a vicious serial killer whose own words tell that story in a way that only a man with the mind of a monster can.

CHAPTER ONE

After Ned was sentenced in Hartford, Connecticut, for murdering a young woman, Carmen Rodriguez, in April 2005, he stood up in court and implored any "reporter" in the gallery to give him two years to study his trial and corresponding documents. After that, he said, he would be willing to provide anyone interested proof of his innocence in the murder of Miss Rodriquez. He said he had been convicted of a crime, Rodriguez's murder, which he had not committed, and DNA results and the evidence of shoddy prosecution would exonerate him one day. He maintained that he was certain of this.

Snelgrove could not claim innocence in the murder of Karen Osman, or the vicious attack on Mary Ellen Renard, because he had admitted committing those crimes. He was sentenced to sixty years (essentially a life sentence for a man in his forties) for Rodriguez's murder. She was discovered stuffed inside several layers of plastic garbage bags, which had been meticulously stapled closed, on the side of the road in Rhode Island, just over the Connecticut border. It was at a location sixty miles from where she was last seen (in a bar that Ned Snelgrove frequented every night, that is, up until the day Carmen disappeared). Inside that bag, Carmen's bones told the story of her being hog-tied and thrust into the bag like a rag doll. She was identified by only a small section of skin on her shin that had not decomposed, and, remarkably, a tattoo that cops sketched out and sent to police departments across New England. Otherwise, there was nothing left to Carmen but a bag of bones attached to her skull and long mane of brunette hair, all held together by the ropes binding her.

At the 2005 sentencing hearing, in which forty-four-year-old Ned Snelgrove ranted and raged about his wrongful conviction, thereby filling the classic role of the narcissistic serial killer who needed to take the opportunity to speak his proverbial piece, the judge blasted Snelgrove. Judge Carmen Espinosa said: "I have been doing this for many years, talking to psychiatrists and psychologists who try to explain why people do what they do. But sometimes people are just bad, beyond redemption, and you are one of them. All we can do is warehouse people like Mr. Snelgrove to make sure they don't hurt anyone again."

Powerful words from a powerful and respected woman

of the bench, which angered Ned. The judge had rattled his cage pretty well, and the contempt he had for him was evidentacross his face. If this had been a cartoon, cue steam protruding from Ned's ears at this moment.

Judge Espinosa, who, at various intervals, had sparred with Ned throughout his trial, concluded by stating what every law enforcement officer and prosecutor that knew Ned or crossed paths with him at some point had told me as I wrote my book: "The court is convinced that if he ever gets out on the street, he will kill again."

I have said this before, and I am not the first person to utter it, that some people are just plain evil and there is no rehabilitation that can turn them back into human beings. Lacking a conscience, they walk the earth simply to hurt people.

Ned Snelgrove is one of these inhumane people.

After being convicted for Carmen's murder, Ned flaunted his arrogance and contempt for the court during his sentencing. When Judge Espinosa finished, Snelgrove stood and addressed her. A professor type (his nickname in prison) with large tortoise-shell glasses, a chip on his shoulder the size of Gibraltar, reading from a piece of paper in his hand, his voice crisp and sharp: "You used my past convictions as a substitute for evidence," Ned began as the gallery gasped at Ned's utter display of hubris and flagrant self-absorption. "Things that happened seventeen years ago," he continued, referring to Karen Osman's murder and a subsequent twelve-page letter he wrote to the judge during the time frame of that case (which I'll get to later on in the piece), "are totally unrelated to Carmen Rodriguez. This conviction will never stand [on appeal.] So go ahead and sentence me to life."

He took a deep breath. Looked up at the judge, squarely, sporting a smirk. "And I'll see you again in a couple years when my conviction is overturned."

After a bit more back and forth, Ned made his declaration to the journalists in the courtroom gallery.

I wasn't in the courtroom that day, but I did write to Ned. The basis of that first letter and my subsequent investigation into Jane Goodwin's murder was the impetus for the "Dance With the Devil" episode of DARK MINDS.

Here is the letter which began the process:

February 3, 2007

Dear Mr. Snelgrove:

Forgive this brief intrusion. Allow me to introduce myself. I'm a nonfiction book author. I've penned seven books, several of which were best-sellers. (I've enclosed a brief bio for your convenience; you can also visit my author Website at www.mwilliamphelps. com)

The purpose of my letter is rather simple. I followed your case. I've done some preliminary interviews. I've read some of the documents. I'm interested in your case, particularly your story.

I'm just digging in here and wanted your input and maybe some direction regarding where to go with my investigation. I like to look into every aspect of a case and query beyond what was presented in court. I've found there are always two sides to a story. I was wondering if I chose (I haven't really decided yet) to write a book about your case, would you be willing to be interviewed by me?.

Let's be honest: I had ulterior motives when I wrote it. I knew Ned's type. I had written several books about serial killers by then ("Every Move You Make," "Sleep in Heavenly Peace," "Perfect Poison"). I understood how the mind of the monster works. One detective I interviewed before writing to Ned, a cop instrumental in solving Carmen's murder, explained, "My gut feeling was that Ned … was basically telling us that, you don't know how I did it … but you know that I did it … and he was happy with that. It was almost like a cat and mouse game. He knew we knew he did it."

Ned wasted little time contacting me. Several days after sending my letter, I received five pages of what was the beginning of a relationship, if it can be called such, between a writer and a serial killer.

It was one that would not end amiably.

Here, then, in its entirety, in his own handwriting, is Ned's response to my first letter. One incidental note I'd like to add is that the highlighted portions of Ned's letter are not mine; they're his. This would become a common theme of Ned's: pointing out certain words in his letters and the documents he sent; writing cryptic notes in the margins; and sending along strange pieces of cardboard (like bookmarks), inserted into certain sections of a stack of papers to point me in a certain direction and to point out his perceived "wrong-doings" by cops and the prosecutor. Please note how Ned personalizes the letter at the end, letting me know (subtly) that he (thinks) he knows where I live. Ned was obsessed with a few key phrases (of which he would continually remind me), and he opens his first letter to me with one of his favorites:

*For a better look at the letters and pictures in
this book, visit http://wbp.bz/mrpg*

PAGE ONE OF FIVE

EDWIN SNELGROVE JR. #297891
CHESHIRE CORRECT. INST.
900 HIGHLAND AVENUE
CHESHIRE, CT   06410

MR. M. WILLIAM PHELPS
INVESTIGATIVE JOURNALIST
P.O. BOX 3215
VERNON, CT   06066

MONDAY, FEBRUARY 19, 2007

MR. PHELPS:

I did not kill Carmen Rodriguez.

With that in mind, and at the risk
of being perfectly blunt, thank you for your
letter of February 3.

There are so many aspects of my
case, I have no way of knowing how
your curiosity was first piqued, and therefore
I don't know how to react to your interest.

So, can you please tell me more about what you referred to in your letter? Whom have you talked to in "preliminary interviews"? What are "some of the documents" you've read?

Also, I am curious to know if you have ever written any non-fiction about prosecutors and/or detectives in Connecticut who have quite obviously lied and encouraged perjury in witnesses in order to help secure a dishonest conviction. My case is replete with documented examples.

A dishonest prosecution notwithstanding, the jury in my trial did not base their verdict on any of the Carmen Rodriguez evidence. As a matter of fact, the physical evidence found on the victim's body did not match me, according (transcript, January 14, 2005) to a lab technician's testimony. Even the world-famous Dr. Henry Lee,* during two hours of testimony, could not bring himself to state that there was a connection between the evidence and the defendant (transcript, January 19, 2005).

No, all the jury needed to know about were my previous convictions during the eighties, and all the exculpatory evidence was white-washed from their evaluation. Heck, even the Sentencing (April 15, 2005) featured statements from the victims' families from twenty years prior. Indeed, this entire Carmen Rodriguez fiasco was an opportunity to have me re-convicted and re-sentenced for punishments I had already endured. Why would it be necessary or appropriate to invite people from the <u>eighties</u> to speak at the Rodriguez Sentencing?

One small, insignificant detail that the judge said the jury did not need to know about: someone else <u>confessed</u> to murdering Carmen Rodriguez before committing suicide (transcript, Jan. 28, 2005, outside the presence of the jury).

Finally, I won't be able to visit the author Website you mention. There are no computers here.

Thank you again,

E F Snelgrove

EDWIN SNELGROVE JR. #297891

* The gist of Dr. Henry Lee's testimony was, paraphrasing, "after studying the lab reports, the photos, and the materials found at the crime scene, it is my professional opinion that the murderer, whoever it was, did this, and the murderer, whoever it was, did it in a particular way, and the murderer, whoever it was, must have done these things in this order, blah blah blah." Dr. Lee never said anything like "I believe the defendant is guilty," or "the evidence points towards the defendant." (transcript, January 19, 2005)

P.S. Is "MARK'S BIG RIBS", a restaurant on Route 83 in Vernon, still in business? I think that was the name... right across the street from a gas station? Not far from Interstate 84?

For a better look at the letters and pictures in this book, visit http://wbp.bz/mrpg

CHAPTER TWO

The book I ended up writing about Ned's crimes and my relationship with him was published in 2009. Titled "I'll Be Watching You," the book was re-issued by my publisher to coincide with the March 2012 debut of the DARK MINDS episode about Ned. For that side of the story, the book is a good resource. This e-book is more of a continuation of what has happened since the book was published, along with a few details about what went on behind the scenes as we filmed the episode while I began to chip away at a theory that Ned Snelgrove murdered a Newark, New Jersey woman, Jane Goodwin.

As I was researching and writing my book, I became close to several sources. One of which is irrefutable as a Ned Snelgrove source, and I wish I could reveal the name of this person, but for the record, I understand why he or she has asked for anonymity, and I respect that.

As my research began, a name kept popping up: Jane Goodwin. I had heard this name several times while talking to several different sources in New Jersey. At one point, as I turned to John Kelly, my profiling partner on DARK MINDS, and asked if he had ever heard of Ned Snelgrove, John even said he knew of the name Jane Goodwin being connected to Ned.

Small world, I thought.

Jane was beautiful. She embodied the spirit of the tough and strong-willed single woman of the seventies and early eighties, fending for herself in what was a male-dominated and male chauvinist world. Jane lived alone in downtown

Newark, New Jersey. It was 1982, and just two weeks prior to her murder in late August, Jane had started a new job training on Hewlett Packard computers. At the time, Ned also worked for Hewlett-Packard in New Jersey, and was involved with training people on the complex mystery machines. There is no doubt in my mind that Jane and Ned crossed paths. Rutgers, where Ned went to school, was a five-minute drive from Jane's apartment. Jane was several years older than Ned, and she also had large breasts (two distinguishing characteristics, at the top of a short list, that all of Ned's victims had in common).

"[Ned] could be placed at a training seminar that Jane attended," one law enforcement source told me, with two others backing it up.

That was all I needed to hear. The thing about Ned is, if he knew you and you later became a murder victim, there can be no doubt that he did it. The fact that a woman with large breasts was stabbed to death in the manner that she had been AND that she had crossed paths with Ned Snelgrove is not a mere coincidence.

The summer of 2012 marked the 30-year anniversary of

Jane Goodwin's murder.

"I was told first that she was stabbed," Jane's mother, Aletta, told me. "And I thought, *OK,* she walked in the door and somebody stabbed her, you know. I wanted her to have suffered the least pain and I thought if that's what happened, I thought, Thank God, she didn't know what happened. But then I found out she was also strangled and then I thought ... she suffered."

I'd like to give a bit more background on Ned before I get into the schematics of Jane's murder and how Ned's handprint and signature are plastered all over the matrix of this brutal crime. All of Ned's victims had large breasts. Ned was known as a "breast man," but not simply in terms of him having a particular liking or fascination with women with large breasts (which he certainly did, but not solely in that way). Ned's fixation and obsession with large-breasted women also included the element of seeing those women, he once admitted in a letter, immobilized and unconscious. This was Ned's MO: to render a good-looking, large-breasted female (usually older than him by many years) unconscious (through strangulation), so that he could then place her limp body on a bed or another place that was to his liking, and then strip her naked (very important) from the waist up, which exposed her large breasts so that he could, I began to find out, pleasure himself while stabbing the woman in the chest.

This fantasy of seeing women like this has been inside Ned's head, he once admitted, since the third grade. He recalled having these fantasies, can you imagine, while learning to read and write. Other kids in his class were dreaming of Matchbox cars and playing in the mud, and little Neddy Boy was picturing his teachers—providing they had large breasts—unconscious and propped up on a bed, ready for him to do what he wished. This seems remarkably profound. If it had not come from Ned's mind onto a a letter he wrote to a New Jersey judge, I would have had trouble believing it myself.

So we have a very distinctive signature admitted to by a serial killer. What's important to understand is that this is behavior no other killer would have (or, before Ned was caught and admitted to it) could have mimicked with exactness. I am convinced of that. This sort of crime scene signature is Ned's all the way (unless, that is, we're talking about a copycat killer).

In Karen Osman's murder , to which Ned admitted and gave a fairly detailed, if not bizarre, account, corroborated by the evidence left behind at the murder scene, Ned had strangled the young, beautiful and very large-breasted woman, torn open her blouse and bra, exposed her breasts, and then proceeded to stab Karen around her breasts in what is believed to be a (semi) star-shaped pattern. The quote that stands out to me from Ned about this crime is as follows: "I felt her throat in my hands." He said they had been horsing around on Karen's bed and the next thing he knew, he was strangling her and had no idea why or how it came about. "I could not stop my hands from squeezing as hard as I could," he said.

Ned did not touch the bottom half of Karen's body. She was found (horribly, by family members) with her pants on, posed with her arms out to her sides (in the manner of a cruxifiction pose), her back up against the side of her bed, her chest a mess of blood and stab wounds. The crime went unsolved for several years. Law enforcement had Ned on their radar, of course, and had already questioned him. This was during an era before the DNA/forensic technology we have today, and Ned had a viable reason to have left DNA all over Karen's apartment, because they had dated shortly before her murder, although they were estranged at the time the murder took place. Also, Ned, because he is a bit more intelligent than your average serial killer, was able to play cat and mouse with the cops, outsmart them, and dodge any heat that was first on him for the murder.

Nearly four years after Karen's murder, unable to control himself, Ned struck again. I would argue here that Ned, like any serial killer displaying the same pathologically fantasy-driven thought processes, did not stop attacking women during this time, but simply made several mistakes with this "next" victim and was caught.

Ned's next victim, Mary Ellen Renard, forty-four years old, a newly divorced New Jersey mother, happened to go to the wrong singles dance on August 1, 1987. She walked directly into the clutches of a monster. Ned spied Mary Ellen alone at the bar and approached her. In a performance straight out Ted Bundy's playbook, after Mary Ellen left the bar alone and realized her car wouldn't start, she turned around, and guess who was standing there, waiting with open arms to help her out?

Ned did get Mary Ellen's car started. I could never nail down any supporting evidence or admission, but I am certain that Ned somehow managed to find out where Mary Ellen's car was parked. They had spent over an hour in the bar talking and hanging out. Perhaps he had slipped out into the parking lot after telling her he had to use the restroom, and then he may have fixed her car so that it wouldn't start. Ned had planned to kill Mary Ellen from the moment he met her. I know this because Ned was honest with Mary Ellen about where he worked, where he went to school, and his real name. Later, Ned talked about how he had botched this murder and that alone tells me that he was there, at that singles dance, looking for a victim.

In any event, Ned got Mary Ellen's car started and then suggested that he should follow her home just in case something went wrong with her vehicle along the way.

Mary Ellen thought about this. Her instincts were undoubtedly speaking to her as she hesitated. But, nonetheless, she said, "OK."

When they got to Mary Ellen's apartment, Ned walked up to the window of her car before she even got out and, showing Mary Ellen his dirty hands, asked if he could use her restroom to wash up before driving home.

Mary Ellen lived on the second story of a double-decker house converted in two apartments. Her landlady lived downstairs, and a set of stairs and a door separated the two apartments.

"I don't know," Mary Ellen said. Again, her instincts were telling her to question this man and turn him away. But she said OK and let him in.

The devil had talked his way into his next victim's lair. Ned was alone with a woman (older than him) with very large breasts, and no one else around. Moreover, no one even knew they were together. There was no connection, as Ned himself would later explain, between him and Mary Ellen. He had her exactly where he wanted her.

Mary Ellen told me she felt bad for the guy. Ned did not come across as some sort of one-eyed green monster resembling a Charles Manson or John Wayne Gacy, or even Gary Ridgway. He didn't have that filthy, skanky serial killer look to him, that most people imagine. He came across as a charmer. He knew how to speak to his victims and knew the right victims to choose. He was good-looking at the time, and even slightly resembled a man who would become one of his heroes, Ted Bundy. He had a boyish appeal about him. Ned was book smart; he had graduated from Rutgers University with honors. Fellow students spoke highly of him. He was a model employee at Hewlett Packard. Anybody (besides Karen Osman's family) who knew Ned said he was a model citizen and nice guy. Ned had that geekish frame of Ted Bundy, not so much weak but almost childlike. He didn't come across heavy-handed or overbearing. He didn't speak much. Many women I interviewed said Ned appeared to come across as shy and introverted.

"Non-threatening," was a quote I heard again and again.

Mary Ellen and Ned walked up the stairs and into her apartment.

After some time, Ned said he had to use the bathroom. Mary Ellen needed a snack of cheese; she had a condition where she needed to eat every few hours in order to keep her blood sugar up.

Ned went to use the restroom; Mary Ellen sat on her couch with a can of soda pop while she ate the cheese.

When Ned came out. after an oddly extended period of time, Mary Ellen reported that she immediately saw a different person. Ned had an awful stone-faced look about him, as if he was a different man altogether. He was quiet and had withdrawn deeply into himself. It was as though Dr.

Jekyll had gone into the loo to transform himself into Mr. Hyde.

Ned had essentially walked into the bathroom and turned himself into that psychopathic killer he would soon write about. Ned needed those moments alone in order to change into this "other person"—that meandering menace to society that liked to see big-breasted females unconscious and unable to move, spread out for him so he could do as he wished. This was the fantasy Ned had obsessed over since grade school. He crossed over inside that bathroom, preparing himself for the reality of bringing that fantasy to life. Serial killers live inside their fantasies day and night. When one can manifest that fantasy into reality, it becomes overpowering in a way they have a hard time not only controlling, but later explaining. If he was a drug addict, you could say that Ned walked into the bathroom, took out a bag of dope, prepared the spoon, heated it up, and placed the solution inside the syringe. Walking out and facing Mary Ellen, he steadied himself enough as he willed the poison throughout his veins.

"Serial killers," John Kelly likes to remind me, "are addicted to murder They are unable to stop killing in the same way that a drug addict cannot stop shooting dope."

As Snelgrove exited the bathroom, first staring down at the carpet and then up at Mary Ellen with a transfixed look of abnormality, he attacked her without speaking a word, making a move as though he wanted to kiss her, but then strangling Mary Ellen to unconsciousness while they struggled on the couch.

The details of the next thirty minutes or more are chilling and replete with the textbook behavior of a serial killer fitting Ned's psychological wiring. My book, "I'll Be Watching You," details every beat of this scene and I don't want to simplify that evil moment in Mary Ellen's apartment by summarizing it here. It's a complex series of events that speak volumes about who Ned is as a serial murderer and psychopath. I'll just end here by saying that Ned wound up straddling Mary Ellen on her bed, her blouse and bra open (her pants left on, of course), as he touched himself and stabbed Mary Ellen repeatedly in her chest.

Remarkably, Mary Ellen Renard survived—and the story of how is utterly incredible. In short, she woke up while Ned, after ripping open her blouse and tearing off her bra, was straddling and stabbing her in the chest repeatedly. As she came to, Mary Ellen recalled a self-defense technique she had read about in a magazine and instinctively gouged Ned in the eyes with her fingernails. He screamed like the coward he is and jumped off which was enough for Mary Ellen to be able to get up and run for help.

Mary Ellen Renard is an extraordinary woman—a survivor.

CHAPTER THREE

Ned was eventually arrested for attempted murder and sexual assault on Mary Ellen, mainly because she knew his name and where he worked, and therefore could In a surprising example of how Ned's so-called intelligence plays into his career as a serial killer, Ned told his lawyer that he wanted to, on top of copping a plea in Mary Ellen's case, admit to the murder of Karen Osman.

What? Admit to the murder of a woman the cops are not even asking about any longer? It seemed preposterous. Had Ned lost his mind? Had he wanted to come clean and show some remorse for his crimes?

"I could not believe this," someone close to Ned later told me. "But then, as we discussed it, I understood."

Ned Snelgrove, Mr. "I-Didn't-Do-It," wanted to admit he had murdered his former girlfriend, Karen Osman, when he was no longer even being questioned about the murder, and there was no evidence linking him to that case. To those involved on the legal side, it made little sense.

"For a defendant to come forward and admit to a homicide that had been open for many years with no prospect of being solved," the prosecutor in charge of Mary Ellen Renard's case told me, "that's extraordinary."

Or was it?

Ned had thought this through. I was told by someone close to him that Ned decided to the plea because he didn't want to face the iron crunch of Lady Justice if (and possibly when) she caught up to him while he was behind bars serving time for the crimes against Mary Ellen. Ned knew he was not getting out of the case against Mary Ellen. He was going to serve time for stabbing and sexually assaulting her. The way Ned began to think was: What if forensics tie me to Karen's murder somewhere down the road (while I am in prison serving time for Mary Ellen's case) and there is no escaping a guilty verdict?

Undeniably, if that was the case, Ned would be tried and charged separately for Karen's murder. Ned figured, what the hell, I'll roll the dice and plead it out, forcing the prosecution to put both cases together, and take a sentence for both cases, which he calculated would potentially put him behind bars for less time than if tried separately.

Faced with the fact that they had no evidence against him in Karen's case, the prosecutor decided to make a deal with the devil. After reportedly talking it over with Karen's family, Ned was allowed to plead out to both cases at the same time.

Ned was ultimately sentenced to twenty years. He knew, however, that in the state of New Jersey, you walked into prison with "good time served," meaning, a twenty-year sentence was actually eleven (you got your nine years good time served the day you started serving your time). Based on your behavior behind bars, days were *added* to your sentence, not taken away. Therefore, although Ned had received twenty years, he was walking into prison with eleven years to serve on that twenty-year sentence. (Sounds confusing, I know.) Every time he misbehaved, a day or more would be tacked on to his eleven years, pushing him closer to that original twenty year sentence.

The system seemed to work backwards, yes, however, knew the system and worked it to his advantage.

"I've never met a more model prisoner," a professional at the prison where Ned did his time told me as we filmed episode eight of DARK MINDS, "Dance with the Devil."

"No kidding," I said.

"Yeah. Ned was a great guy. Really nice prisoner. Great with numbers."

Lest we forget: we're talking about a ruthless killer of women, I thought. What nerve. To say that Ned was a nice guy. It was akin to, as I saw it, spitting on the graves of his victims. By a prison employee, no less.

I was at that jail, East Jersey State Prison, formerly known as the infamous Rahway State Prison, established in 1896 as the first reformatory in New Jersey, to conduct an interview with Fred Schwanwede. He prosecuted Ned for Mary Ellen's attack and also took Ned's confession of Karen Osman's murder after making that plea deal with Ned's attorneys.

"Ned is dangerous precisely because he didn't look like a bad guy," Fred told me as we stood in front of the prison on a day so hot and humid that it was hard to breathe. "We all go to the movies, we watch TV shows, and you always see the same actors playing the bad guy because they look like bad guys. They have that kind of face. Ned was just the opposite. Ned had the kind of face that you say to yourself, Eagle Scout. He was a handsome guy. He was a personable guy, very bright. None of the alarms would go off. He didn't have any characteristics that would raise a woman's awareness to a level that she would defend herself against him."

What struck me about Fred and his passion for prosecuting Ned back in 1987-88, was how deeply engrained Ned Snelgrove had become inside the psyche of this retired prosecutor. Here we stood, nearly thirty years later, in front of a prison, talking about Snelgrove, and Fred was spouting this stuff off as if he had prosecuted Ned the day before. It was incredible to hear how Ned had influenced this prosecutor's life over the years.

Staring at Fred, listening to him, I thought about my own experience with Ned and other serial killers like him, and considered how you can never forget evil. It has a way of getting under your skin and you either cave in to it, or learn to fight it any way you can.

Eleven years after Fred Schwanwede was able to secure a confession from Ned Snelgrove in Mary Ellen's case (Ned, of course, blamed Mary Ellen for bringing on her attack, telling a fairytale about Mary Ellen coming onto him) and got him to admit to Karen Osman's murder, Ned Snelgrove collected his things from prison. He combed his hair, now gray, one last time in the mirror inside his cell, said goodbye to his mates, and walked out of prison a free man.

"He ran back up to Connecticut," one prosecutor in Hartford told me. "He was afraid New Jersey might figure out a way to put him back behind bars."

Indeed, after a short time staying at a sleazy motel, Ned moved in with his parents. He set up a bedroom in the basement of their Berlin, Connecticut, home, just a skip off the Berlin Turnpike, nearby where the motel had been located.

Schwanwede was mortified, as were Ned's victims. After all, this monster had admitted to having a significant problem with women and once had even written that as long as he wasn't around women he would be okay, had been released. In a letter Ned had written to the judge before his sentencing in 1988, Ned did something unprecedented. He talked about what goes on inside the mind of a monster. For some reason nobody can explain to this day, Ned Snelgrove wrote to the judge who was going to be sentencing him, describing the fantasies he'd had since he was a boy. Portions of this remarkable twelve-page document are worth publishing here:

*For a better look at the letters and pictures in
this book, visit http://wbp.bz/mrpg*

Thurs., 4/14/88
(ELEVEN PAGES)

The purpose of this statement is to describe
what happened in the aggravated manslaughter
of Karen Osmun in middlesex County on
December 24, 1983 and the attempted murder
of Mary Ellen Renard on August 2, 1987, in
Bergen County, N.J.

Both incidents occurred because of a
strong sexual arousement I have had since
I was in grade school. For unknown reasons (I
never thought it was a problem until the middlesex
County case) I get enormous pleasure from seeing
a good-looking female become helpless. Whether it
is ~~seeing~~ seeing a
pretty girl asleep in person or seeing a girl
faint or get killed in a movie or TV show,
I cannot even come close to describing
the feelings I get. My heartbeat rate increases
until I think my heart is in my mouth,
I get ~~~~ slightly dizzy, my hands sweat and
there is an enormous sexual arousement. I
can remember having these feelings about my
teachers ~~~~ as early as second
and third grade, but I somehow knew
enough not to talk about them to
anybody. Every time I see a girl I
am attracted to, whether it is in ..

179

person, TV, movies or photographs, instead of
simply "undressing her with my eyes", as
most men describe themselves doing, I
always imagine strangling her or lifting her
over the head, carrying her limp body onto
a bed, ~~and~~ undressing her, and arranging
her arms and legs in some ~~kind~~ of
seductive pose. This is what is going
through my mind every time I look at
or talk to a female. For over twenty
years now, this has constantly been reinforced
in my mind, mentally rehearsing ~~doing~~ it
dozens of times a day. I will go out
of my way (stay home from a party, stay up
all night for the Late Show) to see a
movie like "Psycho" (the shower scene), "Frenzy,"
"No Way to Treat a Lady" (starring Rod Steiger),
"The Boston Strangler," and most James Bond
films (where at least one beautiful female spy
is ~~killed, usually~~). I sometimes wonder ~~make~~ what
it would be like to have an EKG machine
~~attached to~~ monitoring my heart rate while
I sit and watch some of these shows.
When I am alone with a girl, this is what I
am always thinking about. I even think about
this — fantasize about it — when I am in
bed with a girl, constantly telling myself

"no, no!" Ninty-nine out of one hundred times, I am able to restrain myself, (although there have been a few very close calls). It is like two people inside of me, one wanting the anything to hit or strangle this girl I'm with, the other knowing that it is wrong, ~~everything~~ fighting to stay in control. ~~Except there two can the incidents in~~ Except for these ~~three~~ incidents I'm in jail for, I always managed (sometimes it was very difficult) to control my feelings and my hands. This is why it was so shocking for my friends and coworkers when I got arrested and charged with ~~these~~ ~~time~~ crimes — I have been with many different girls, from college and work and I am very popular. Everyone who knows me thought there had to be some kind of mistake, that I ~~would~~ would never do such a thing. These feelings have never been a problem in any social setting (work, parties, etc.) I it is when I am alone with a girl that the heartbeat, the sexual arousement and the dizziness become OVERWHELMING! Until I actually killed a girl (December 1983), I never considered that there was a serious problem, as long as I was perceived as an intelligent, pleasant adult at college or work.

( )   ( )

what happened in Middlesex County is as follows: On Saturday night, December 23, 1983, I was at a Christmas party with friends from college (I had graduated ~~in May o~~ from Cook College of Rutgers University in the spring of 1983). Karen Osmun, a girl I had dated, from June 1981 to August 1982, happened to be at the party. We had each driven to the party alone, each in our own cars, and ~~each~~ did not know the other would be there. It would not have mattered if we had known ahead of time; we were still friendly since breaking off our relationship. (This is not what the Prosecution will say; the police believed from the beginning that this death was the result of a heartbroken boyfriend. It is true that Karen had ended our relationship fifteen months before her death, but I was over that; it had nothing to do with ~~the death~~ what happened ~~it~~ in her apartment that night.) Karen and I were leaving the house at about the same time, but we were not actually "leaving together." We were parked close to each other, and ~~I~~ was driving right behind her all the way home, since we lived right around the corner from each other, in New Brunswick, (the Party was in Piscataway). I decided at ..

For a better look at the letters and pictures in
this book, visit http://wbp.bz/mrpg

the last minute to stop at her house instead of going home. She invited me in; she was not surprised to see me, because she knew it was my car behind her coming back from the party.

When we got inside, we started kissing, and she had taken her shirt and bra off when my heart started racing and these scenes in my mind began to take over, as usual. We were rolling around on her bed, and at one point, we rolled a little too far, and we fell off the bed, with me on top of her, with my hands on either side of her face. I remember at this point not being able to breathe too well, and my hands just wrapped themselves around the bottom of her throat. It was like one continuous motion, with my hands just ending up on her throat as her feet were still coming off the ~~edge~~ edge of the bed. I remember thinking "I'm actually doing it this time." I can't ~~describe the~~ ~~feeling I had as I felt her throat in my~~ ~~hands. I~~ I know this is sick, and I'm embarrassed and ashamed to be writing about it like this, but I can feel that adrenalin racing through my heart, hands and legs just thinking about it. It is like a combination of an electric shock and having someone sneak up behind you and scaring the daylights out of you. It's ~~so~~ ~~hard~~ ~~to~~ describe these feelings... It is like I just ran up three flights of stairs. It is like I have just taken a whole bottle of pep pills and something inside me wants even more, to make the heart, the dizziness, the shortness of breath to increase even further. ~~something inside me~~ likes these feelings. (I've never taken illegal drugs). ~~by the way~~

Anyway, I found out that strangling a girl in reality is not like in the movies. It is practically impossible to kill someone with your bare hands. You'd have to be a football player with huge hands to really be able to do it. I held Karen's throat, pressing down with my thumbs, for as long as I could, but she was still sputtering, her eyes closed, her tongue stuck out of her mouth, lying on the floor making terrible, animal-like noises. Looking down at her, naked from the waist up, I remember all those feelings that drove me to do this disappeared, she wasn't going to die, I remember thinking, she's going to wake up and call the police"! At this point I panicked. I went into the kitchen, found a steak knife, went back

( )   ( )

to Karen and stabbed her in the ~~back~~ abdomen. ~~~~ I was so scared at this point, and she was ~~~~ just lying still, making those noises, I just wanted her to stay quiet. The feelings were completely gone. Blood and stabbing and yellow mucus coming out of her mouth were never part of my sexual fantasies. That ~~ruined~~ ruined ~~it~~ it for me.

I was always the prime suspect in this homicide, but the police never had anything but circumstantial evidence, so they never were able to charge anybody. I felt terrible from then on. I tried to commit suicide the next day: I swallowed a whole package of sixteen sleeping pills and a bottle of iodine, but I didn't die. I couldn't eat or sleep ~~~~ ~~~~ ~~~~ I promised myself I would never do anything like that again.

You can see that these feelings ~~get in the~~ ~~way of logic, they~~ are so strong that they get in the way of logic. The prosecutor Fred Schnannede, is probably going to ~~tell the~~ Judge that I am a cold-blooded, heartless killer. If I were a cold-blooded heartless killer, would I have chosen a former girlfriend for a victim? Of course not! Karen just happened to be the unlucky girl to be with me when I lost control of these feelings. The fact that she was a former girlfriend had nothing to do with it, as you can see by the fact that I did the same exact thing to a lady I had just met on the night of August 1, 1987 (the Bergen County incident)...

You would think that after actually killing someone, I would have tried to get professional help. But it was such a terrible experience, and I was so thankful to have not been arrested, that, even though I would _still_ get those sexual and violent urges, I had convinced myself that I would never allow myself to lose control ever again.

A very similar scenario occurred on the night of Saturday, August 1, 1987. I had met a lady named Mary-Ellen Renard at a bar, in Clifton, spent a few hours with her, and she invited me to follow her back to her apartment in Elmwood Park. Once in her apartment, pretty much the same thing happened. I had undone the top half of her dress and taken her bra off. She was laying on her back on the couch, and I was on top of her when I could not stop my hands from squeezing her throat as hard as I could.

For a better look at the letters and pictures in this book, visit http://wbp.bz/mrpg

"I told the parole board that Ned Snelgrove was the most dangerous defendant that I have ever dealt with in the criminal justice system," Fred Schwanwede told me. "I believed he might do something like this again whenever he was released. Even if he was released after twenty years there was a real danger that he was going to do something like this again."

Fred was not some sort of prophet, or able to see into the future. This was the impression of the prosecutor and just about every other law enforcement person that had ever had any contact with Ned.

Not even two years after Ned was released, while living with his parents in Connecticut, he found himself back in prison facing murder charges. This time for the murder of Carmen Rodriguez, whom Ned had met at a bar he hung out at in Hartford.

In the "Dance with the Devil" episode of DARK MINDS, I explained what happened to Carmen as I stood in the spot where we believe Ned drove to kill her: "So this is the Berlin fairgrounds [just a skip from where Ned lived with his parents]. This is where families come, have fun, eat cotton candy. And this is also where Ned Snelgrove brought Carmen Rodriguez for her last ride. They come down this street right here and Carmen thinks she's just going to party a little bit with Ned. And they pull in here and Ned drives back to those woods over there and he starts in with Carmen and he grabs her around the throat and she gets away and she runs into the woods. [While] running for her life ... Ned tackles her. He drags her back to the car ... where he puts her in the back seat, on a tarp and he starts stabbing her. And when he's done, he hogties Carmen, puts her in garbage bags, puts her in the trunk of his car, and then he takes back off and he heads out to Rhode Island."

Ned is an animal. He kills women. He will never stop.

Carmen had to pay the price for all those women Ned would have continued to murder had he not been caught for her murder six months after she disappeared.

This thread of the story leads us back to the beginning.

Re-enter Jane Goodwin and my literary dance with Ned.

I kept hearing Jane's name pop up in conversation as I interviewed cops and attorneys and prosecutors and people who knew Ned in New Jersey while I was writing "I'll Be Watching You."

"You have to look into Jane's murder," sources said again and again.

What I didn't know was that Jane's mother, Aletta Goodwin, was also in search of someone to look into her daughter's murder. Aletta, even before reading my book (in which I never specifically identified Jane)already had Ned Snelgrove on radar for Jane's brutal slaying, particularly ever since she, not long after Karen was murdered, contacted Karen Osman's mother and learned something remarkable about Ned.

CHAPTER FOUR

Aletta is one of those women you feel, after sitting and speaking with for a time, that you want to help anyway you can. She's gentle, yet opinionated, outspoken, and educated. She's getting older, Aletta explained to me,so she needs to know, before the white light appears, who murdered her daughter. I didn't make any promises, but I told her that I would do my best to find answers.

As Aletta read my book, she took notes. Lots of them. She wrote in the margins. She sketched things out on a piece of paper. She believed that I was correct about what several others had also thought: that Ned Snelgrove killed her daughter.

I told her it was only my opinion; I had no conclusive, tangible proof. I also said that a cold case detective from Essex County had contacted me and I had worked with him to help him try and prove Ned killed Jane, but the case is still open.

"I know," she said. "he contacted me, too."

I then asked her about that conversation she'd had with Karen Osman's mother not long after Karen's murder. Why had she reached out to her? What led her to think there was a connection between Ned, Karen, and Jane?

Turns out Aletta had reached out to Karen's mother after reading about Karen's murder finally being solved.

"I wrote to her and said I really know how you feel because this just happened to me a year ago," Aletta told me, "and if I can help you in any way, please contact me. So she did, immediately."

Karen's mother told Aletta that she had always suspected that Ned had killed Karen. One of the reasons why Karen had broken it off with Ned was because her family had impressed upon her their distrust of Ned and their perception that he was strange.

"There was something about him," Karen's sister told me. "You could sense it when you were around him. Finally, Karen even picked up on it at the end and let Ned go."

While Karen and Ned were dating, the Osman family had noticed what they later came to believe was Ned's demonic nature. They had observed Ned closely whenever he was with Karen and knew something was terribly off.

As Aletta and Karen's mother chitchatted, Karen's mother dropped a bombshell.

"Well, the thing that sticks in my mind the most," Aletta explained to me, "is, she said that she saw Ned Snelgrove on

August twenty-something, sometime during late August and that he looked like he had been through something very bad, he looked terrible. He was pale and looked sick and, ah, and that would be around the time that Jane was killed."

I had already looked into this possibility while writing my book. Karen's family had told me the same thing, that there was a time right around the week that Jane Goodwin was murdered when Ned seemed spooked, and was looking over his shoulder, as if in fear of being caught for something. The behavior was enough to rouse suspicion in them and they remembered it all those years later.

This seems to fit with Ned's evolution as a serial killer. When he murdered Karen (which he always claimed was his first kill), Ned seemed to be very structured and certain about what he was doing. He didn't, in other words, come across as a man killing a woman for the first time. The crime scene told that story. It never appeared, as he claimed, that he'd killed Karen in a fit of rage he couldn't control, or went into some black out, murdered her, and then hurriedly taken off from the scene. The crime scene seemed almost staged to some extent; and certainly did not appear to be the work of a killer who was still experimenting or unsure of himself. In my opinion, Ned had a plan going into that murder, and he carried it out. Killing Jane some time before he carried out Karen's murder would explain the comfort level obvious at Karen's murder scene.

Jane lived on the bottom floor of a three-story, small (for Newark), red-brick apartment complex close to the corner of North 12th Street and Davenport Avenue in downtown Newark. Her apartment, as the crow flies, was a 2.8-mile hike from the Rutgers campus where Ned hung around. Newark today is not the Newark of Jane's day. When we were there in XXX YEAR filming the episode, the streets were coated with a layer (or glaze) of filth, garbage literally lined the sidewalks, and the traffic on Davenport seemed to never let up. Cops were everywhere. People were everywhere, keeping to themselves, many of whom were locked into the technology in their hands, talking on a cellphone, or conversing with friends on the corner. I didn't get a "community watch" feel while in Newark. I'm sure there are sections of this city where residents band together and keep an eye on one another, just not where we were.

In Jane's day, this particular section of Newark was more secluded and laid back. There were half as many people. At night the streets were dark, poorly lit, especially where Jane's apartment was located. Although, that said, crime rates back then were higher per capita than they are today, Newark being one of the cities with the highest crime rates in New Jersey year after year. Anyone could have followed Jane into her apartment, attacked and murdered her. It could have been a random act of violence. Looking at the remnants of the crime scene, at least the way in which they were explained to me during my investigation (I have not seen reports because it is an open case, but have spoken to law enforcement), and the particular signature attached to this murder, including evidence that Jane and Ned could have crossed paths several times throughout their days, I am led to the conclusion that I cannot exclude Ned as a suspect in Jane's murder.

In fact, if I look at everything that has been made available to me, it points to someone who had at least known Jane enough for her to be willing to invite him into her apartment. The fact that two wine glasses were discovered on her kitchen table, with a bottle of wine nearby, suggests that Jane was not murdered by a random act of violence or that this was a crime of opportunity. It suggests that Jane invited her attacker inside and they were close enough for Jane to feel comfortable enough to make an offer of wine.

On that Friday morning, August 20, 1982, Aletta called Jane, as she was in the habit of doing with all of her grown children, every other day. Repeated calls brought no answer. Over the course of the day, Jane's mother grew increasingly concerned, leading her to call her two other daughters and explain the situation. This was so unlike Jane, even though she lived on her own, she always answered her phone and consistently told the family if she was running off somewhere.

Jane's sisters also called with negative results. After not being able to reach Jane, the sisters took a ride over to the apartment and knocked on Jane's door.

Jane was a "meticulous" person. She liked to keep things clean and tidy. When one of her sisters, after not getting an answer at the door, peered in through an open window, she saw that Jane's living room was in disarray, and knew immediately that something was wrong, and suspected that something terrible had taken place inside that apartment.

Some family members of murder victims have expressed to me during interviews a certain feeling, or "sixth sense," they've had at times. It's a strange, but strong, sensation of something being terribly wrong. It happens with some siblings and family members of murder victims before they even know a tragedy has occurred. I recall the day I was told that my brother's wife had been found murdered. I took the call. Moments later, my brother, who was out shopping for food, walked through the door. He and my sister-in-law were estranged at the time. They had not been together for a few weeks. He was living with me. He took one look at my face and, literally dropping the groceries on the floor, said, "She's dead, huh?"

He knew. I wasn't crying. I was stunned, more than anything.

Yet this sixth sense is baffling to me in some respects. Perhaps it could be compared to what twins describe when the other is in distress. I don't understand it, but it's real and I believe it. I have heard it over and over and experienced it myself with my brother's wife's death. Family members say things like: "I knew something happened to her. I had this feeling she was in trouble and I was never going to see her again."

In any event, this is the part of Jane's story where conflicting accounts come in to play. Jane's sister had a key to Jane's apartment but she didn't want to use it because she was scared to go in. Additionally, as one report claimed, the door into Jane's apartment had been tampered with, as though someone had broken in, which heightened th e sisters' alarm.

Somewhere around eleven p.m., Jane's sisters called police.

The cops said they'd only come out if the sisters waited. They worked it out and the police arrived at 12:30 a.m.

Jane's sister spoke to a newspaper reporter the following day, recalling what happened next, saying, "It was a nightmare."

Jane was found stabbed to death.

A source close to the case tells me that Jane was found with her breasts exposed, stabbed in the chest, and also strangled. She was apparently clothed from the waist down. The door tampering could have been staging done by Jane's killer. What's more, and this is where it becomes something of a lock for me as to Ned's guilt, if the information I obtained during an interview with someone close to Ned is true: I was told a business card belonging to Ned was found around the corner from Jane's apartment on a nearby lawn not long after Jane's murder. My source for this is indisputable. This person was certain of this fact.

If that information is true, which I believe it to be, I have to ask myself: What are the chances that Ned Snelgrove did not have something to do with Jane's murder?

CHAPTER FIVE

The pen pal relationship Ned and I shared lasted close to a year. I routinely asked Ned to put me on his visitor's and/or phone call list so we could discuss his case at length person to person, but he ignored my pleas. Ned is a control-freak type of killer: He won't face someone who is going to challenge him. He's afraid that he'll give himself away with a look, a particular stare, or even a slip of the tongue. Detectives tried to interview Ned on several occasions, but described him to me as a man who would not engage you in person. Ned learned this from studying his hero and mentor, Ted Bundy (a relationship I will explain in more depth momentarily).

So, for months Ned and I wrote. I played this bizarre game with Ned, not sharing with him (and why should I, really—he's a scumbag killer and deserves nothing from me or anyone else!) exactly what I was thinking. Ned had developed a theory,or some sort of odd belief,that I had walked into his life to rescue him. That I was going to take his case and prove a miscarriage of justice, same as he had implored a journalist to do two years before after his sentencing. (I had never told Ned I was going to do this—I might have hinted, now that I think about it, but at the end of the day, it really doesn't matter.) The problem I ran into was that the more I studied the evidence, the more I believed Ned had not only attacked Mary Ellen, nearly killing her, murdered Carmen Rodriquez and Karen Osman, but in my opinion I believe he murdered Jane Goodwin and several other women. I had a detective tell me that he had been looking at Ned for potentially several other murders with similar patterns all throughout New England, but could not nail anything substantial down. The fact that this detective had spent months looking into this side of Ned's life told me something. Off the record, this same cop said he believed Ned was responsible for at least two additional murders between the time he got out of prison in 1999 and 2001, when he abducted and murdered Carmen.

During that eleven-year period Ned spent behind bars in New Jersey for Karen's murder and the attack on Mary Ellen, he wrote pages and pages of letters to an old friend of his. The content of these letters—a lot of which later became part of Ned's Hartford, Connecticut, court case—was astonishing. Ned's friend saved the letters because he was going to write a book one day with Ned's blessing and input. They talked about this in the letters, both agreeing they needed more "drama" (more murder, in my opinion, is what they meant) in order to up the ante of Ned's story and make it more salable.

On a whim, the Connecticut State Police, while investigating Ned for Carmen Rodriguez's murder, took a ride to visit Ned's so-called friend, simply to find out what he knew. They didn't have a clue as to the amount of information they were about to unearth after asking him if he still had any of the letters he had Ned had shared over several years.

Ned and his friend had an ongoing chess match throughout many of the letters, but they also discussed Ned's obsession while in prison with Ted Bundy. The original title of the Ned Snelgrove DARK MINDS episode was "Better Than Bundy." The reason for that was simple: Ned believed that by studying Bundy's mistakes, he could, in turn, when he got out of jail, become better than Bundy at stalking, abducting and murdering women. Why this friend never turned the letters over to the police in real time, while Ned was talking about all of this madness, baffles me to this day.

Ned studied every nuance of Bundy's life. Bundy made errors, Ned was convinced, which sunk him. Ned resigned not to make those same mistakes once he got out andto, as Ned wrote, "pick up when I left off."

In speaking to his friend about Mary Ellen's attack, Ned explained how meeting Mary Ellen and getting into her apartment (like a Bundy copycat) "**was** the perfect situation." The way Ned talked about it, you could almost sense how erotic and gratifying this would have been for Ned if his original plan had fallen into place.

Mary Ellen became a *situation* in Ned's way of telling this story. As 13, our serial-killer expert consultant on DARK MINDS, might say, Mary Ellen was nothing more than an object for Ned to gratify his sick needs. She was not a person, but a situation to control, to do as he wished with.

What happened during that "situation," Ned wrote, was what put him behind bars that first time.

"I botched it all up," Ned wrote to his friend. "She didn't die! If she had died, my name wouldn't have even made the suspect list, because she had just met me that night."

Ned went on to call Bundy "stupid **after the fact**. He kept maps, schedules and pamphlets of the hotels, brochures of ski resorts he visited. He even purchased gas with credit cards (stupid!)."

Funny thing is, when Ned got out later and murdered Carmen Rodriguez, he made these same mistakes.

CHAPTER SIX

I grew tired of playing games with Ned Snelgrove. As I began to wrap up the research portion of my book in 2007, I hit him with one last letter which I hoped would twist his arm behind his back and make him reveal some of his innermost thoughts about why he kills. I did it knowing full well it wasn't going to do much more than rattle his cage.

Still, it had to be done. I'd been playing Kick The Can with the guy. We both sensed there was this 800-pound gorilla between us, but had avoided it for whatever reason. I was getting something out of Ned, and he was getting something out of me. Ned had always explained himself, throughout his run as a killer and afterwards, on his terms. He had never allowed someone to question him specifically or directly. He never wanted to be in a position where he had to answer questions that made him uncomfortable.

This is why I call Ned a coward. I've spoken to serial killers that are (dare I say) at least "man enough" to answer questions. As an example, look at 13 on DARK MINDS. Here's a guy who tells it like it is, no matter what. Whether 13 or other serial killers lie to us as researchers is not the issue here (that is a separate argument/discussion). Ned always dodged the questions that pried into his personality, especially dealing with the past. He didn't want anybody to know what he was thinking unless it had to do with the stock market (his cellmates claim he was a master at picking stocks) or the Boston Red Sox (a sports team he was obsessed with).

During the research and writing process of "I'll Be Watching You," I had developed a snitch on the inside, a man who testified against Ned in court during his trial for Carmen's murder. My snitch claimed on the stand that Ned had given him a blow by blow account one day of killing

Carmen Rodriguez. On several occasions, I met with this man inside the prison where he is serving time himself for murder, just as recently as a few months before writing this e-book.

I recall the first letter I got from this guy, after writing to him and asking if he'd be willing to tell me what he had told jurors about Ned. I wanted to sit in front of him, stare into his eyes, and decide for myself if what he had to say held the truth which the jury in Ned's case obviously believed.

In his first letter, my snitch said, "...There is much more [about Ned] that you need to know. There are more murders that he told me about and he gave me detailed information about who and where and how he did them."

Here is a portion of that same letter:

August 1, 2007

Dear M. William Phelps,

I am very interested in giving you all the input I can on this case. There is much more that you need to know. There are more murders that he told me about and he gave me detailed information about who and where and how he did them.

*For a better look at the letters and pictures in
this book, visit http://wbp.bz/mrpg*

My snitch told me Ned bragged to him about several murders he had committed in and around the Hartford region. Many of the women he had first stalked, he had met through a door-to-door meat sales job he had at the time he murdered Carmen. I should also mention that Ned allegedly tried grabbing a girl off the streets of Hartford before he abducted and murdered Carmen. He was brought up on charges of kidnapping in that case, went to trial, but was acquitted of the charge. There were several women Ned had called on during his meat-selling days that police later spoke to. They claimed Ned acted strangely while in their house. One even said Ned kept returning to her house without being asked, kept calling and calling her, and only stopped after her husband waited for Ned one day and gave him a warning about coming back.

The idea that Ned had killed many women throughout New England after being released from prison in 1999 played into a letter that Ned wrote to me near the end of our correspondence. In this particular letter, Ned went on and on about how he "did not kill Carmen Rodriguez." He said my snitch was full of shit and making it all up so he (the snitch) could get a break in his sentence.

That, I must admit, is buyable. The fact that a snitch came forward and bartered with prosecutors over information he had about a so-called serial killer on trial did raise some eyebrows at the time. Prosecutors and police checked out the snitch's stories, however, and proved that there were details in what he had reported that had never been made public (this is one reason why cops like to keep certain facts of cases close to the vest).

I did the same. I also interviewed him in prison and gave him my carotid artery test to see if he was lying. The carotid artery test, of course, is from "Meet the Fockers." In the popular series of films, Robert De Niro's character Jack Byrnes, an old CIA man, could tell if you were lying by watching your carotid artery as you spoke; if it beat rapidly, you were nervous and likely bullshitting. I'm joking, obviously, about using this method on my snitch. But looking into the snitch's eyes as he spoke, watching his hands, listening to the details, going back and checking those details out one by one, I felt the same as the detectives: he was being honest.

Ned wrote to me in a peculiar way about Carmen's murder, trying to convince me, I can only assume, that he didn't do it. Yet he revealed several interesting details about his psyche within this series of letters. He belabored the point of how the medical examiner could never determine an actual cause of death in Carmen's case (true) because her body was so badly decomposed. He even listed several of the differences between Karen's and Carmen's murders, as opposed to Mary Ellen's attack, and sketched out a quasi-chart listing all of the variations in each case.

You must understand something about Ned's letters to me. They were banal in every way possible, and proved how structured and obsessive-compulsive this serial killer was during his reign of terror. He'd send me a letter, for example, and then a day later, I'd get another letter asking if I had received the one previous and if the staple in the right-hand corner he had purposely placed there had been disturbed. This would have been a telltale sign, Ned explained, that someone had tampered with the letter. But he didn't stop there. Each letter always came with a small card with questions he had designed and created himself in pen: Did you receive my last letter? Was the staple disturbed? There'd be actual check boxes made by Ned, with "yes" and "no" above each box. He'd implore me to send the card back ASAP. Strange, indeed, but also quite telling if you're someone studying these types of sexual sadist killers and their behaviors.

Getting back to what I was explaining about Ned and one of his charts pertaining to the differences between Carmen's murder and the other girls, here, see for yourself what I mean. Have a look at one of Ned's bizarre "charts." He even talks about himself in the third person, which is a tell-tale sign of emotionally distancing himself from these crimes.

Jersey N·OSMUN 12/23/83	New Jersey MARY ELLEN RENARD 8/1/87	Connecticut CARMEN RODRIGUEZ ?
Former girlfriend of Snelgrove's.	Met Snelgrove that night.	A mere acquaintance. Snelgrove was a steady customer at KENNEY's; Rodriguez was an occasional customer there and a small-time prostitute.
Snelgrove was not invited to follow her home.	Snelgrove was not invited to follow her home.	Asked for a ride in Snelgrove's car.
Drove herself to her own apartment.	Drove herself to her own apartment.	Did not drive herself. Was dropped off a block away by Snelgrove.
Deceased	Did not die.	Deceased
Strangled and stabbed.	Strangled and stabbed.	Cause of death completely unknown
Topless but fully clothed from the waist down.	Topless, but fully clothed from the waist down.	Was found completely naked but wrapped in a garbage bag.
Was left in her own apartment.	Was left in her own apartment.	Found many miles from her home, outdoors.
Snelgrove was the last to be seen with Osmun.	Snelgrove was the last to be seen with Renard.	Contrary to what police say, Snelgrove was not the last to be seen with Rodriguez, MEDICAL EXAMINER's report of Jan. 7 '02 says she was dead for at least "two months," which does not reconcile with the date on which Snelgrove was seen with her (Sept. 21, '01). Surely she was with someone, doing something!
Time between being with Snelgrove and time of death was accounted for.	Time between being with Snelgrove and time of assault was accounted for.	Time between being with Snelgrove and discovery of the crime scene is wholly unaccounted for. Rodriguez was missing for three and a half months, while MEDICAL EXAMINER's time of death estimate accounts for only two months.
No trauma to teeth.	No trauma to teeth.	Was struck in lower right canine at time of death, according to the lab. No mention of this from Pascual.

For a better look at the letters and pictures in this book, visit http://wbp.bz/mrpg

He focused on the testimony of a doctor who, according to Ned, got it all wrong. Ned's entire argument here became:

Just because I killed before and promised to kill again when I got out of prison, it doesn't necessarily mean I did it in Carmen's case.

"He was upset because we proved Carmen's case against him," said one detective. "He thought he'd covered every base with Carmen's murder, but we got him and he was pissed."

No professional could determine the cause of Carmen's death, indeed—which I would argue was Ned's plan from the moment he convinced Carmen to go with him and then tortured and murdered her somewhere in the darkness of the woods on the grounds of the Berlin Fair in Connecticut, but a few mere miles from where he lived with his parents at the time.

In the second part of that same letter, which was even more bizarre than the chart-like portion, Ned could not let go of the idea that the cops and the medical examiner could never figure out how Carmen was murdered, thus, in Ned's mind, excluded him as a suspect in the crime. After all, Ned wrote, "… other causes of death [for Carmen] that cannot be ruled out: why weren't they mentioned in the autopsy?" He listed the ways in which Carmen COULD have been killed. I wondered, staring at this poorly written document, which had obviously been scribed in a fit of rage over him being figured out (and exposed), what type of sick person would think of the following ways to kill another human being?

- Gunshot through soft tissue (no bone damage)
- Electrocution
- Drowning
- Forced starvation as result of being held captive
- Forced dehydration as result of being held captive
- Hard blow to the temple (no skull damage)
- Heart attack brought by external, traumatic event

The only conclusion I could come to was: only a person who has done it!

The thinking process of this man is alarming, yes; but also quite illuminating and obvious. He had gone to great lengths to come up with different ways to kill another human being.

So the question had to be: Had Ned practiced these various ways of murder? Was he sending me a direct message, describing to me some of the additional ways he had killed? Serial killers, at least the ones I've interviewed and built professional relationships with, love to send subliminal messages. They get off on speaking between the lines to see if we can figure it out. I mean, "heart attack brought by external, traumatic event"? Who else but a killer (someone who's done it already) could think of that?

My bet is, despite the narrative my snitch gave cops of Ned stabbing and strangling Carmen to death, that Ned used one of these methods to kill Carmen, and then told the snitch that he had stabbed and strangled her.

CHAPTER SEVEN

According to a law enforcement source, there was a woman found dead not too far from where Ned had an appointment to sell some meat in Massachusetts, just over the Connecticut border. I was told she had been murdered in her bathtub. The tub had been filled with acid or bleach or a combination of the two. This was an extreme way to kill someone. Cops didn't really connect Ned to this murder because it didn't fit his normal MO of breasts exposed and stabbing and strangulation.

But given what Ned had written to me, I would suspect

that Ned Snelgrove, unlike many serial killers, experimented with several different methods of murder, especially AFTER having that particular M.O. attached to him all those years. Ned is right when he says we don't know, other than what a snitch has told us, how Carmen Rodriguez was murdered.

What we do know, however, is that Ned Snelgrove was responsible for Carmen's death.

The one rock-solid piece of evidence in all of this, the absolute undeniable fact which convinces me that Ned murdered Carmen Rodriguez, turned out to be a piece of evidence offered at Ned's trial in Hartford, Connecticut which was ultimately prohibited from being entered into the record. The prosecution could not get it in. It was too "controversial" at the time.

A rather high-profile, well-known forensic expert had testified outside the jury about conducting ballistic-like tests on a few staple guns found in Ned's basement bedroom apartment inside his parents' house (where he went to live after getting out of prison in 1999). Yes, ballistics can be conducted on staples and staple guns, and, according to this expert, each staple gun fires a different staple, thus leaving behind a fingerprint, if you will, of that staple. It's much like that unique spiral, candy-cane-shaped pattern on a bullet that matches the inside of only one gun chamber.

How does this play into Carmen's murder?

The bags that Carmen's body was found in, a series of several black plastic leaf/garbage bags placed inside each other for reinforcement, bags which, I should note, were then matched to bags purchased near Ned's home, had been meticulously stapled. Law enforcement believed he had done this so that animals would not get into them, so that Carmen's body could deteriorate on its own time without being disturbed by nature or wild animals. You can see the bags in this photo here, taken after Carmen's body was discovered six months after she went missing by a guy walking along the roadside collecting garbage. The white dot on top of the bag is Carmen's skull.

For a better look at the letters and pictures in this book, visit http://wbp.bz/mrpg

That forensic expert had proven that the stapler (pictured below; and look closely, you can see the hair I'll discuss in a moment) in Ned's bedroom was the only stapler in the world, in his opinion, that could have fired some of the staples used to seal the bag Carmen's body had been found in. Moreover, a pubic hair belonging to Ned was found on that particular stapler which was uncovered in Ned's bedroom along with a cache of other bizarre items.

Included among articles about famous serial killers and videos of Ted Bundy and true crime books found inside Ned's bedroom was a set of Styrofoam mannequin heads (pictured here). Law enforcement believes that Ned used them to "practice" various methods of killing. The Styrofoam heads, incidentally, were found underneath Ned's bed and he blamed his nephew for marking them up and putting them there. As you can see, one of the heads is pristine and made up nicely, while the other is marked with pressure point areas to choke (the Adam's apple, distinctively), and different areas of the skull to strike and knock unconscious.

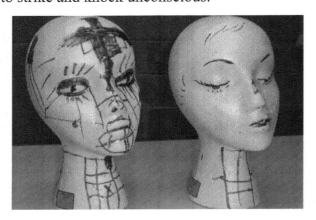

Typical Ned behavior is obvious in these items if you look closely. Thus, combined with the evidence presented in Carmen's case, what do these items of Ned's tell us about how he kills?

Ned was pleasuring himself as he stapled that bag containing Carmen's body. That is about the only conclusion I can come up with. The Styrofoam heads, well, I'll leave that up to the imagination. But let's be clear about one thing: all this man thought about was killing women. How he did it, fundamentally, we could argue all day long.

CHAPTER EIGHT

As recently as January 2012, I have received e-mail from women who have had brushes with Ned and feel that they have narrowly escaped death. One woman e-mailed with a story about Ned that I had heard no fewer than a dozen times since "I'll Be Watching You" was published in 2008: "In 1986, while a Rutgers University … student, I was drugged and nearly attacked by Mr. Snelgrove. This encounter has weighed on my mind for 26 years, in fact I have dreamt of the event on-and-off for as long. …"

Over and over, I have heard this same basic story. Ned means it, trust me, when he tells us in his letter to the judge that he cannot handle himself around females. There's a switch inside Ned that goes off when he sees a large-breasted woman he is attracted to. It's not a normal reaction. He doesn't feel an attraction. He doesn't want "get to know" the women.

Ned wants to kill her.

And then pleasure himself after the murder in some sick, twisted ritual that has been hard-wired into his mind since grade school.

While working on the book, I was resolute in finding out why Ned is the way he is. Sure, Ned was seemingly born a sociopath/psychopath, but somewhere in childhood the wires in Ned's brain were crossed and he began to merge feelings of violence and sex into one basic, violent need. He fantasized about this fetish of seeing good-looking women rendered totally incapacitated for his evil pleasuring ever since he was in the third grade (or even sooner, he himself tells us). A kid that age doesn't have those sorts of thoughts unless he witnesses the behavior repeatedly, generally in person, not in photographs or film.

I beat this point to the ground, gumshoe-wise. I asked everyone and anyone who could have possibly had insight where Ned would have developed his rather bizarre methods of killing and sexually assaulting women, and where his fantasies are rooted.

A law enforcement source finally started talking one day about it. That source told me: "Look, I was wondering the same thing—we all were. Where did Ned pick up this behavior?"

Apparently, through some investigating, the story goes that someone (an adult I won't name) took young Ned on several peeping-tom missions around the neighborhood. That alone would screw a child up enough to make him question his relationship with females and view females as objects for his sexual gratification. Ned's vision of sex and women in general would have been touched by filthiness, sexual confusion and sadism. We can all likely agree on that, if what this cop told me is true.

But where does the masturbation within the context of violence against women come into play?

Assuming the peeping tom that took Ned along masturbated in the bushes of those neighborhood women as

Ned looked on, we can clearly come to the conclusion that Ned Snelgrove, from an early age, began to associate sex with this type of personal, sadomasochistic behavior that puts women at the center of exploitation and humiliation. Maybe the women being peeped on weren't showering or undressing, but were sleeping. This theory—and that's all it is until Ned talks, and he never will—seems to be the most logical based upon what Ned himself has written.

All that said, as I wound down my relationship with Ned, I sent him that letter I knew would twist his arm and rattle his cage. Allow me to present it here before I share Ned's interesting and rather threatening response:

October 3, 2007

Hi, Ned:

Received your latest letters and your notes to your lawyer. Thanks!

You wrote: "Am I just imagining all of this ... Am I just stamping my foot, crying 'foul' for no good reason? Please tell me what you think."

Well, Ned, since you asked ... it's time, perhaps, that we stop this game between us.

There's a theme to your letters I need to point out: I find that you say the same things over and over without offering much proof-positive evidence to support your claims. Just rhetoric, in other words. No substantial evidence. Calling someone a liar does not make that person a liar—evidence does. I have yet to see any *evidence* that proves any of your claims. I have studied police reports and trials for my entire career (tens of thousands of pages and dozens of cases). I am considered an expert in this field. In none of the papers you've sent have I seen any *evidence*—

just your "interpretations" of the facts.

I need to address a few things. One, thanks for the permission slip to quote your letters to me. Appreciated. Second, I do *not* need permission from you—just to be clear—to quote the letters you wrote [to your friend]. They are part of the court record … and, as you likely know (you claim to be a smart guy), I have "fair use" copyright laws on my side and many of the letter excerpts were reprinted in newspapers across the country. Thirdly, I do, in fact, quote from those letters throughout my book.

To ask me to buy into your idea that there is no pattern, no "signature," surrounding the three victims—Mary Ellen Renard, Karen Osmun and Carmen Rodriguez—is quite a stretch on your part. This has been, however, another theme of yours: that Carmen's murder was "different" from the other(s) in NJ. The theory is (and I have quoted several well-known serial killer profilers who have tracked you for 20+ years), that, after studying Ted Bundy, you *changed* your m.o. That is what the prosecution is quoted as saying.

Furthermore, to claim that the "pick up right where I left off" quote from [your friend's] letters pertains to you going back to Hewlett is, to quote you, "laughable." Come on, Ned, do you expect me to believe that? Do you expect *anyone* to believe that after eleven years in prison for two vicious crimes, your goal, your dream, was to return to HP? You didn't return to HP, did you? And you didn't move in with your parents right away, as you told me.

You moved into a seedy Berlin Turnpike motel and, according to a source of mine, started killing again right away. You never went back to HP.

I could go on and on contradicting your notes and theories, but I'll stop here.

I need to ask you some "hardball" questions and offer you the opportunity to respond. I think it's only fair since I've been interviewing you (through our correspondence) now for several months.

My questions:

1.) Explain what you mean by "responding to questions" posed by [your friend]? (That's not what he says, by the way.) Certainly, you don't expect me to believe that everything you wrote to [your friend] was a response to a question he asked. I feel [you] were gloating, bragging, etc.

2.) Where do you think your thoughts of harming women and posing their bodies come from? You said it was there since the second and third grade. Explain that for me a bit more.

3.) One of my (professional) sources tells me that you told him/her that you're a breast man—which makes sense, seeing how your victims were attacked and left exposed from the waist up. How do explain this behavior? Where is it rooted? Were you ever sexually abused? Why is it, you think, that in your mind you equate this type of violence with sexual gratification?

4.)How many other women—if any—have you

murdered or harmed? Sources I've spoken to (many different sources, mind you) claim the number could be five, six, even ten more? Would you like to go on record as being the most prolific serial killer in the Northeast? Or do you deny all of this?

To expand on this question: If you have murdered other women, don't you want to give those families out there waiting, wondering, a bit of closure? I've spoken with people in Essex County, NJ, and Baltimore and other places (you know what I'm talking about!), some closure would help them cope with the loss. [Here I am referring to the Jane Goodwin case and another murder committed in Maryland while Ned was down there that bears striking similarities to his confirmed kills.]

5.) A final statement from you: what is it you'd like to say? Give me a direct quote that you want printed—a sort of statement from Ned Snelgrove to all of his critics and law enforcement.

6.) Why did you never put me on your visitor's or phone list?

7.) I've interviewed [the snitch] at length, visited him several times, what would you like to say about [his] claims? As you know, he claims that you have committed other crimes, beyond the Rodriguez matter.

Please don't take offense to any of these questions. As a journalist I need to ask them.

You asked me if I have interviewed any of

the jurors. Well, I cannot say. I've done over 100
interviews for this book. Many of my sources have
asked to stay anonymous. I have to give them that
right.

No notarized letter is necessary. What you sent
is fine.

Finally, you asked if I am "dumbfounded" that
a prosecutor (in your words, the prosecutor in your
case) could lie?

No prosecutor lied in this case, Ned. I've studied
all the data. I've spent a long time reviewing all of the
documents and statements and interviewed scores of
people connected to the case. Don't kid yourself into
thinking that you're going to get someone to believe
that there was a conspiracy against you. It's simply
not true. Although probably impossible, you need to
study your case objectively and then you'll see what
I mean.

If I don't hear from you by October 15, 2007, I'll
consider it a refusal to respond to my questions. ...

Ned did not respond in the timeframe that I had given
him. Although, I should say in all fairness, I had plenty of
time to spare. I was simply pushing him. But on October
29, 2007, Ned did speak. He was two weeks late, but I was
able to get him to respond to my rather outspoken letter,
nonetheless. Here is what Ned sent me (note the absurd,
structured boxes denoting "beginning of quote" and "end of
quote"):

BEGINNING OF QUOTE

"M. William Phelps's own logic discredits the theory that he claims 'profilers' have formulated. Case in point, if I were guilty of unsolved crimes, then, according to Mr. Phelps's prior reasoning, [my friend] would have produced written boasts and critiques pertaining to them, comparing them to the misdeeds of Ted Bundy. As it turns out, [my friend] Mr. Phelps and all his 'sources' and 'experts' come up completely empty on this point, a main pillar upon which Mr. Phelps attempts to build his thesis." END OF QUOTE

For a better look at the letters and pictures in this book, visit http://wbp.bz/mrpg

My book came out and I didn't hear from Ned—at least not right away. Then, one afternoon, I pulled up to my P.O. box, opened it and, while whistling the day away and pulling out all of my mail, there was a letter from Mr. Snelgrove.

I was overjoyed. This was going to be Ned's analysis

of my book about him. I was hoping he'd read it, took notes, and then sent me his annotated analysis so that I could perhaps catch him in one of his many lies and psycho-pathetic theories.

I didn't open the letter in the post office. I must admit I wanted to savor the moment. It sat on the front seat of my car as I drove home—still whistling—staring back up at me.

Finally, I got up the nerve, I guess you could say, to open it. By then I knew it wasn't much, simply because it was very thin; maybe a page, two at best. By nerve, what I mean is, Ned had gotten to me. He had, as my criminal profiling partner on DARK MINDS, John Kelly, says, "penetrated my psyche and gotten under my skin." As Kelly explained, I had invited this. I allowed my emotions to control the relationship. I make no apologies for that. This is how I am. I react. I don't allow scum like Ned Snelgrove to tell me what, when, where; I stand up to him. This may not be the right approach, but it is the victims' advocate's way of sending a message to psycho-killers that they don't matter. Victims and their families are what matter here. I owed Carmen's and Karen's families that much. To stand up to Ned Snelgrove was to spit in his face, something I would do without hesitation if given the opportunity.

I don't recall exactly where I was when I read Ned's letter, but as I opened it and read the salutation, I laughed, and then understood that Ned's flair for the dramatic was what he was going after:

"Dear Hunter S. Thompson," Ned wrote.

Ah! You got me, I thought. I had never fashioned myself after the gonzo journalist, had really never read anything ever written by Thompson, had never seen the Johnny Depp movie about him, "Fear and Loathing in Las Vegas," and never thought, for the life of me, anyone would ever compare me to this man. But once I thought about it, yeah, well, OK, in some respects … maybe.

Ned, with his Dear Hunter, was of course referring to me blindsiding him with that last letter of mine. He was saying that I had hit him with a sucker punch, as if he wasn't expecting it. But I beg to differ: Ned knew that I was not some sort of newspaper reporter answering to a bunch of white shorts keeping a tight leash on me. He understood that I was my own man and person.

Believe it or not, Ned didn't say much. He simply gloated about an article he had read in *The New York Times*, which he was now encouraging me to seek out and read myself. That article, if I had the balls to read it, would explain, Ned suggested, what was going to be his reality someday soon.

He did not tell me what the article was about, so I became a bit frantic driving down to the library to go in search of it. If it was some sort of article depicting how a prisoner had escaped and killed someone he'd had an ongoing feud with, well, I might want to take that to the prosecutor in Ned's case and present it as evidence that Ned was threatening me. But Ned, as I have said, is a coward. He's a small man, with a weak mind, and no guts.

Here is Ned's entire letter:

CHESHIRE CORR. INST.
900 HIGHLAND AVENUE
CHESHIRE, CT
06410

SUNDAY, FEBRUARY 22, 2009

HUNTER S. THOMPSON
P.O. BOX 3215
VERNON, CT
06066

HUNTER:

For a long time now, you have despaired of not being acknowledged as a "crime expert" among other writers and/or police investigators.

I have a suggestion that will help you to take a step towards obtaining the status you've coveted all your life.

Obtain a copy of the NEW YORK TIMES from Sunday, February 8, 2009. Turn to page 26. Read the article at the top of page 26. Now, re-read the last paragraph.

Maybe you'll learn something.

E F Smlgrove   297891

*For a better look at the letters and pictures in
this book, visit http://wbp.bz/mrpg*

Ned attacked me personally in the letter, beyond letting me know vis-à-vis that *The New York Times* article that DNA would one day bust him out of prison and he would then stand atop his soapbox and scream to the world, *you see, I did NOT kill Carmen Rodriguez.*

The headline of the article, "NEW EFFORTS FOCUS ON EXONERATING PRISONERS IN CASES WITHOUT DNA EVIDENCE," explained where Ned was coming from. That last paragraph he refers to in his letter has to do with a quote from an expert in wrongful convictions, who said: "One thing we've learned by studying these cases and litigating these cases is it could really happen to anybody....Nobody is immune."

That is the final paragraph Ned asked me to read and "re-read again ..." so that, he wrote, "Maybe you'll learn something."

He's an idiot and stupider than I thought if he actually believes what he wrote in that absurd letter to me.

All of Ned's appeals have been exhausted. He will NEVER get out of prison. He will spend the rest of his miserable life in the sex offenders unit of the Connecticut prison that houses him, because if they put him in the general population, there will always be someone ready to attack him. In fact, it has happened a few times.once by a relative of Carmen's who just happened to be incarcerated in the same jail as Ned).

Likewise, Ned will never grant Jane Goodwin's mother the satisfaction of telling her that he committed that crime because it is not in his nature to feel empathy or sympathy. Ned does not care what people feel. He is emotionless, in other words, just a shell of a human being.

All of this is my opinion and alleged by me, I might add here!

As recently as 2011, a cold case detective contacted me about Jane's murder and Ned's possible involvement. Jane's murder is not just some sort of investigation I have embarked on by myself, or dreamt up by talking to sources on my own. Ned's name is attached to it and has been for decades.

This cop came up to Connecticut to visit Ned and ask him questions about Jane's murder.

Ned refused to speak to him.

I was told the cop held up a photo of Jane in the window of the room where Ned sat and waited.

Ned looked at the photo, turned, and walked away.

If you're interested in reading the complete story of Ned's life and crimes, my publisher has re-issued my book about him, "I'll Be Watching You."

EPILOGUE

Jane Goodwin's murder, like most of the unsolved cases I profile on "Dark Minds," is solvable. With the way in which DNA works today, we could hear down the road that Ned had nothing to do with Jane's murder and it was a random act of violence by another predator. That conclusion would not surprise me. My point with profiling Ned for this crime is that I cannot exclude Ned from Jane's murder. Until I can exclude him, based on what we know about Ned and his crimes and close contact to this case, we have to include him.

A major goal of the "Dark Minds" series is to put the victims' stories out there so that, hopefully, it will encourage people to come forward with information they might have in these crimes. My job is not to solve cases. I am not a cop. For me, this is about gathering information. It doesn't matter how insignificant or significant you think the information you might have is. Let the cops sort it out. Murder victims matter. They had lives before the devil's claws hooked into them. Their lives were not disposable. They should NEVER be forgotten. Help the authorities solve this case. Give Jane's family some peace and allow Jane's memory the honor that it deserves.

She deserves justice.

If you want more information about "Dark Minds" (or you have any tips for this case), please go to the Investigation Discovery website: *http://investigation.discovery.com/* or visit the "Dark Minds" Facebook page: *http://www.facebook.com/pages/Dark-Minds/1924938008815468?skip_nax_wizard=true*

THE EASTBOUND STRANGLER
BEHIND THE SCENES OF INVESTIGATION
DISCOVERY'S "DARK MINDS"

*"Here I was, out of my office, doing what
I did best: hunting murderers."*

Atlantic City, New Jersey

CHAPTER 1

THEY WERE WALKING along a service road between the Atlantic City Expressway and Black Horse Pike, in Egg Harbor Township, New Jersey. The dirt road was deserted, garbage strewn all over the place. Weeds ran waist-high and thick. The oddly fragrant juxtaposition of seawater, car exhaust, and filth permeated the air. On one side of the dirt road they could see the back walls of the sleazy weekly/monthly/hourly motels; on the other, they could see a small drainage ditch, about fifteen feet across, a few feet deep, feeding into Lakes Bay maybe a half-mile upstream. Cars whizzed by on the expressway, while the train tracks between the thruway and the small chasm of slowly running water provided an avenue for the incoming locomotives transporting gamblers, well-wishers and runaways into Emerald City.

The last thing the girls expected to see while going about their day was a dead woman. Her bare feet stuck out of the brush, her head pointed toward the water, and her clothed body fit to the contour of the sloping bank. Her eyes, cast to the east, were wide open and cloudy, like fish in supermarket snow.

"Me and my friend were taking a walk on the path by the railroad tracks," one of the girls said to the 911 operator. "There's a dead woman down there."

It was November 20, 2006.

That call ultimately led local authorities to the bodies of four dead women. Apparently, the work of the Eastbound Strangler, as he would soon be known, had been exposed—and the hunt was on.

From the best law enforcement could tell, one of the dead women had been strangled. Another died of asphyxia. But two additional bodies were in such a state of decomposition that figuring out their causes of death with any precision would be mere guesswork. Each female had been left along that slight bank formed along the drainage ditch just outside Atlantic City with her head facing toward the city. Each was fully clothed, except for shoes and socks. Three of the victims were said to be prostitutes, and all were reportedly drug users. An early news report concluded that they were found approximately sixty feet from one another and that their deaths had been spread out one week apart.

I didn't believe that report when I heard it, and confirmed my suspicions after being on the ground, talking to police sources and seeing an aerial photograph of the bodies and how they were spread out.

First, the girls were not equally spaced apart, as if a killer was sending a cryptic message by placing them *exactly* sixty feet from one another. Second, who could say that the two women whose bodies were so badly decomposed had been murdered? There was, after all, no evidence (other than an assumption) that they had been killed in similar fashion to the others.

What interested me initially was that a law enforcement task force had spent upwards of 200,000 man-hours investigating this case (an investigation that is still open) between 2006 and 2011 and no arrests had been made. With that kind of attention put on a case and still no viable perpetrator sitting behind bars, my first thought was that I was dealing with a potential structured serial killer with above-average intelligence—but, maybe, not as smart as he (or them) had seemed to be at first glance. On balance, at least in a lot of the cases I have studied, there is some luck involved for these guys. And killers, like machinists and accountants, get better at what they do the more they do it.

"We find what works best," one infamous serial killer told me, "and we stick to it."

IT HAD BEEN AT least twenty years since I had taken a trip on a train. After shooting an episode ("The Valley Killer") of "Dark Minds" in New Hampshire, Vermont, Massachusetts, and Connecticut, I opted for the train from my office in Connecticut to Atlantic City, N.J., knowing that I had a tremendous amount of travel in planes and automobiles ahead of me for the duration of the series shoot (eight episodes). I felt it would give me time to think. Here I was, out of my office, doing what I did best: hunting murderers. The ride would allow me the opportunity to get into the mindset of this perpetrator and begin—as I had been trained to by my serial killer profiling mentor, John Kelly—to *think* like him.

"There's a good chance," Kelly told me before I left, "you'll come face to face with the guy you're hunting down there. I believe you are going to be sitting and interviewing him. You better be ready for that."

Kelly had worked this case back in the day. It was the profile his company had written that tagged this killer as the

Eastbound Strangler because of the Atlantic City Expressway along the ditch where the women had been found, along with the sensationalized theory that the girls' heads were facing east for a reason only the killer knew. It seems to me that most high-profile serial killer investigations, once the media sinks its claws into the case, take on a construction of their own. There needs to be, for some reason, a diabolical killer with deep-seated ulterior motives rooted in his psyche at play. It's that ticking-clock syndrome that Hollywood has injected into the mix over the years.

I believe that some people are just fucking evil and like to watch people suffer, for no reason other than their own sick, psychological needs being met within the madness they create. It can be that simple.

Kelly had contacts. He knew Atlantic City. He grew up and lived in New Jersey most of his life. Kelly had been in the business of catching serial killers for twenty years and had worked with the New Jersey State Police and FBI on several high-profile cases, including the Green River Killer, the Unabomber, and John Wayne Gacy, to name only a few.

Thinking things through as I traveled from Connecticut to Atlantic City, the one item that stood out to me most—beyond, that is, realizing how looking at the underbelly of most major cities from the viewpoint of a train is akin to staring into the bottom of a Dumpster—was how proficient this killer had been. He was presumably able to kill four women, transport their bodies to a rather busy area of Egg Harbor Township along the Black Horse Pike, just on the outskirts of Atlantic City, and place each girl methodically in a precise position.

All without being seen.

He knows this town, the terrain, the ebb and flow of the area, I thought. *Where cops hang out. And where they* don't *hang out.*

Kelly met me at the train depot in Atlantic City and drove us to one of the major casino hotels. It was cool that day. Sunny. As soon as I got into Kelly's car and we made our way toward the city, I could sense some childhood memories bubbling. As a youngster, I vacationed here with family. That was the in the late seventies and early eighties. Atlantic City's heyday. There were money and bright lights and happy people gorging themselves at the buffets, blowing college-fund money and mortgage payments on the slots, and going to those silly cabaret shows in the ballrooms of the casinos. The beaches were clean and vendors were friendly and helpful. The taffy was sticky and salty. The riffraff was hidden away somewhere; you knew they were there, but you never saw them. Tourists came in by the thousands, and the casinos had money to burn.

It was that smell—musty and reminiscent of week-old garbage—that brought it all back for me as soon as we approached the Boardwalk. The stench had never left this place, I realized as I got out of the car.

Maybe, I considered, *the city hadn't changed.*

Wishful thinking. The truth was: the Indian casinos of Connecticut and Pennsylvania had drained the life out of this place. It was a dead zone. The city's upkeep had suffered. It appeard that nothing had been updated or repainted. The strip, Pacific Avenue, had a dirty and unkempt feel to it, like an abandoned building overtaken by weeds. The hotels were empty. The band names in lights (Chicago, Tony Orlando & Dawn, etc.) told the story of entertainers who perhaps should have retired long ago, but were still milking fizzling careers. Residents looked tired, sick, and as if waiting for a demolition ball to tell them the city was closing, and to evacuate while they could. I thought about how Sammy Davis Jr., Joey Bishop, and Frank Sinatra once called this place home while they played to sold-out audiences at the

Resorts Casino for weeks on end. Now, I looked around and saw such A-listers as Don Rickles (a man I could have sworn was dead, but who, in fact, turned 90 the year of this publication), and the big draw of the week, Seth Meyers.

Atlantic City, I realized, *had* changed. This was not the city of my youth. The life had been sucked out of this place. The sun shone, but it felt dark and gloomy all the time, as if a depression had consumed the entire town and its people. I could see how these murders had not surprised residents, because it seemed like the kind of place in which a serial murderer could thrive. When you do what I do long enough, and you come into a town, you can almost sense the evil looming in the infrastructure. And here, where gambling, drugs and prostitution were all that was keeping the city from imploding, that darkness, so oppressive and evident, was what I had come to embrace and settle into.

CHAPTER 2

JOHN KELLY SPORTS A swath of silver-white hair that works for him. He looks the part. Kelly, an addiction specialist/ therapist by trade, has a congenial demeanor that makes you want to open up and talk about yourself. Kelly has been a friend and mentor for years. He's one of the best people I know, and I love the guy. He thinks differently than me, especially where it pertains to profiling serial murderers and crime scenes. It's one reason we make such a great team. Kelly's cause is to educate the world about child abuse and how it greatly influences children to grow into violent, self-loathing adults, and sometimes even serial killers. How can one argue with a guy whose lot in life has become spreading the word that child abuse is the worst disease there is, and the fact that nobody is really doing much to put an end to it.

"Not every abused child grows up to be a serial killer," Kelly likes to say. "But every serial killer we study tells us he's been sexually abused."

It was nice to see Kelly in Atlantic City under these circumstances. We were here to help catch a monster. Kelly's role, along with a friend he had brought along, a big guy with a big gun, was to watch my back for a few days and make a few introductions.

Most of my memories of Atlantic City, probably because of the emotional place I was also while here in search of a serial killer, involved my oldest brother Mark, his better half Diana, my mother and father, and our summer vacations in this boardwalk town and gambling haven. The adults would drink, gamble and fight; I would find a game room and somebody to buy me some booze so I could have my own little party under the Boardwalk. It was interesting to me, as I took in the city for the first time in nearly thirty years, how my life had come full circle. Here I was in Atlantic City, investigating a presumed serial murder case in which several of the victims were alleged to be prostitutes. Diana, my brother's common-law wife, had been not only like these women, but she was also murdered (in Hartford, Connecticut, in 1996) by what we at first believed was a serial killer (her case remains unsolved).

I call Diana my sister-in-law because it's characteristic of her role in our lives. She and my brother, although they were together some twenty years, never officially married. That's because they could never stay sober long enough to see it through. Diana was a fixture in our lives. She and my brother, who died some years after her, left three kids—my niece and two nephews. Their lives were a tragedy.

During her best days, Diana was a beautiful woman with striking blonde hair (nearly down to her waistline), a round, baby face, blemish-free skin, and a cheerful, entertaining demeanor. She was the life of any party. She loved Stevie Nicks and, in many ways, resembled the popular singer in looks and in life. As I worked myself through what we had to do in Atlantic City that week, I had to ask myself: *Was I here for Diana? For my family? Or to perhaps rectify childhood memories? Was I trying to right something that had gone wrong in my own life?* Sure enough, we had been at war, the three of us, myself versus Diana and my brother, when she was murdered. If I were being honest, I would say I actually despised her at the time she was killed. It had even gotten to the point where I had taken her and my brother to probate court and won guardianship of their kids in a custody battle. But that's a story for another time.

I had to remind myself that I was in town to film an episode of "Dark Minds," a real-life dramatic true crime series I had created myself and worked on for years with John Kelly. Yet, as I began talking about my feelings with Kelly, who is also a forensic psychotherapist, I had to wonder not only what answers I'd find for myself to satisfy my own demons, but whether both purposes were intertwined. I mean, this is what I do. Crime is my life, so to speak.

"You're in the game now, Mathew," Kelly warned me. "Take it easy. Always remember what Friedrich Nietzsche warned: 'When you stare into the abyss, the abyss stares back.' Be prepared for that."

John Kelly was worried about me; I kind of liked that. It was comforting.

CHAPTER 3

WHAT DID WE KNOW about these women and their deaths? For me, all murder investigations have to begin with the victims. I was once told to look at every murder victim as the bull's-eye on a target and within the ripple effect of rings around the eye, you would find the answers to the mystery. It all begins by analyzing and searching the framework of the victim's life. It doesn't take Columbo to figure out that if you trace the final steps of a murder victim's life, wherever it leads, you are going to run into her killer sooner or later. By the same token, however, you have to be prepared for *any* answer, whether or not it fits into your preconceived notions—and we all have them—of the crime.

With a series of murders that all *seem* to be connected, profilers and investigators look for patterns. The ages of the four victims here did not take on any sort of similar shape.

KIM RAFFO, the last known victim of the Eastbound Strangler, was a 35-year-old wife and mother of two from Florida. (Atlantic City is one of those cities where no one who ends up in trouble or dead is actually from there.). According to reports (and an interview I conducted with Kim's husband to confirm), Kim was born in Brooklyn and moved to Florida during the 1990s, where she remained until the bug of drug addiction bit her. She had volunteered with the Girl Scouts and the local PTA. Kim's passion was cooking. She was enrolled in a cooking class at a technical school in Florida, where she met a drug user who allegedly introduced her to cocaine and heroin. As her love affair with drugs began, so did an extramarital tryst with her new cooking partner. I say *allegedly,* because I suspect that Kim Raffo was dabbling in drug use before meeting this guy. Something tells me there is more to that end of her story than has been told.

When Kim fell victim to the drug-fueled way of life (addiction, I have always said, is the most prolific serial killer on the planet), her husband, Hugh Auslander, a carpenter, took the kids and left. Kim and her boyfriend (the drug-using cook) took off north and settled in Atlantic City, where Kim worked as a waitress, Hugh told me, before turning to prostitution to feed her habit.

Found along the bank of that drainage ditch near the Atlantic City Expressway, just in back of the Golden Key Motel, Kim Raffo was dressed in a Hard Rock Cafe tank top and pants (probably jeans). Unlike the other dead women, Kim's tiny body was found before decomposition had set in, possibly within twenty-four hours of her death. She had been strangled with a rope or cord.

The parallels between Kim Raffo and Diana, my sister-in-law, are nearly indistinguishable—right down to how Kim was killed and the life she fell into leading up to her death. My sister-in-law, who was murdered in Hartford, was found dead inside an apartment building. She was five months' pregnant. Her killer had placed a pillowcase over her head and strangled her with a telephone cord. Diana was a drug addict, same as my brother Mark. At the time she died, she was doing what she needed to do to feed both their habits.

"Kim was just this wonderful person who got hooked up with drugs and never turned back," Raffo's former husband, Hugh Auslander, told me. "I tried repeatedly to save her, pick her up and take her out of there, but she always went back to Atlantic City."

Change Atlantic City to Hartford and Kim's name to Diana, and the same could be said by me and the rest of our family.

Hugh admitted he had taken Kim into Atlantic City several times (a statement that baffled me). They had once moved to Long Island together where he said Kim got sober for a period of time. But, he added, Kim ultimately went back to her boyfriend in Atlantic City, to sell her body for drugs. There's a missing link here somewhere, because although Hugh had taken the kids away from Kim in Florida, the children ended up in foster care, and Hugh never got them back. Hugh told me that he and Kim, when they lived in

Long Island, were no more than "friends helping each other out." Kim and Hugh had parted company in Long Island during the late summer once Kim took off, saying she had some "unfinished business in Atlantic City." They agreed to meet up again.

Instead, Kim wound up dead.

I asked Hugh why he would allow Kim to go back to the city, knowing what she was going to do.

"When she was ready to get help," Hugh said, "I always told her I would be there for her and pick her back up."

Listening to Hugh describe the final months and days of Kim's life, I couldn't help but think how life, and the people around her, had let Kim down. When she crossed that line into heavy daily drug use, she couldn't find her way back on her own. She needed someone to step up and take control. In some ways, I felt Kim suspected she might end up dead one day, one way or another, just as Diana must have.

It takes only one stumble, a slip and fall, to throw off the course of their life. When you're dealing with drugs like crack cocaine and heroin, you have to take into account how relentless these poisons are. Drugs first encompass and then strangle your soul. They do not want you to get back on your feet. They tell you when to eat, when to sleep, how to think, what to wear, who to have sex with, who to steal from, when to shower, —all things that those of us who aren't addicted to drugs are able to make choices about in our daily lives.

As I've said, Kim and Diana could have been the same person, which is one reason I cringe when I hear people talk about prostitutes and street girls as being "easy targets" for serial killers. While it does make them more vulnerable, such talk seems to imply that their lives lack importance, as if being on the street was a choice they made easily or because they wanted to. Many people look down on drug abusers who sell their bodies to feed their addictions, and

I even understand why it's easy to be so cynical. It's in the same vernacular as, ignorantly mocking overweight people. There are those who are convinced that overweight people could help themselves if they chose to do so. So it's no surprise to me when society at large seemingly doesn't even seem concerned about a street girl who turns up dead in a ditch. I get the dichotomy of the human mind and spirit which sometimes causes a struggle for some of us to love those who need it most.

Many would have you believe that law enforcement feels the same, which could be erroneously interpreted as the reason many of these crimes go unsolved for so long. But that line of thought is patently unfair. Cops want to solve these cases as much, probably more, than anybody else, save the victims' families. Victims of murder are victims, period. I am reminded of something John Kelly once told me: "Have you ever met a 10-year-old girl playing with Barbies that dreamt of growing up to be a drug-addicted prostitute?"

Cops (the good ones!) think this same way.

In the eyes of most people in law enforcement, there is no distinction between a mother in suburbia who's been swiped from the parking lot of a supermarket and a hooker from the streets of Atlantic City who's found dead in a ditch. Sure, there are exceptions. There are bigoted and , corrupt cops who don't treat street women with respect and violate their human rights whenever they can. But those types of cops truly are rare, as you'd find out in the field asking around.

So I'm not talking about the *exception*, I am focused on the rule. The problems arise when cops begin to investigate and realize quickly, same as I did, that investigating these types of deaths/murders becomes a rather intricate maze of walking through the sticky underbelly of a city steeped in crime, corruption, drugs, gambling, all of the extraneous criminal activity which envelops the crimes of prostitution and drug usage. People are scared to come forward. They don't want to be arrested for the crimes *they're* committing. This type of obstacle can stall an investigation.

TRACY ANN ROBERTS, just twenty-three, grew up in New Castle, Delaware, a quick surf south of Atlantic City. Tracy's body was found in the drainage ditch not far from Kim Raffo's, facing the same way and posed (a word I use cautiously) in the same peculiar positioning, according to several reports. Tracy had lived in Philadelphia for a time before heading to Atlantic City to work the strip club circuit. Her story was a familiar one: Tracy got herself involved in drugs and turned to the Atlantic City streets to work for money to feed her habit. Friends and fellow working girls called Tracy "the young, pretty one." She lived in the same run-down area of seedy rooming (crack) houses as Kim Raffo, located near the Resorts Casino close to South Tennessee Avenue and Pacific. It's an area known to locals as "The Track." Kim and Tracy were also friends.

According to one report, authorities found Tracy wearing a red hooded sweatshirt and a black bra. A source told me she had been clothed from the waist down, except for her shoes and socks. Tracy was said to have been dead for as little as a couple of days or as long as a week, but we just don't know for sure. Kim Raffo's body was found by the two girls walking along the service road which was parallel to the drainage ditch, and that led to the discovery of Tracy's body, as well of as the other victims. It has always been *assumed* that Tracy and the others were there all along, but their killer (or killers) could have kept the bodies elsewhere and dumped them when he wanted to (or at the same time he dumped Kim's body).

In looking for patterns, new evidence, and information that will point you in the direction of a viable suspect in a serial murder case (as opposed to some person of interest that everyone is hot on), you cannot *assume* anything, especially the obvious. Serial killers *want* you to think in that frame of mind. They *want* you to believe the lies they tell with a crime scene. Crime scenes left behind by serials, a majority of them, anyway, are almost *always* staged to some extent. That is, unless the location represents, out of necessity, a dump-and-run (or kill-and-run) scenario.

This particular location outside Atlantic City was no dump-and-run site. It is tucked away in back of a strip of seedy motels and, if you're not from the area and don't know it's there, you'd be hard-pressed to simply come upon it and choose it as a recurring dump site. Locals know of this place. Area working men and women know about it, too. Cops are familiar with it.

There is no doubt that this killer knew the area very well. The dump site, in relation to the Atlantic City area and the lifestyles of the victims, says something about who this animal is, why he chose these types of victims, and why he chose a dumpsite near water.

"In the shadow of evil, a feeding frenzy takes place among those who stumble upon the art of murder," one infamous serial killer told me recently. We've been corresponding through the mail and talking via phone. This is not the same killer known as "13," I should point out, whose voice and insight you hear on "Dark Minds."

Further, he added, "Our experiences dictate how we kill. We *learn* from our experience."

Based on our developing profile, the guy we're hunting in Atlantic City is not some sort of married, working man (hiding in plain sight, much in the same manner as, say, BTK or Ted Bundy). This is obvious in his choice of dump site. At first blush, you might want to place him in the same pool as the Green River Killer, Gary Ridgway, but first impressions and comparisons to high profile serials are always a slippery slope.

Consider for a moment what my man on the inside said: Once something works for a serial, he sticks with it. Until, that is, a turn of events (such as those girls stumbling on Kim Raffo's body) changes things. At that point, as an investigator, I'd have to ask myself: *Did the Atlantic City killer leave Kim's body out so it* could *be found?* Kim's body was left closest to one of the service road entrances into the drainage ditch. It was almost a certainty to this killer, unless he's a total moron, that by leaving Kim's body where he had, she would eventually be found. Moreover, a back door exit which connected to a room at the Golden Key Motel led directly out to where her body was found.

What if he was back there, searching around for the perfect spot to place his latest victim, staging his scene the way he wanted, and someone came upon him and he had to dump Kim's body and get out of there quickly?

BARBARA BREIDOR, at forty-two, was the oldest of the four dead women. She had been raised in Pennsylvania, but came to Atlantic City to rent a house in the hamlet of Ventnor, about three miles southwest of Atlantic City, reportedly so she could run her family's Boardwalk jewelry store. With business not what it used to be along the now crumbling Boardwalk, with a beach on one side with sand almost too dirty to walk on, Barbara moonlighted as a cocktail waitress. That is, before "a longtime drug problem worsened and pushed her into prostitution," a news report claimed.

Barbara had been dead, by some accounts, for as long as two weeks when she was found. Forensic testing concluded that she had a "lethal level of heroin" in her system at the time of her death, and yet authorities claimed they were unable to determine how she died. Wearing blue jeans and a long-sleeved zipper shirt, Barbara was also reportedly missing her socks and shoes.

MOLLY JEAN DILTS was the Eastbound Strangler's presumed final victim (or his first victim, if you look backwards at the timeframe in which the women died). Molly, at 20, was a chubby-cheeked, perpetually smiling, young girl with dark hair and a cheery manner. Everyone along The Track adored the young girl. She had left her home, and her child, in Pennsylvania after being busted on charges of harassment and underage drinking . She had also suffered a series of additional hardships, including the suicide of her brother, and the loss of her mother, who died while waiting for a heart transplant. The stress of life was too much and Molly found herself on the streets of Atlantic City, at first working as a fast-food cook. Molly was never arrested for prostitution in Atlantic City, though there were reports that several girls reported seeing Molly working the streets. Molly's toxicology results showed no traces of drugs, but she had been drinking heavily before her death. Dressed in a denim miniskirt, a bra and blouse, Molly had died about a month before she was found.

I mucked around that drainage ditch and along the service road, snooping around, getting wet, with hundreds of ticks stuck to my jeans like prickers, not to mention snuggled clingingly to my arm hair. I was looking for some sort of reason other than the obvious as to why these girls could have been placed *there* (specifically), and why, if Molly had indeed been there a month, no one had seen her (or any of the others) in all that time. Billboards hug the bank of the drainage ditch. Any worker changing a light bulb, or putting up a new billboard poster, could have looked down and spotted the bodies. There are also train tracks along the bank on one side of the water. How many thousands of people, I wondered, had traveled by here on those trains, staring out the window and perhaps thought they'd seen a body, but wrote it off as their mind playing tricks on them? Why hadn't a train conductor reported seeing anything?

One possible answer: the bodies hadn't been there as long as the ladies had been dead.

Perhaps the women were killed elsewhere, and kept for a period of time before being dumped. Perhaps Molly and Barbara died of causes other than murder *while* in someone's company. Law enforcement has never publicly said that a serial killer was working in Atlantic City. Nor has anyone officially said that these four women were the victims of *one* killer. Or even said that they all were murdered.

Still, we look for patterns, and there are several present here. So far, three confirmed prostitutes and one fast-food cook who was addicted to alcohol and had been seen working the streets. All were found in the same general area, facing the same way. All were barefoot. All worked in the same general street area of the city (The Track). All likely knew each other.

What stands out to me the most? The fact that they were all found barefoot. And that their heads faced the east toward the expressway and Atlantic City.

I spoke to Dr. Ed Merski, a psychologist and expert in the taboo-ish field of fetishes. Merski, a friend and colleague of Kelly, explained that the man I am hunting could have a foot fetish. The combination of foot fetishes, prostitutes, and a tendancey towards violence can produce a man with a sadomasochistic personality who can turn ugly and deadly with the blink of an eye. Add substances to that (and I believe, as John Kelly has told me, most serial killers are drug addicts and/or alcoholics), and we have the makings of a dangerous psychopath who preys on women he can *easily* convince to get into his vehicle for party purposes.

If so, the no-shoes, no-socks evidence is not, I am certain, a coincidence. However, as far as all the girls' heads facing east and that being some sort of ritualistic message, I am more inclined to believe, based on what law enforcement has told me, that this is nothing more than a result of the tide and the water current flowing out with the ebb and flow of the water table, pushing all their heads in the same direction.

CHAPTER 4

THE ONE COMMON THREAD that emerged as I hit the streets along The Track and began talking to several working girls was that this city, perhaps like no other, has a mysterious pull. It lives and breathes and sucks you in, consuming your every sense. A lot of the girls I spoke to agreed. Atlantic City, they told me, was a well, and once you fell in, it turned darker and deeper as you moved along your way toward hitting the bottom.

"Like a magnet," said one woman, whose face was pockmarked with sores, and whose arms were so speckled with bruises and scars from cutting herself, that it was hard to find a clear patch of skin untouched by the street life. "This city gets a hold of you and doesn't let go."

Looking at this woman, sizing up her life, I was brought to tears. Like many of the women along The Track in Atlantic City, she has children, some of whom she hasn't seen in years. There is anguish there, recognizable in her eyes, that runs so deep that no drug can numb its throbbing ache. I am convinced it is why she cuts herself. And cutters, I know from research I've done, are screaming for help. This girl standing in front of me, a veteran of this tortured life along the road to hell, wanted to get out, but she just couldn't pull herself from beyond the hole long enough to stretch out a hand. Her story tore Kelly and I apart. Personally, I wanted to pick her up and take her away, drop her off at rehab, and give her a fighting chance. Curtis Sliwa, however, I am not, and I know my place and limitations. John Kelly, an addiction specialist with connections, told me I could offer her a free stint in rehab, but she refused, saying, among other things, "Now is not the right time."

We talked about the murders. She knew two of the girls. There were tears in her eyes as she recalled last seeing them.

"You don't fear this guy yourself?" I asked. "I mean, there's a serial killer out there, who hasn't been caught … he won't stop … he *cannot* stop. That doesn't *scare* you as you work the streets?"

More tears. She looked away, collected herself, and then looked me straight in the eye. "Fear? I don't have fear any more. I don't know what it is."

When you lose your sense of fear, I thought, *you're finished.*

This woman referred me to a former street girl. I spent the better part of the next three days, along with my producer, trying to track her down after being told that she had answers, and that she had been in a motel room with Kim Raffo the night before Kim was found dead.

"You need to speak with [Jane Doe]," my scarred source on the street told me. "She has a story to tell."

I ended up interviewing a host of others along The Track, including one hooker who told me she had been choked by a john who was acting weird, and liked to play with her feet.

"How'd you get away?"

"I maced him."

"And yet you still get into cars?" I asked.

Her explanation was sobering, if not startling. "Yes. But I look inside the vehicle first," she explained. "If the guy is wearing a tie and suit, wedding ring, and there is a baby seat in the back, I know two things."

"What's that?"

"He'll be quick," she said with a smile, "and he won't hurt me."

"What if the serial killer I am hunting is using a baby seat as a ruse?"

She didn't have an answer.

CHAPTER 5

I MET WITH FORMER Atlantic City police officer Jim Hutchins at the drainage ditch to discuss the case. Hutchins, a tough looking, shaved-headed, straight-talking "Joysey" man's man, was frank and honest to the core.

There had been a rumor that a Muslim could have been the Eastbound Strangler, as a potential explanation for the seemingly ritualistic significance of the heads facing east (toward Mecca, presumably). A person of interest had even been hauled in and interviewed. When you size up this theory in accordance with the evidence, not to mention the fact that certain Muslim customs demand for the dead to be buried without shoes or socks, it begins to look (and feel) pretty accurate. A local reporter had broken this thread of the story, and once word hit the streets, it took on its own life.

I must say, I bought into this, a little bit, when I first heard about it. This sort of theory fit the Hollywood version of this case that I had in my head. However, in all reality, it was not practical, much less reasonable, given the totality of the evidence available at that point.

"Those are theories," Hutchins told me as we stood down by the drainage ditch on one of those days when the rain just kept coming down. The weather got so bad that we moved into my rented Suburban to finish our conversation. "I think the obvious answer could be that the tide made all of their heads face that particular way. It flows out into the Back Bay eventually," Hutch continued, pointing in that direction, "and follows in between the tracks and Route 40, so there is movement. You can make a case that the water moves, forcing the faces (heads) to go east." Hutchins looked over at the water. Then back at me while answering his own question: "I would say, yes."

In studying this idea, standing by the water with Hutchins, I agreed. If this was a ritualistic set of murders, set up by a rogue Muslim who was perhaps looking to send a message that Mecca is being violated by the filth of the street girl, and her sordid sex-for-sale lifestyle in support of her drug addiction, he would have made it more evident in the way in which the girls' bodies had been staged, if, in fact, the bodies had been deliberately *placed* in this way. In other words, he would have, most likely, set the scene to give it a more apparent Hollywood flair.

Hutchins and I also talked about the maintenance-man theory. At one time, cops were hot on a man I'll call John Doe. His reputation has been destroyed so badly that one newspaper referred to this person of interest as the "fifth victim." Slit-eyed, with an eighties haircut that was almost a mullet, thin lips, and a solidly built frame, John Doe seemed like the perfect suspect. He worked maintenance at the Golden Key, which is directly in front of where the girls had been found. The back of the Golden Key faces the drainage ditch, its yellow walls easily visible through the brush, and there are several doors exiting Golden Key rooms which lead *out* to the dirt road just before the drainage ditch. John Doe also spent some time living at the Golden Key, a one-level, skanky motel where you can get a room for fifteen dollars a night. This place, and several others like it dotted along Black Horse Pike, catered to the girls and their johns. Reportedly, Kim Raffo had partied at the Golden Key the night before her body was found, We'll talk more about this later on in this piece, as I verify this fact with a girl who had been with Kim that very night.

As a maintenance man, John Doe did repair work around the Golden Key motel. He knew several of the girls and had "helped them out," I was told. In one interview, John Doe said he remembered the day he thought his life was over, when an Atlantic City homicide detective cornered him and said, "We know you did it." He had first come under suspicion, on the day Kim's body was found, after he pointed out to law enforcement that he had located a shoe on the roof of the Golden Key and thought it could be important to the case. It was theorized that perhaps John Doe was hanging around the murder scene because he was the killer. It has been established that some serial killers like to do that: watch their work as cops explore and look for clues. Law enforcement believes that it's part of the high for serials, as much a part of the criminal elementas the stalking and killing. I think this is an overblown profiling analysis generated by the Hollywood version of the serial. In reality, after serials kill, they get as far away from the scene as possible.

"I often left the state for a few days," one infamous serial killer of eight women told me.

Not long after making that comment to police about the shoe (and a call into police from his angry girlfriend), John's truck was impounded and a house he had fixed up and lived in was descended upon by law enforcement, and torn apart in the search for evidence.

John Kelly was hot on this guy as person of interest, and still is, in some ways. This is the guy Kelly had warned me about sitting down with, face to face.

Anyway, authorities found nothing linking John Doe with the dead bodies uncovered in the drainage ditch in back of the Golden Key. Despite thata DVD with photos of a nude underage girl, his girlfriend's 15-year-old daughter, was found. It was said to have belonged to John Doe.

John insisted that his girlfriend was so pissed off at him that she had set the entire thing up, taking the photos, calling the cops, and planting the evidence to make it look like he was a sex-crazed maniac who photographed kids and killed prostitutes. Items of a pornographic nature, which the media had deemed "kinky sex tapes" and "sex toys," were eventually found in John Doe's truck. His rationale for all this was something to the effect of: *Can't a guy have a sex life and fantasize?*

If John Doe actually took the photos of his girlfriend's child, and I'm not convinced he did,it would indicate the psychological mindset of a man who favors younger girls. Girls who were "clean and untarnished." This is not the same person who would kill prostitutes. Moreover, cops hadn't found any porn related to foot fetishes inside his truck. It is unlikely that he would be capable of changing his fondness for bare feet within his pornographic fantasies; such thought processes become too ingrained. He would, I think, use the porn as an accelerant to ignite his foot-fetish fantasy, and not having located any porn of that nature in his truck, would seem to indicate a lack of support that he was the perpetrator of those crimes. Dr. Merski keyed on this when we interviewed him.

On paper, however, it all seemed a plausible theory, so John Doe was arrested for possessing the DVD of his stepdaughter. The main reason for getting him into the interrogation suite, however, was to ask him about four dead prostitutes found behind a building where he had once worked.

After months of investigating John Doe, he was released. John Doe remains free from charges today.

Did he do it?

I asked Hutchins.

"I don't think so," Hutchins told me off-camera. "Doesn't fit."

I agree, it didn't when you looked closely. I spoke to several people who knew John Doe personally and he was no more a murderer than he was a sex addict with violent tendencies, according to them. The cops, I was told, needed to fit a square peg into a round hole and were trying to find the right lathe to turn it into the proper shape.

Not quite sure I believe that, either, but sometimes you have to question how law enforcement goes about things, especially if you're trying to reignite a cold case. There is also the pressure of a high-profile investigation to take into account. The media coverage of a case like this is a tremendous strain on investigators and gets in the way of their case. Pressure is put on the prosecutor's office to come up with answers.

"I know, personally speaking," my serial killer (not 13) on the inside told me, "law enforcement, for good reason, places misinformation in the media."

I don't ever want to be accused of questioning police tactics or ethics, because they have their own reasons for doing things. I simply like to look at an investigation from a different perspective. The cops know more about John Doe than I do. I am basing my thoughts, opinions and observations on what I know and the people I have interviewed about him.

"[John Doe] helped people," one former friend of his told me, "he didn't kill people."

"His girlfriend set him up," said another.

John Doe eventually volunteered to take a polygraph and DNA test.

"In my mind," John's attorney told reporters after news broke that he wanted to take those tests to clear his name, "he was either completely not guilty, or the dumbest serial killer on the planet."

At one point, John Doe was going to talk to me on camera, but then something came up. My producer and I had a difference of opinion regarding the motivation behind the cancellation, but I felt in talking to John's lawyer that John was not blowing me off. Furthermore, I had no gut instinct that John Doe was my guy. If he was, he had done a damn good job of hiding evidence and thwarting a major offensive by the police, who went after him with magnifying glasses and aggressive forensic strategies but came away with nothing. I'm from the old school of thought that you can burn evidence and wash DNA away with bleach, you can hide the trophies you take from your victims, but you cannot get rid of *everything*. It's impossible. They tore apart John Doe's truck and home to the point where it was rendered unlivable. With that kind of search, if you come up empty, there's a reason for it.

Martin Siegel, a respected attorney who once represented John Doe, claimed his former client wasn't "treated fairly by the system."

I agree with this, the "system" being the local media, which is why I changed his name for this piece, though John Doe's real name was all over the news.

As John Doe sat in jail, a man came forward and wanted to admit to the murders, but, that man later said, "The prosecutors blew me off."

There are plenty of nutcases that like to take credit for murders, especially the high-profile ones. For that reason alone, each "nut" has to be looked into. You cannot just write them off. As of now, I still have no opinion about this guy who came forward. I do know, which I am getting to soon, that the name of a viable suspect or suspects was given to police.

The bottom line is that if cops had anything on John Doe, or the guy who came forward, and I mean any discrepancy in an alibi, a sketchy timeline, a single piece of trace evidence, even any halfwit eye-witness, either of them might be in jail awaiting trial for these crimes. But as of this writing, John Doe and the other guy are both free men.

CHAPTER 6

WHAT INTERESTED ME THE MOST as my time in Atlantic City wound down (we have about week to film our interviews; but spend weeks and even months looking into and researching the cases we cover) was the fact that once the heat was on and Kim Raffo's body led to the discovery of the other three bodies, "Boom," John Kelly said. "The murders *stopped*."

(Presumably, I should add to Kelly's comment.)

John Kelly has an opinion about this, saying, "Serial killers live to kill and kill to live. He cannot stop. He's addicted to killing."

So, although the bodies stopped showing up along that drainage ditch—and I'm told they did a complete search up and down miles-long sections of the drainage ditch from helicopters, looking for additional bodies with heat-seeking equipment—it doesn't necessarily mean the killer (or killers, as we are about to explore) actually stopped.

The theory we all agreed on was that our guy in Atlantic City was scared off. Even "13," our serial killer on the inside and consultant on "Dark Minds," said the same thing. Once this particular dump site was discovered, the killer either moved his show somewhere else ("13" believes that the new location is Oak Beach, Long Island), found a new dumping site in the Atlantic City region, or wound up in prison on another charge and was forced to stop.

This led some back to John Doe's trail.

Then, as the end of our week came, I began to think that perhaps I was not going to find out anything more than anyone else had managed to do. The source I was hoping to talk to, the person my cutter/prostitute friend had told us about, kept calling and then blowing us off. I was frustrated. I knew she had something big.

But as we packed to leave, the call came. She was finally ready.

"The end of the Boardwalk," the source told my producer over the phone. "Out of the way."

She didn't want to be seen talking to us. A camera crew shooting a crime series causes a ruckus and people become engrossed and interested in what you're doing. We had caused somewhat of a stir while in town all week. Everyone knew why we were there and crowds were coming out to see us. There was even one night, as cameraman Peter Heap was capturing some images of the Boardwalk at dusk, when we came close to getting into a fight. Being violent is not a general practice of mine, and has not been since junior high and high school. But assholes are assholes.

Most of my team is Australian. My production company is based in Australia. For the time we are on the road shooting the series, we travel together and live like family. Anybody who has ever worked in documentary television knows what I'm talking about. You eat every meal together, work together day and night, laugh, get pissed off, and travel in the same vehicle for weeks at a time. You become close. You watch one another's back. I consider my crew, Peter, Jared

Transfield, Colette Sandstedt, and Jeremy Adair,like family, and I love each of them dearly.

Anyway, as Peter was mounting a shot of the Boardwalk, some idiot came up and started asking stupid questions. I told him (nicely) to please find our producer, who could explain everything to him (even though she was running around doing a thousand other things).

Peter didn't say a word. He has that kind of patience.

This clown persisted. He reeked of alcohol. He was acting tough and being belligerent and rude. I noticed him, as he maneuvered around us, making remarks to some of his buddies sitting off to the side, that he'd once had a broken nose. The evidence remained, it was twisted and pinched, like a boxer's.

We ignored him as best as we could. I asked again, "Please, dude, just leave us alone, let us do our work. Our producer will be back soon and you can speak with her. We have all the permits required to shoot here."

He mumbled something.

Then, as Peter spoke up and asked him kindly to go away, the guy picked up on Peter's accent and, like some of the ignorant, bigoted a-holes we meet along the way, he said something about Englishmen and how England was "this and that."

"Wrong country," Peter said. "I'm Australian."

My blood was beginning to boil. It had been a long week. I was tired and frustrated. The city itself was weighing heavily on my emotions. I'd had enough. I needed to get out of Atlantic City. I felt dirty.

I looked at him.

"What are *you* going to do?" he said, noticing my angry gaze.

So I approached him. I told him to move away and let us alone.

"Did he just call me an asshole?" the drunk said to me, pointing at Peter. It was obvious he wanted a piece of Peter and was trying to start something.

Peter had not said a word.

"I need you to step back," I said.

He looked at me strangely.

Then he repeated the asshole comment again—and this time, it flipped a switch in me.

I snapped.

As he moved toward Peter, who was still shooting, I stuck my chest in between and asked him if he wanted his nose broken—again!—and that I'd be more than willing to oblige. "You've pushed me too far now" I said, charging at him. "I'm finished with you."

He backed away and left us alone.

A quarter-mile down the Boardwalk, we came upon two drunks sitting on a tourist trolley car, drinking, saying things to passersby, laughing. One of them got up, a big sonofagun I wasn't about to tangle with, and turned around as we walked by, dropped his fly, and took a leak off the side of the Boardwalk. Mind you, this was at about six in the early evening, with hundreds of people out strolling along. He had some words for us, but we ignored him and moved on.

Further down the Boardwalk, some dude snarled angrily when Peter pointed the camera in his direction. He threatened to make big trouble, in the form of ass-whippings for all of us.

"He's probably on a most-wanted list somewhere," I said, and we high-tailed it out of there.

This was the vibe, the atmosphere of the city, we had felt just about every day while we were there. It was as if the totality of the city's filth built up like a coat of wax all over my body, no matter how many times I showered. Atlantic City, by the time we were ready to leave, had gotten under my skin like an allergic reaction. I felt a substantial gloom pushing down on my back, doing its best to force me into a place of desolation. Maybe it was the facts of the cases we had been investigating. Perhaps talking to all the street girls, seeing firsthand the terrible lives they led and the current hell they were living in, was getting to me. Or perhaps it was memories of my past bubbling up? Was I trying to reconcile my feelings about Diana? I felt a twinge of remorse as I recalled once saying to her during a heated argument, "I wish you would just go away and never come back!"

That's what happened. We have to be careful what we say to people we love, however ostensibly.

Whatever the case, by the time we were ready to haul ass out of town, I was wishing we had left days earlier.

But then the call came. My source was ready to give up the goods. She obviously didn't want us to leave the city without hearing her story, which, as things would turn out, left us with our jaws on the ground.

CHAPTER 7

SHE WAS YOUNG. In her twenties, I'll say, and leave it there. She was dressed in a hoodie and clean clothes. She wore makeup, smelled nice or clean?, and had a smile that only someone with a length of sobriety could manage. She had been off the streets and sober for over a year. In fact, the night before we met, she had gone out to see her first concert.

"I couldn't have done that if I was using," she said.

She was scared, for sure. Terrified that the story she was going to tell would endanger her life more than it had already. Nonetheless, she proceeded to explain to me how she came to be with Kim Raffo the night before Kim was murdered. This was a startling revelation, given that it had never been reported.

I had no reason not to believe her. She seemed very sincere, and I could tell that she wasn't looking for the fame of being on television. She didn't want her name to be used, although we know who she is. She wasn't looking for anything other than for the truth to be told. She stated that she had tried once before to tell this story and it fell on deaf ears.

As context, I need to explain that as a production begins, we have all types of people coming forward, each wanting to tell us their story related to a case we are covering. I get calls from people who claim to have all sorts of insider information about cases. We, as production crew filming a nonfiction television series, need to carefully assess the credibility of each source we interview on camera. We don't, in other words, take just anybody off the street to speak about a case on-air. We take our work seriously. I treat this series and the way I conduct myself in the same way as I do when I research a book. I am a journalist first, and as such I am trained to question people and their motives.

My source said she was partying that night and met up with Kim at a motel. They had been picked up, although at different times, by the same two black guys in a van and driven to a seedy motel room on the White Horse Pike (not the Golden Key, which is located on the Black Horse Pike) under the lure of all the free drugs they wanted to do. When they arrived, there was a third john, a white guy, waiting for them.

The white dude was sketchy and wired. My source stated that he acted strangely from the moment she entered the room.

But walking in, she saw someone else.

Kim Raffo.

Our source reported that Kim looked bugged out, panicked and terrified. The white guy was a freak, acting weird and smoking crack and putting his hands around Kim's neck. He and the other men said derogatory things to all the girls, calling them "whores" and "sluts."

My source claimed she was frightened for her life.

"What else did you see when you arrived at that motel room?" I asked. This was the "money" question, I had been told. This girl, such a brave soul, had supposedly seen two of the other girls whose bodies were later found along the drainage ditch, but they were allegedly dead at the time she saw them. That is the story I wanted to hear about.

Our source continued, explaining that Kim Raffo was seated on one bed in the motel room. On the other bed were two "bodies."

Bodies?

"They were lying still on their backs, and they had a sheet covering them. The whole time we were there, they never moved."

Kim appeared to be pretty much frightened out of her mind. My source asked Kim what in the hell was going on.

"I don't know," Kim said. "They weren't there when I went to sleep." Kim had obviously passed out or spent the night in the room with the white guy. After she awoke, she noticed that there were two bodies in the bed next to hers, both covered by a sheet, only their hair sticking out.

I asked my source who she believed those bodies were.

"Barbara [Breidor] and Tracy [Ann Roberts]."

She was certain of it.

I asked her about the white guy. *How* was he acting strange? What type of sex did he want?

"... [T]o massage your feet ..." she said.

After a time, the guys decided that the party was going to

move to another motel. One of the black guys stayed behind with the purported dead women in the other bed.

"And the rest of us," my source explained, "… we went in the van and we went and got another room."

From that first motel room, they (my source, Kim, the white guy, and one of the black guys) traveled to a motel on the Black Horse Pike. The Golden Key.

When they arrived, the white guy said, "I need to leave and take care of something."

He took off.

A while later, he returned.

"And that's when," my source explained, "it started to become a really scary situation."

CHAPTER 8

FOR THOSE WHO have survived the attack of a serial killer, at least the ones I have ever interviewed, a similar scenario is described about the moment when, seemingly all of a sudden, the attacker violently unleashed his fury. They talk about how this person suddenly morphed into a different human being all together. Not just in the way he acted, or his vocal patterns, but also in the way his face and his persona changed entirely. He is now in the kill zone, somebody else who is able, willing, and ready to do the unthinkable.

Effectively, he *is* someone else.

I asked my source what happened next inside that Golden Key motel room. "This glaze came over his eyes [the white male] and he just kept repeating, 'I did something in my past … I did something in my past.'"

After things became physical, with the men treating

the women roughly, groping them, and saying harsh and degrading things, my source grabbed her things and convinced the men to let her leave.

Kim Raffo stayed behind.

Her dead body was found within the next twenty-four hours behind that same motel.

My source said that she went to the police, told her story, and gave them the names of the men she and Kim were with that night.

The police told her they checked it out and released the men because they didn't have any evidence to hold them. The police, according to her, believed those three men had nothing to do with the four dead women. This was, incidentally, around the same time period when John Doe was in custody, my source pointed out. In fact, my source claims, as she was being taken from one police station to another after giving her statement, that the cop driving her called her a liar and, naming John Doe specifically, said, "We *got* our man!"

All I can do is report what I find. My source told me several more things about the police that I don't feel comfortable including. They are serious accusations that go beyond the scope of what I do, but I believe her. The look on her face, the tears in her eyes, her body shaking as she told me this story, with her gaze never once looking away, told me she was scared for her life. She had no reason—and nothing to gain—from coming forward to tell me this story. She wouldn't give me the names of the cops she dealt with, so her motivation wasn't to get back at them.

Given all of this, what do I think?

Rewinding a bit, going back to the beginning of our production, I believe we came face to face with one of these guys while we were shooting along The Track early in the week. As we sat in our rented black Suburban waiting for information, with the doors wide open facing the sidewalk, a guy walked by and gave my female producer a look that scared her to the core. This dude was serious. He had a girl with him that he was manhandling in a "come on, let's get out of here" kind of way. He was black and fit a description I was given by my source, off-camera, of one of the guys she was with that night.

Do I think my source spent part of her night with the killers in this case?

I do. I also believe that after Kim Raffo's body was uncovered, these guys left town, perhaps started dumping bodies at another location, or wound up in jail on drug charges. (I heard that they might have taken off to the Midwest somewhere.) The idea that these guys are the same perpetrators dumping bodies in Long Island has been played in the press and even "13" has mentioned this as a theory on the episode of "Dark Minds" we produced for this case.

I believe the Long Island theory is *possible*, but not highly probable. I don't know enough about Long Island to make a professional comment/judgment. (The Long Island case, by the way, is a possibility for season two of "Dark Minds.")

What I can say is that there are people involved in this case that know more. But for some reason, they refuse to open up.

EPILOGUE

THIS CASE, like most of those I profile on "Dark Minds," is solvable. A major part of what I do in the series is akin to John Walsh's purpose in "America's Most Wanted." I need people to come forward if they know something. My job is not to solve cases. I am not a cop. This is about information-gathering for me. It doesn't matter how insignificant or significant you think the information you might have is. Let the cops sort it out. These girls matter. They had lives before the devil's claws hooked into them. Their lives were not disposable. Help the authorities solve this case. Give these families some peace and allow the victims what they deserve.

Justice.

If you want more information about "Dark Minds" (or you have any tips for this case), please go to the Investigation Discovery website: *http://investigation.discovery.com/* or visit the "Dark Minds" Facebook page: *http://www.facebook.com/pages/Dark-Minds/192493800815468?skip_nax_wizard=true*

DEAD PEOPLE WON'T WALK AWAY
INSIDE THE REAL WORLD OF FORENSIC SCIENCE WITH DR. HENRY LEE

DURING THE SUMMER of 2005, as I was working on my fifth book, *Murder in the Heartland,* I started collecting research for a future project I had thought about doing for years. From my own work as a nonfiction crime author, conducting well over 500 interviews, with scores of different people from all walks of crime, I knew first-hand that the work forensic scientists and crime-scene investigators did out in the field on a daily basis was vastly different from the CSI-type of fictionalized crime drama we see on television. It doesn't take a crime expert to figure out that a television show, such as CBS's "C.S.I.," and the real world of forensic science and crime-scene investigation are in no way alike. A lot of the television crime shows dramatize investigations to make the shows more appealing to viewers. I understand this. In doing my research, however, I planned on leveling the playing field a bit in order to show readers the true differences, so at least one could watch these shows with a bit of optimism and truly enjoy the experience of being entertained.

While conducting interviews for that project, which I titled *CSI Confidential: Inside the Real World of Forensic Science,* I met and spoke to some of the most qualified, intelligent forensic experts in the world. One of my first interviews was with renowned forensic scientist Dr. Henry Lee. Most people, I think, view Lee as an extremely bright scientist who just happens to have his own show on Court TV, and appears, at times, on cable television to discuss the latest high-profile murder cases.

That is, I guess, a fair description.

But from the moment I set out to talk with Dr. Lee, I decided I didn't want to write about the same personality we have all come to know (and love) from his books and television appearances. I wanted to write about the man behind the microscope, and to get his principal views on forensic science: where it is today and where it will be tomorrow.

IT WAS A HAZY, hot and sticky June morning when I drove down to the West Haven, Connecticut, campus of the University of New Haven to meet with Dr. Henry Lee. The first thing that caught my eye after stepping off the elevator onto the fourth floor of the Dodds Building, located at the bottom of a hilly patch of land near the campus police station, was an unassuming blue-and-white sign tacked to the wall directly in front of me: "Dr. Henry C. Lee, Founder and Professor, Forensic Science Program, University of New Haven."

The sign, in its academic directness, aroused my curiosity. Continuing on, alas, it occurred to me that "The House That Henry Built" would have been a more appropriate introduction, because everything about this unfamiliar world of simulated decomposing corpses, blood spatter, and DNA that I was about to step into was the brainchild, in some form or fashion, of the man they call "the father of forensics." Indeed, Dr. Lee, over the course of four decades, has established several innovative ways to figure out what happened at a crime-scene, and has solved thousands of cases others might have thought were unsolvable.

Immediately to the right of the sign is a hallway, a long, narrow corridor separating the entire floor of the Forensic Science National Crime Scene Training and Technology Center from the Forensic Training Center. This hallway, I soon find out, will be an important part of my visit, metaphorically representing the separation between the forensic science side of criminalistics and crime-scene investigation. Contrary to what many people think, based on how television generally fuses both into one, there are major differences between the two.

On one side of the hallway is Dr. Lee's renowned crime-scene training center, complete with several replica crime scenes (living room, kitchen, bathroom, bedroom), right down to the life-size mannequins—stabbed, shot, bludgeoned to death, strangled—spread randomly throughout like crash test dummies or victims of a plane crash. On the other side are several laboratories (fingerprinting analysis, DNA, trace evidence) which students and state police recruits use to sift through mock evidence, learning hands-on how the forensic science side of crime-solving works under pseudo-real conditions.

Striking to me, is that within the entire building, there is only one official classroom, a low-ceilinged, dark room with no windows, containing a few desks and chairs, a chalkboard and a podium. It was the only hint that this place, a celebrated academy of crime-scene and forensic science education, is, first and foremost, a school.

Wherever you look inside the building are reminders—letters of thanks and praise, crime-related relics Dr. Lee has collected over the years—of how important the work is, not to mention how many people depend on the results Dr. Lee produces. After all, Lee is to the crime world what Donald Trump is to the world of real estate: an icon, a pillar of knowledge and success, with world-wide recognition. Lee's friends and colleagues will tell you that, like a rock star, he cannot walk through an airport, restaurant or shopping mall—anywhere in the world—without being mobbed by fans clamoring for a photograph or autograph. For a man in near perfect physical and mental shape at the age of sixty-seven, it would be a mistake to place Lee in a celebrity box and view everything he has accomplished through the lens of the high-profile cases he's been involved with. Primarily, Lee exemplifies humility and grace, and appreciates the fact that people respect the work he does.

By occupational definition, Lee is a criminalist, more specifically a forensic scientist.[2] His greatest skills include being able to recognize trace evidence where others cannot, preserving and identifying it while individualizing, evaluating and studying it. On his Court TV show *Trace Evidence*, Lee showcases perhaps his greatest skill of all, the one characteristic that separates him from just about anyone else in his field: crime-scene reconstruction—a division of criminology[3] that, like a martial artist, Dr. Lee has mastered with a profound sense of perfectionism, professionalism, and expertise.

But to categorize Dr. Lee wouldn't be fair. On balance, he is also a forensic scientist who can find that single human bone chip the size of a pencil shaving in an acre of topsoil, as he did in the "Wood Chipper Murder" case in 1986. In

---

2   A criminalist is a "specialist in the collection and examination of the physical evidence of a crime." Dr. Lee, of course, is involved in many different aspects of forensic science and crime-scene investigation.

3   "The scientific study of crime, criminal behavior, responses by law enforcement, and methods of prevention."

the southern woods of Connecticut, Lee then ordered the excavation of a wooded area near a lake where he believed Richard Crafts, a pilot, had murdered his wife, Helle, a stewardess, dismembered her body with a chainsaw, secured her body parts in plastic bags, and then ran those bags through a wood chipper to cover up what was one of the most brutal crimes Lee later admitted he had ever seen.

Eventually, Lee's instincts paid off. In total, "2,660 strands of blond hair (bleached), 69 slivers of human bone, 5 droplets of human blood, 2 teeth, a truncated piece of human skull, 3 ounces of human tissue, a portion of a human finger, 1 fingernail, and 1 portion of a toe nail"[4] were found in the woods, along the embankment, and in the lake where Crafts discarded Helle's dismembered body. Through early blood comparison testing, blood spatter evidence, fabric and hair analysis, along with good old-fashioned gumshoe police work, the prosecution was able to place Crafts at the scene of the crime. Lee also discovered several "reddish-brownish stains" on the mattress Helle and Crafts used to sleep on, which, when later proven to be Helle's blood, combined with hair fibers, additional blood stains, and wood chips found in the trunk of Crafts's car, was enough to convict him. Because Helle's "body" was never recovered in full, Lee said, the Wood Chipper Murder conviction was groundbreaking in a sense that it moved the "American justice system away from the notion that there has to be a recognizable corpse before we can prove that a murder has been committed."[5]

Thus, the Wood Chipper murder became one of the signature moments of Lee's early career, yet was only one of 6,000 cases around the world he has solved in a career

4   Quote is from *Cracking Cases: The Science of Solving Crimes* (Prometheus Books; 2002), by Dr. Henry Lee and Thomas O'Neil.

5   Quote is from *Cracking Cases: The Science of Solving Crimes* (Prometheus Books; 2002), by Dr. Henry Lee and Thomas O'Neil.

that has spanned some 46 years. Dr. Lee makes it clear that it matters little to him whether he is investigating a junkie found dead in the gutter, or a high-profile murder that has garnered media attention from around the world.

"Even a burglary," he suggested, "is important to the victim. You come home and someone has violated your privacy. That person wants you to solve the case as much as a murder victim's family. You certainly can't say homicide is more important than burglary." In his book, *Cracking Cases: The Science of Solving Crimes,* co-written with journalist Thomas W. O'Neil, Lee further explains this core belief: "My life's credo is to work to discover the truth."

WHEN I SAT DOWN to interview Dr. Lee, it wasn't the first time the two of us had met. Although it was brief and casual, I was first introduced to him in Manhattan at a party for one of his best friends and distinguished colleagues, Dr. Michael Baden. As I learned that night, however, any encounter with Dr. Lee turns out to be a memorable experience.

A torrential rain had started about three o'clock that afternoon—and never let up. What should have been a two-hour drive for me into New York City from my home in Connecticut turned into a four-and-a-half-hour-white knuckle clash with Mother Nature.

Lee was seething with frustration over having run into the same driving conditions when I stuck out my hand and introduced myself. "Nice to meet you, doctor," I said as he was heading for the exit door. The party had just started. He and his wife of 44 years, Margaret, had arrived only minutes before. I was curious about why they were leaving so soon.

"This rain," steamed Lee, "is horrible. Do you know it took me four hours to get down here?"

"Yeah, I can relate to that."

After shaking my hand, he waved to a few people in the crowd, smiled cordially, and left what was a surprise party for Dr. Baden, who hadn't even arrived yet.

As I mingled my way through the party, I couldn't help thinking: *There goes this world-renowned forensic genius, idolized and glamorized, a pivotal player in the JonBenet Ramsey, Chandra Levy, and O.J. Simpson cases, upset by weather conditions, like an average Joe.* Lee could have, I'm sure, taken a limousine to the party. Instead, he chose to, like he does wherever he goes, drive himself. To say the least, this wasn't the image I had held of such a prominent man of science.

When we sat down at the table in Lee's campus office that June morning, a year or so after Baden's party, I asked him how he was getting around these days. I mentioned the party and wondered why he had driven himself. It might seem trivial to begin a conversation with the former Commissioner of Public Safety for the State of Connecticut and Chief Emeritus for Scientific Services, the same man who is responsible for creating the forensic science laboratory in the state of Connecticut, about his choice of transportation, but as I was about to find out, Lee's answer would explain everything I needed to know about why he has been so successful at anything he applies himself to.

"In early days," said Lee, "when I was Commissioner, I had three sergeants who drive me everywhere, you know, eight hours each shift. Sometimes they are so tired I have to drive them back and bring them home." He laughed. "I was the only Commissioner to drive my drivers."

Being unable to keep up with Dr. Lee is an understatement. The day I was with him, a Monday, began at seven in the morning for me, but Lee had already put in about four hours of work at home, he said, by the time we sat down at 9:05 a.m. After our interview, he explained, he would attend two meetings, then head to New Jersey to consult on a murder case, back to Rhode Island that evening to consult on a second case, then back south into New York City the following day to make an appearance at a book release party for his friend Nancy Grace. In between, he would be working in the lab on several different homicide cases.

"That's certainly a full week—"

"You didn't let me finish," he interrupted. "After the party, I need to be in Utah, then Palm Springs, California, a day after that. I'm testifying in two different murder cases."

"My goodness ..."

"Then it's off to Taiwan to consult on a serial killer case."

I'm speechless.

He smiled, saying, "I'll be back home on Sunday night for dinner."

This is the essence of Lee's life; he sleeps four or five hours a night and "eats very quickly," adding, "My wife says I'm 'like a vacuum cleaner.' Five seconds, boom, I'm done—and she's not even finished cooking."

Yet, it is a knack he has for prioritizing his work and managing his time, he said, which allows him to function as, say, five different people.

"It's pretty easy, actually. We are all equal. You have 24 hours in the day"—he points at me and then at himself—"as well as I do. That's one thing God gave all of us: 24 hours. But how you use those hours is what separates us." He then picked up a file on his desk to explain his point more clearly. "Some people take a letter, look at it, put it on the opposite side of their desk. And then later that afternoon they pick up same letter and look at it again and put it on the *other* side of desk. Then pick it up *again*...and end up rearranging things and getting nothing done. I have long objective, medium objective, short objective; along with what I *want* to do today, things I *have* to do, things that, if I had time, I *would* do, and things I *wish* I could do. You see, things you have to take care of, you do. But things you can put off," he shook his index finger at me, "you simply put off—and, hopefully, they go away."

There were times in the early part of his career when Lee could, he added, run four, five or six meetings simultaneously. He'd dart from one meeting room to the other, say a few words, and then move on to the next, as if he were some sort of superhero.

As I waited for Lee earlier that morning in the reception area of his office ("He always runs just a little bit late," his secretary told me), a nondescript room with concrete cinderblock walls painted white and a cork-board ceiling saturated with water stains and damaged tiles, the pipes above his secretary's desk dripped water on the carpet below. It was a subtle reminder that forensic science and crime-scene investigation don't necessarily take precedence at universities, police departments, or government agencies. Like anywhere else, the Forensic Science National Crime Scene Training and Technology Center, a lab and forensic program Lee created himself, struggles with funding issues the same as any other lab in the country. Lee was quick to point out that many people believe the high-profile cases in which he's been involved (and which made him famous) have lined his pockets. That the O.J. Simpson case, for example, along with work he's done on other famous cases, and for police departments throughout the world, have fattened his bank account.

In the O.J. case, Lee was asked by Bob Shapiro, one of O.J.'s lawyers, at the urging of Dr. Michael Baden, whom Shapiro had also hired, to join the defense team soon after Nicole Simpson and Ron Goldman's bodies were discovered. It also turned out to be the day O.J. took off on his infamous white Bronco adventure. In fact, Lee and Baden were in O.J.'s house when O.J. and Al Cowlings bolted. Lee admitted later that he had never heard of O.J. Simpson before Shapiro's call. For the most part, Lee and Baden were hired to conduct a forensic examination of O.J.'s body, review any forensic testimony and examine all of the prosecution's evidence against O.J.

Interestingly, Lee has strong opinions regarding the way blood evidence was collected from O.J. and the crime scene. He maintains that much of the blood was "contaminated and rendered unsuitable for proper DNA testing." Lee provided shocking information that "1.5 cc of blood was missing from the known amount" of samples taken directly from O.J., and EDTA, a chemical preservative used by labs, was uncovered in blood samples "taken from a pair of socks found in" O.J.'s bedroom and "in the blood taken from the ... gate" at Nicole Simpson's condominium.[6]

Regardless of the O.J. debacle and the heated debates that ensued afterward, Lee didn't take any money for the work he did: "I asked O.J.'s lawyers to write a check to the *lab*. It's all about the lab. The work. We need things, you know." Indeed, out of the $150,000 Lee was paid for his consultation services, he donated $80,000 to the forensic science program at the University of New Haven. The remaining $70,000 went to the State Police Forensics Laboratory in Meriden, Connecticut.

Then he told me how much he charges the State of Connecticut annually for his services: "One U.S. dollar."

**

WHEN LEE ARRIVED IN the United States in 1965, he had but $50 in his pocket, and spoke only four words of English.

6   The quotes in this paragraph were taken from *Cracking Cases: The Science of Solving Crimes* (Prometheus Books; 2002), by Dr. Henry Lee and Thomas O'Neil.

He and Margaret had been married for three years. With a yearning to earn a Ph.D. in science, he viewed what America had to offer as an opportunity. Growing up in China was not an easy way of life, even though Lee's father had been born into an affluent Chinese family. As China became entangled in the mess and horror of war, Lee's mother, An-fu Wang-Lee, migrated to Taiwan with 10-year-old Henry and his siblings. Lee's father, Ho-Ming Lee, had to stay behind, but promised to meet up with the family later that same year.

On January 27, 1949, as Ho-Ming boarded a ship in Shanghai harbor, excited and determined to reunite with his family, the ship came under shell attack, and Ho-Ming, along with scores of his fellows, was killed.

It was a devastating blow to the family, both emotionally and financially. With little income coming in, An-fu Wang-Lee and her children, now alone in Taiwan, became among the country's millions of poor.

"I would go days and nights without food," remembered Lee.

Yet he doesn't view the experience in retrospect as a dark part of his life; instead, he believes the hardships which he and his family endured instilled integrity and honor in him.

Unlike most of his colleagues, Lee comes from a police background, which is what feeds his incredible knowledge of crime-scene investigation-reconstruction, and allows him to essentially be both: crime-scene investigator and forensic scientist. In 1960, he graduated from the Central Police College in Taiwan with a degree in Police Science. I was told the Central Police is one of the foremost training facilities for cops in the world, because of the strict discipline taught to recruits and the attention required to be paid to respect, detail, and work ethic. From there, Lee went to work for the Taipei Police Department for several years, becoming its youngest captain at the age of 22. It would be a job that, little did he know then, would lay the foundation for what would ultimately garner him respect from the law enforcement community worldwide.

Lee speaks with an articulate sense of confidence, and has a knack for explaining even the most complex criminal issues in basic, layman terms. Despite his encyclopedic knowledge of all things criminal, it's "patience," he insists, that "is the key to my work." A continuing education doesn't hurt, either, he explained. "I've been in this business forty-six years now, and every day I'm still learning. The day you feel you know everything, that's the time you retire."

Lee's job, beyond even anything else, is to uncover the truth, regardless of which side of the law it supports. There have been times when he has been called into assist in cases to aid the defense but ended up helping the prosecution's case. "We are not judge and jury," he said, leaning back in his chair, opening a bottle of spring water. "We don't judge people. We find *truth*."

"No caffeine?" I asked, surprised to learn he doesn't fuel his Type-A personality with caffeine and sugar, to keep the machine working all those hours.

"No, no, no," he said, handing me a bottle of water. "You drink up. Water is what keep me going. Water and tea. You should drink water or tea only."

Sitting, listening, I thought maybe I should heed his advice: Lee himself looks not a day over 50 and, obviously, has the energy of a 20-year-old.

As he talked, I couldn't help noticing that just about every inch of wall space in his office is covered with some sort of award, recognition, certificate of appreciation, or letters written by former presidents, clients, high-profile lawyers, entities ranging from the FBI to the International Homicide Investigators Association, to Bill Clinton, to the late Johnnie Cochran.

"Everybody," Dr. Michael Baden told me once, "loves Henry."

"This is just a small representative sample of the awards I have received," remarked Lee, glancing at the wall, humbly taking pride in what he has been able to accomplish. In addition to the awards tacked to his office walls, he said, are about "800 to 1,000" more at his home. "I get two or three a day sometimes," he added. "I don't know why, but Michael [Baden] and I have dozens of honorary doctorates from colleges all over the world." He shrugged and raised his eyebrows, then shook his head as if in a moment of disbelief at all the attention thrown at him.

It was easy to tell, though, that the credit Lee is most fond of is the Medal of Honor he received from Ellis Island in early 2005 for his efforts, achievements, and pioneering work in science as a Chinese immigrant.

"It's a prestigious recognition of my work," he said. "I feel very honored they've recognized the *work*. This country is most wonderful country. If you work hard, you can have chance. I work my—literally—ass off. Seventeen, 18 hours a day, every day, and [today] people think I'm stupid. All my friends say, 'You made it, Henry.' I say, 'It's no secret; just hard work.' Unless you have last name Rockefeller, Kennedy, or Trump, door won't open for you. For us," and he again pointed to me, then to himself, "we have to work hard."

For an immigrant who juggled four jobs for several years while earning a bachelor's degree in forensic science at John Jay College of Criminal Justice in Manhattan in 1972, on top of raising two kids with Margaret, the honor is certainly well- warranted.

It wasn't long after Lee graduated from John Jay College that he studied for his Ph.D. in biochemistry at New York University and moved his family to Connecticut, where he immediately accepted an offer to take a faculty position at the University of New Haven.

The program at the college he presides over is split into two different criminal categories, he explained. "One is forensic science, which is criminalistic, just laboratory work; and the other is forensic investigation, with emphasis on crimescene."

This is, Lee pointed out, the major difference television fails to accurately portray. Most forensic science/C.S.I. television programs integrate the two into one. That's not how it is in the real world, Lee stated firmly. During an appearance on the Larry King Show in 2002, along with the cast of *C.S.I.: Crime Scene Investigation*, Lee said the "public is dying for reality shows. Many times, by second commercial, you guys already found clue. We have to work years—*years*—before we found any lead."

More than anything, it's the work itself that fuels Lee's craving to continue, despite it being his fifth decade behind the microscope.

"You see, when you talk about forensic work, you talk about passion. You cannot replace passion with *anything*. If you just take job, nine to five or eight to four, you're just technician. If you take this seriously and treat it as profession, then you don't feel tired."

In other words, it's not work if you love what you do.

"I work during the day in the laboratory," he said, describing one of his average days (emphasis on average). "Then task force meeting. Then go to courts. At night, I go to lectures, crime scenes, dinners. And again, day after day after day, many people think I'm stupid."

Stupid?

So, within the snap of his fingers, we were back to the notion of Lee's circle of friends and family urging him to stop working so hard. His kids especially, he said, tell him that there are easier ways to make a living, and they have a good point. Lee could jump on the lecture circuit bandwagon and earn millions of dollars per year. As I sat there, he said his secretary was booking lectures, speaking engagements and seminars for the year 2008 already.

"In 46 years, I would not change a single day. Every time someone talks to me about a case, even a homeless person, a person in gutter,it is as important to me as the billionaires, the O.J.s, Chandra Levys and JonBenet Ramseys."

Endurance and persistence are Lee's sixth and seventh senses. His dogged determination, while sometimes having to investigatea case for years, is what ultimately solves them. On one occasion, while he was at home suffering from a 104-degree temperature, the Connecticut State Police called. They had a murder scene in the town of Newington (about an hour's drive from Lee's home) which they needed him to take a look at immediately.

"But I can't even walk," he said.

Apparently, the crime scene couldn't wait. Fifteen minutes later, an ambulance was at Lee's door carting him to the scene on a gurney.

He ultimately solved the case by linking DNA, from a cigarette butt he discovered in an ashtray, to the victim's ex-boyfriend.

When he talked about patience, Lee spoke from experience. Think about taking an entire car windshield, shattered into pieces, and bringing it back to the lab to reassemble, piece by painstaking piece. Thousands, perhaps hundreds of thousands of pieces of glass which required being put back together again like a puzzle. It can take weeks, months, but it could provide the one missing link in solving a case which a forensic scientist has been working on for years.

One of the toughest parts of the job, Lee admitted, are

the phone calls from sheriffs, cops, prosecutors, police chiefs and, especially, the families of victims, all putting pressure on him to solve a particular case.

"I lecture to my students: You have to have integrity, objectivity, and be able to take the pressure. Otherwise, you are going to end up like a rubber band."

"A rubber band?" I ask, thinking...*Okay, here we go, here's that philosophy rant I was warned he could sometimes go off on.*

Lee smiled. "Yes, r-u-b-b-e-r b-a-n-d. When the rubber *band* gets pulled too hard, it breaks. Or worse, you lose your elasticity. Many good forensic scientists burn out, just from the lab work alone, which can be tedious and boring."

The worst are vacuum cleaners, he said. Sifting through a vacuum cleaner bag to find clues (hairs, glass, carpet fibers) can turn a good forensic scientist into a madman.

"The dust alone!"

Forensic toxicology is another monotonous job. Among other duties, toxicologists "aid medicolegal investigation of death and poisoning." But many spend their days simply testing drugs.

"Packet after packet after packet," noted Lee.

Serologists, too. Their job is to study bodily fluids and DNA retrieved in rape kits, to examine panties and undergarments, looking for saliva, hairs, fibers, blood, and semen.

Lee has done it all.

"In the early days, I would joke around and tell people I have probably seen more pairs of panties than anybody in the world."

We both laughed. But here, after a moment of humor, Lee talked about an important facet of the criminalist's job that often goes overlooked, which incidentally is one of the major differences between the forensic scientist and the crime-scene investigator. "Besides biological evidence, the forensic scientist should be looking for damage done to panties," he said more seriously. "Any rips, tears.or unusual worn spots. Sometimes, when they're right out of school with no investigative experience, they just look for DNA, for blood, and forget the other aspects."

That is one of the reasons why Lee and his staff are involved in cross-training crime-scene investigators with forensic scientists: to shape and mold what could be, in the future, super investigators that understand and realize how to recognize evidence when they see it. It's a pragmatic view of criminalistics; a way to educate crime-scene investigators and forensic scientists on how to find that hidden piece of evidence when no one else can.

For example, a CSI team shows up at a murder scene. The air conditioner in the apartment is on. Did the victim turn it on? Or did the murderer turn it on to throw off time of death? What about a cigarette butt found in an ashtray? Was it planted? Or left behind by the perpetrator unknowingly?

These are questions crime-scene investigators must ask themselves as soon as they arrive on-scene. Lee said the truth about what happened is always in the details—the smallest details—and that some crime-scene investigators ignore those details, thus leaving key pieces of evidence behind.

As for detectives, one of Lee's goals has been to make the street-level law enforcement community appreciate and understand forensic science so the two can work together for the common good of finding the truth.

"It's not necessary for detectives and police to become forensic scientists," he explained. "But they have to know the potential of what the science can do to assist their jobs."

Take the seemingly simple task of a crime-scene investigator or detective putting in a request to the laboratory.

Maybe a cop has found a gun and needs the lab to dust it for fingerprints. Sounds like a typical request, right?

"Collecting evidence properly is the first key," said Lee. "Then they can make a request at laboratory for certain tasks. Let's say, for example, you find gun at scene. The grip of gun is carved and bumpy with wood grains, and really has no smooth surface. So you send to lab and say, 'I want fingerprints and DNA.'

"The lab is going to laugh at you."

It's the surface of the gun grip. It's far too coarse to yield any type of fingerprint the lab can extract, which is another misconception generated by television: that a fingerprint can be extracted from *any* surface.

Blood is another source of evidence that has to be looked at with an experienced eye. Suppose a victim's body is sent to the medical examiner for an autopsy. The medical examiner takes off the victim's shirt, which is saturated with blood, and sends it to the lab requesting DNA testing be done.

"You don't have to do DNA on that," added Lee. "We *know* that's the victim's blood. You can do 400 samples on such an item and come up with the victim's DNA every single time. Meanwhile, that single drop of blood on the victim's leg or thigh can be whole case—and someone could have missed it."

That's why, he pointed out, the entire team, right down to the medical examiner, should be educated in forensics and crime-scene investigation. If everyone misses that one drop of blood, or the medical examiner mistakenly washes it away post- mortem, a murderer can go free.

At times, Lee asked medical examiners and crime-scene technicians why they would, after converging on a crime-scene, flip a victim's body over, or move a body so quickly after arriving on the scene.

Most of the time, the answers Lee hears fall along the

lines of: "We wanted to determine the victim's identity and to see if there were any injuries on the victim's face."

"Dead people," said Lee, again laughing, "won't walk away. Once you turn, move or touch a victim's body, the chance for contamination exists." All aspects of crime-solving have to "bridge together," he concluded. "It's about educating everybody involved."

**

MURDERERS ARE GETTING SMARTER. Whether it is because crime has been pushed into the forefront of society's daily viewing habits, or simply because criminals watch television shows, study law enforcement procedural books, and learn from them. Either way, Lee told me, "We have to be smarter than they are."

It's the only way to beat them.

Among Dr. Lee's numerous accomplishments, in the early 1970s he started the first forensic science program for the Connecticut State Police. By himself, he created a "Major Crime Squad" concept for the state police. Major Crime Squads investigate all major case investigations, crimes such as homicides, sexual assaults, armed robberies, and arsons, which are split into several groups and spread throughout the state of Connecticut. In addition to primary responsibilities of investigating violent crime, all squads serve state attorneys' offices and assist and support police departments throughout the state.

Before Lee arrived in Connecticut, the forensic laboratory supporting the state police was located inside the men's room of the state police's Meriden barracks. At his disposal, Lee had a fingerprinting kit, magnifying glass, and one drawer in a file cabinet inside a ten-by-ten area of the restroom. Today, the Connecticut State Police Forensic Science Laboratory in

Meriden is a state-of-the-art, 38,000-square-foot facility—all because of Lee's remarkable vision.

When we first sat down to talk, Lee handed me one of his books. "That's one of my bestsellers," he said. "Read it when you get a chance."

"I will," I said, not looking at it, instead just slipping it into my briefcase as we chatted.

When I got into my car after the interview, I took the book out to look at it. To my surprise, the entire text was Chinese.

As I sat there shaking my head, laughing at Lee's obvious penchant for sarcasm, I knew then why so many people have said he is one of the most personable, human, friendliest people they have ever met. It's his sense of humor and smile. Both are magical. I recalled his giving me a little smirk as he handed me the book. It was his way, I guess, of allowing me a rite of passage into the intriguing, yet entirely misunderstood real world of forensic science.

**Coming Soon From WildBlue Press:
BETRAYAL IN BLUE by BURL
BARER, FRANK C. GIRARDOT
JR., and KEN EURELL**

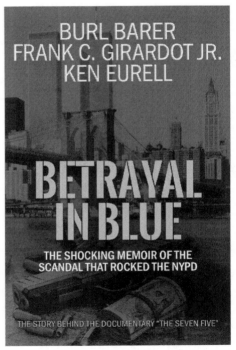

Read More: **http://wbp.bz/bib**

BETRAYAL IN BLUE

They Had No Fear Of The Cops Because They Were The Cops

NYPD officers Mike Dowd and Kenny Eurell knew there were two ways to get rich quick in Brooklyn's Lower East Side. You either became drug dealers, or you robbed drug dealers. They decided to do both.

"I promised my wife that we would make a lot of money, and that she had nothing to worry about. I LIED!"

Dowd and Eurell ran the most powerful gang in New York's dangerous 75th Precinct, the crack cocaine capital of 1980s America. These "Cocaine Cops" formed a lucrative alliance with Adam Diaz, the kingpin of an ever-expanding Dominican drug cartel. Soon Mike and Ken were buying fancy cars no cop could afford, and treating their wives to levels of luxury not associated with a patrol officer's salary.

Then "the biggest police scandal in New York history" exploded into the headlines with the arrest of Mike, Ken, and their fellow crooked cops. Released on bail, Mike offered Ken a long shot at escape to Central America - a bizarre plan involving robbery, kidnapping, and murder - forcing Ken to choose between two forms of betrayal.

Check out the book at: **http://wbp.bz/bib**

More True Crime You'll Love
From WildBlue Press.

Learn more at: http://wbp.bz/tc

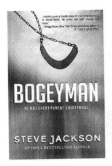

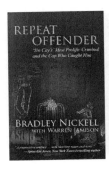
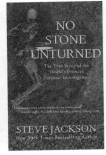
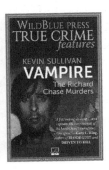

www.WildBluePress.com

Made in the USA
Lexington, KY
23 February 2017